LEON TROTSKY AND THE POLITICS OF ECONOMIC ISOLATION

Soviet and East European Studies

Editorial Board

The National Association for Soviet and East European Studies exists for the purpose of promoting study and research on the social sciences as they relate to the Soviet Union and the countries of Eastern Europe. The Monograph Series is intended to promote the publication of works presenting substantial and original research in the economics, politics, sociology and modern history of the USSR and Eastern Europe.

LEON TROTSKY
AND THE POLITICS OF
ECONOMIC ISOLATION

RICHARD B. DAY

CAMBRIDGE
AT THE UNIVERSITY PRESS
1973

Published by the Syndics of the Cambridge University Press
Bentley House, 200 Euston Road, London NW1 2DB
American Branch: 32 East 57th Street, New York, N.Y. 10022

Library of Congress Catalogue Card Number: 72–91960

ISBN: 0 521 20089 X

Printed in Great Britain by
Western Printing Services, Ltd
Bristol

Contents

To J.D.

Preface

For the use of their holdings I wish to thank the British Museum, the School of Slavonic and East European Studies (University of London), the London School of Economics, the library of Columbia University, the New York Public Library, and the Internationaal Instituut voor Sociale Geschiedenis (Amsterdam). The *Trotsky Archives*, which were essential for this work, were used by permission of the Harvard College Library. For her historical judgement and tireless assistance in the writing, my greatest debt is to my wife. For his bibliographical research on Trotsky I am grateful to Louis Sinclair. The Canada Council and Imperial Oil Ltd. were most generous in their financial support of my research. Olga Crisp, Peter Wiles, Heinz Schurer, R. W. Davies, H. Gordon Skilling, Robert McNeal and Robert Fenn all provided encouragement at various phases of preparing the manuscript. All responsibility for errors of fact or interpretation is of course my own.

R.B.D.

23 January 1973

Part one

The dilemma of economic isolation

The myth of Trotskyism

In the historiography of Russian Marxism the name of Leon
Trotsky is invariably linked with two very famous political
slogans: Permanent Revolution and Socialism in One Country.
Trotsky is portrayed as a dedicated internationalist, who rejected
Stalin's theory of an isolated socialist state in the belief that the
Russian revolution must be 'permanent' in a double sense. In
domestic terms it was to involve a direct transition from the
feudal monarchy of the tsars to socialism, without an intervening
period of bourgeois capitalism. In an international context it was
to be accompanied by a succession of political upheavals throughout Europe, resulting in an international socialist commonwealth.

According to his biographer, Isaac Deutscher, Trotsky's differences with Stalin arose from his belief that unless the revolution
burst Russia's national boundaries it would run into a dead end.
Russia was too backward and economically underdeveloped to
achieve socialism by its own efforts. Summarizing the theory of
Permanent Revolution, Deutscher explained that 'Russia's industrial poverty and backwardness would . . . prove formidable
obstacles to the building of a Socialist economy; and only with
the help of the Socialist West could these obstacles be broken
and removed'.[1] George Lichtheim agreed, claiming that Trotsky
thought Russia 'Could only give the signal; it was for Europe to
accomplish the main task'.[2] In the same connection Robert V.
Daniels wrote that a socialist regime could not endure in Russia
alone. For its consolidation access would be necessary to the
industrial resources of a socialist Europe.[3]

Despite the evident consensus among historians the Trotsky–
Stalin dispute continues to raise problems. Stalin first enunciated
the doctrine of Socialism in One Country at the end of 1924.
Trotsky did not reply until late in 1926, almost two years later.
In the meantime Zinoviev and Kamenev, Stalin's former col-

leagues, loudly challenged the supposed Leninist orthodoxy claimed for the new theory. Trotsky gave no public indication that he shared such misgivings. In fact, his first inclination was to support Stalin rather than the Zinoviev opposition. How can this apparent uncertainty be reconciled with the seeming lack of any ambiguity in Trotsky's own views? And why did Trotsky fail to support Stalin's critics until after they had been defeated? Finally, what could have persuaded him that a political alliance with Zinoviev might ultimately succeed, without offering a more viable policy than the mere wish for an international revolution?

Alec Nove has recently suggested that Trotsky's confusion might be traced to the question of forced agricultural collectivization. The purpose of the collective farm was to extract from the rural economy the resources necessary to sustain a programme of rapid industrialization. Trotsky's enthusiasm for industrial expansion was not open to question; but at the same time he believed that a large-scale development of socialist agriculture would depend upon a degree of mechanization which Russia could not possibly achieve in the near future. As a result, according to Nove's hypothesis, there was no alternative but to hope that industrial growth might be financed by investment capital supplied by more advanced socialist regimes in the West.[4]

The merit of Nove's proposal is that it stresses an empirical issue rather than general theoretical postulates. But it also points to a further incongruity. Although Trotsky seemed to rule out the comprehensive construction of socialism until after the international revolution, he and his associates were nevertheless the most vocal advocates of steadily increasing industrial investments. This fact suggests one of two conclusions: either Trotsky's position was simply inconsistent, or historians have failed to explain it because they have raised the wrong questions.

The purpose of this book is to show that the latter has been the case. The operative question for Trotsky was not *whether* Russia could build socialism in advance of the international revolution, but *how* to devise an optimal planning strategy, taking into account both the existing and the future international division of labour. To date Trotsky's views on Soviet economic policy have not been studied in detail, nor have they been systematically related to the problem of Russia's isolation from capitalist Europe. When this is done it becomes clear that there were actually two periods when the question of isolation assumed critical economic and political significance.

The first of these periods occurred in 1920 and the early months of 1921, the days of War Communism, when the Bolsheviks realized that the international revolution might not be as inevitable as they had expected. By comparing the reactions of various party spokesmen it can be shown that two more or less coherent points of view emerged in the attempt to define Russia's role in a hostile capitalist world. Although the adherents of the two positions differed on matters of detail, for analytical purposes they can be grouped under two headings: 'isolationist' and 'integrationist'. The isolationists, as the term implies, tended to look upon Soviet Russia as an exile from the world economy; the integrationists, in contrast, believed that, despite the country's unique political order, in one manner or another Russia must resume her previous position in international affairs.

If Trotsky's behaviour during War Communism had been consistent with the interpretation normally placed upon the theory of Permanent Revolution, he would have fallen into the integrationist category. For want of a better alternative he would have subscribed to the widely held view that every possible device must be employed to solicit economic aid from abroad, including both a restoration of international trade and even foreign investments from capitalist Europe. But the evidence shows that he in fact emerged as the central theorist of economic isolation. Recognizing that the European revolution would at best be delayed, he nevertheless saw in War Communism a coherent system of policies intended to achieve a direct transition to Socialism – in One Country. The historic debate with Lenin in 1920–1, concerning the role of the trade unions in a socialist society, resulted from the peculiar proposals for labour policy to which Trotsky's isolationist beliefs led. As an outward manifestation of differing assumptions regarding Russia's role in the world at large, the disagreement actually constituted an implicit discussion of the later question of Socialism in One Country. In consequence, a careful study of this early phase of Soviet history provides important insights for interpreting the later conflict with Stalin.

The controversies surrounding the transition from War Communism to the New Economic Policy (NEP) closely paralleled those of the mid-1920s. But in the interval dramatic changes of opinion took place. The relationship between Trotsky and the 'party line' underwent a complete reversal. Forsaking his earlier opinions, by 1925 Trotsky had become the most consistent proponent of integrationist policies. On the other hand Stalin and Bukharin, in command of the party after Lenin's death, increasingly equated industrialization with economic disengagement from the West. Thus the stage was set for the debate which resulted in Trotsky's defeat and exile.

The causes of this transition deserve close attention. They show that Trotsky's feud with Stalin and Bukharin was only very tangentially connected with the theory of Permanent Revolution. Furthermore Trotsky did not insist, as is so often suggested, that a genuine construction of socialism must await the international revolution. Least of all did he predict that without a socialist transformation in Europe Russia must necessarily stagnate. On the contrary, like the integrationists of the period of War Communism, he appealed for extensive trade links with the West and maximum foreign investments.

He objected, not so much to the notion of Socialism in *One* Country (*Sotsializm v Odnoi Strane*) as to Stalin's concept of Socialism in a *Separate* Country (*Sotsializm v Otdel'noi Strane*). Stagnation would result, he argued, from the deliberate creation of a shut-off, closed-in, isolated economy (*zamknutoe khozyaistvo*); autarchy would be a prescription for disaster. The apparently unaccountable inconsistencies in his political behaviour resulted from these fundamental disagreements over economic policies. A closer look at the real importance of the theory of Permanent Revolution will help to explain the background to this interpretation.

The theory of Permanent Revolution
The earliest complete exposition of the theory appeared in an essay entitled *Results and Prospects*, which Trotsky wrote in 1905–6. Russia was the least highly developed country in Europe; the essay suggested that for this very reason the socialist revolution might begin here rather than in the industrial states of the West. Replacing the feudal autocracy with a more democratic form of government, the first stage of the revolution would be short-lived. After a brief interval the momentum of events would lead to a proletarian seizure of power. Since Marx himself had

foreseen a similar course of development for Germany in 1848, the prediction was not entirely unorthodox. In subsequent years, however, the majority of Marxists had sought to determine the 'ripeness' of various countries for socialism by reference to so-called 'levels' of economic development. Within this frame of analysis it seemed that Russia's backwardness precluded anything more than a consistent bourgeois revolution (although most writers qualified this position by making some provision for the possibility of a simultaneous political convulsion in Europe).

Trotsky believed that this allegedly scientific concern with abstract levels of development amounted to 'hopeless formalism'. It was true that Marx had always insisted on the relation between industrial growth and the political power of the proletariat; but he had not intended that his 'historically relative' remarks should be converted into a 'supra-historical axiom'.[5] Russia's history was unique and could not be assessed according to the criteria applied to other countries. Industry had been financed largely by foreign investments; European capital had brought with it the most modern methods of organizing production; Russia had leapt over the early stages of capitalism. Foreign investment had had equally important political consequences. Motivated by gain, European investors had neither the desire nor the opportunity to play the part of a political opposition within Russia. Bourgeois liberalism was much weaker therefore than in other countries. At the same time, because of its unnaturally high degree of concentration, Russian industry could easily be paralyzed by strikes. The strength of the proletariat was greater than its numbers would suggest, and certainly greater than in Germany or England at a comparable period. For these reasons Trotsky concluded that the attempt to establish a mechanical link between the statistical weight of industry in the economy and the dictatorship of the proletariat was 'a prejudice of "economic" materialism simplified to an absurdity'.[6]

In a chapter headed 'The Prerequisites of Socialism' he elaborated these views, polemicizing with the historian N. A. Rozhkov. Rozhkov had held that a country could only be considered 'ripe' for socialism when the following conditions prevailed: (1) large-scale production must almost completely dominate all sectors of the economy; (2) the leading industrial enterprises must be organized on a co-operative basis; and (3) the overwhelming majority of the population must be conscious socialists. Commenting upon this rigid interpretation of the traditional approach, Trotsky compared Rozhkov with the Marx of 1848: 'Apparently,' he remarked, 'Marx in 1848 was a Utopian youth compared with many of the present-day infallible automata of Marxism!'[7]

Rozhkov was said to have strayed from revolutionary Marxism because of his failure to recognize that the foregoing processes were interdependent, that they conditioned and limited each other. Long before they reached their mathematical limit they would undergo a qualitative change, 'and in their complex combination bring about what we understand by the name of social revolution'. Rozhkov had needlessly inflated the economic prerequisites of socialism, and Trotsky endeavoured to redress the balance. In the first place, he claimed, socialism was possible 'only when the development of the productive forces has reached the point at which large enterprises are more productive than small ones'. Secondly, there must be a class-conscious proletariat. In this context Trotsky added, though, that 'the attempt to define in advance what proportion of the whole population must be proletarian at the moment of the conquest of political power is a fruitless task'.[8] Finally, he noted that the working class must establish its political dictatorship. In Russia only this third prerequisite was lacking.

These highly formal and political conditions need only be mentioned to show how deceptive they were in their simplicity. Before he could prove that a workers' government was feasible Trotsky was compelled to reject any analysis which emphasized the impediments posed by Russia's economic underdevelopment. He did not expect that the transition to a new society would take place instantaneously; in fact he anticipated that nationalization would only begin with the larger enterprises, thereafter continuing as a gradual process. Socialism would not be introduced by a few decrees. Nevertheless, he predicted that the revolution 'will come up against political obstacles much sooner than it will stumble over the technical backwardness of the country'.[9]

The chief threat to the proletarian regime was thought to lie in the danger of a hostile alliance being formed by numerically stronger classes. Measures designed to protect the rural proletariat might bring the great bulk of the peasantry, together with the intellectuals, into conflict with the workers' government. Similarly, the capitalists were expected to react to unemployment legislation and the eight-hour day with lockouts, thus raising the prospect of a broadly based counter-revolutionary coalition. These apprehensions in turn led to the famous conclusion that the Russian revolution must be international if it were to enjoy any likelihood of survival:

Left to its own resources the working class of Russia will inevitably be crushed by the counter-revolution the moment the peasantry turns its back on it. It will have no alternative but to link the fate of its political rule, and hence the fate of the whole Russian revolution, with the fate of the socialist revolution in Europe.[10]

The very fact that Russia's growth had been financed to such a large degree by foreign capital appeared to guarantee that for both economic and political reasons the revolution would not be confined to Russia. A socialist government would immediately repudiate the tsarist debts and begin to nationalize industry. The effects of these policies upon Russia's creditors, especially upon France, would be disastrous. 'There is every reason for assuming.' Trotsky wrote, 'that the financial crisis resulting from the bankruptcy of Russia will directly repeat itself in France in the form of an acute political crisis which can only end with the transference of power into the hands of the proletariat.' If the Austrian and German monarchies attempted to crush proletarian Russia in order to prevent the revolution from spreading, Wilhelm II and Franz Joseph would bring upon themselves a revolution on the part of their own working classes. In one way or another the incendiary impulse would be transmitted abruptly to the leading states of Europe. With proletarian military and political support from abroad the peril of counter-revolution would be averted; the new socialist regime would be secured; and Trotsky's ambitious plans for what seemed to be a premature seizure of power would be vindicated. A number of references could be cited to show that on several occasions before 1917, as in 1906, Trotsky spoke of the need for direct state support from the workers of the West. But as in *Results and Prospects* external support was thought of as a political balancing factor, intended to compensate for the numerical inferiority of the Russian working class.

The theory of Permanent Revolution was therefore irrelevant to the economic debates of the mid-1920s on two grounds. In the first place it was concerned with the capture and maintenance of political power, not with the tangible problems of building socialism. Secondly, it claimed to prove the inevitability of an international revolution. To emphasize the problem of technical backwardness would have been contradictory; to suggest the impossibility of socialism in one country would have been logically superfluous. Trotsky did neither. He argued that Russia was prepared for the revolution and that proletarian aid from the West would eliminate the danger of counter-revolution – nothing more.

Yet in 1930, after his exile, he claimed that he had anticipated Stalin's 'errors' and that he had not believed Russia was 'ripe' for socialism without an international revolution. In his intro-duction to *The Permanent Revolution* he rewrote the history of the pre-1917 period in terms of the following dialogue:

'But do you really believe,' the Stalins, Rykovs and all the other Molotovs objected dozens of times between 1905 and 1917, 'that Russia is ripe for the socialist revolution?' To that I always answered: No, I do not. But the world economy as a whole, and the European economy in the first place, is fully ripe. . . Whether the dictatorship of the proletariat in Russia leads to socialism or not, and at what tempo and through what stages, will depend upon the fate of European and world capitalism.[11]

In the limited sense that *Results and Prospects* had predicted the need for a workers' government to rely upon external support, the assertion had some tenuous validity. Otherwise it was a falsifi-cation for purposes of anti-Stalinist propaganda.

While its intent has been misunderstood, Trotsky's earliest theoretical work did nevertheless contain significant elements of his later quarrel with Stalin. Surrounded by economically stronger enemies, Russia was described as having to choose between two possibilities: either to succumb, or 'to overtake them in the devel-opment of economic relations and absorb a great deal more vital forces than . . . [the country] could have done had it remained iso-lated'.[12] Industrial protectionism and the encouragement of foreign investments had imparted an artificial stimulus to econo-mic growth, proving that history did not necessarily move through predetermined stages in blind accordance with objective laws. Tsarist Finance Ministers had demonstrated that 'the state . . . is

a tremendous means for organizing, disorganizing, and reorganiz-
ing social relations'.[13] Giving the impression that a socialist state
would follow the same historical pattern, Trotsky wrote that a
workers' government would rely 'not merely upon the national
productive forces, but also upon the technique of the entire
world'.[14] If *tekhnika* is translated as 'technology', the inference
would be that Russia would continue to import both 'know-how'
and technical equipment. When he eventually realized that international trade should be treated as an economic rather than a
political question, Trotsky fell out with Stalin over policies of
economic isolation. From this point of view it could be argued
that *Results and Prospects* implied the irrationality of striving for
a self-sufficient economy. But Trotsky's contention that the essay
ruled out the construction of socialism in one country was an
attempt to create a political myth.

The fact that the myth took hold was largely Stalin's responsibility. By endorsing the fiction that Trotsky had unreservedly
and at all times rejected the idea of Socialism in One Country,
Stalin intended to prove that his defeated rival had never ceased
to be a faint-hearted Menshevik, a revolutionary impostor with
no faith in Russia's capabilities. The resulting confusion, per-
petuated by generations of Trotskyists and official Soviet scribes,
has continued until the present. Overshadowed by the doctrine
of Permanent Revolution, Trotsky's other early writings have
been ignored. The most significant of these, for the two major
periods dealt with in this study, concerned the theory of imperialism.

The theory of imperialism

In their attempt to determine Russia's relation to Europe the
Bolsheviks customarily began by endeavouring to project future
economic developments in the capitalist countries. Russia's potential bargaining strength, together with the possible benefits from
various forms of concessions, were thought to be a reflection of
the probable fate of the enemy camp. In Trotsky's case *Results
and Prospects* implied that Russia might benefit from imports of
foreign equipment. The theory of imperialism provided the other
half of the analysis, suggesting the extent to which Europe might
be willing, or able, to continue supplying the products required.
In this respect it was instrumental in answering the question of

what concessions the new socialist government should be prepared to consider.

The most important influence on this aspect of Trotsky's
thought came from the German Marxist, Alexander Israel Help-
hand (Parvus), with whom he had been closely associated in
1905. In the course of the revisionist controversy at the beginning
of the century Parvus had defended Marx's theory of the ten-
year business cycle against the criticisms of Eduard Bernstein.
The suggestion that the theory was no longer realistic was said
to be flawed because Bernstein had overlooked the development
of international capitalism. With the emergence of imperialism,
according to Parvus, crises had assumed world dimensions.
Periodical disturbances in a capitalist economy were unavoidable. The system of privately appropriating production had
resulted in one inescapable defect: capitalism could not provide
markets for the total volume of goods it created. The tendency
towards a state of chronic glut had led to a phenomenal growth
in international trade, breaking down artificial political barriers
between nation-states and causing countries to become increasingly interdependent. Paying low wages, and thereby narrowing
the market, the capitalist countries had been converted into
imperialist powers, recklessly engaged in the conquest of overseas
sources of demand. As Parvus observed, the capitalists 'begin to
push each other out of markets, and their conflicts, when other
means are lacking, lead inevitably to world wars'.[15]

Despite the intimacy of his relationship with Parvus, Trotsky
only became fully aware of the nation-state and the international
economy after he left Russia in 1907 to take up residence in
Vienna. In January 1909, impressed by the anarchy in the Bal-
kans, he wrote that conditions 'for a powerful development of
the productive forces' could not be secured unless a federation
were created similar to that in Switzerland or the United States.[16]
This proposal was a variation on Parvus's earlier appeal for a
United States of Europe. Later, in the summer of 1910, the
failure of the Sofia Pan-Slav Congress prompted Trotsky to
write that a common market was 'the only way out of the nation-
state chaos and bloody confusion of Balkan life'.[17]

The final confirmation of Parvus's findings seemed to come
with the outbreak of the first world war. Trotsky concluded that
the underlying cause of the hostilities had been the inability of

the belligerents to find markets for their entire national product. All his commentaries on the subject of imperialism henceforth started with the view that international trade had rendered the nation-state economically and historically superfluous. The rise of monopolies, the cartelization of industry, the emergence of international financial combines, the rapid expansion of capital exports: all these features of imperialism were relegated to a secondary position in comparison with capitalism's perpetual imbalance between production and effective demand. On 31 October 1914 Trotsky explicitly attributed the war to the fact that the productive forces had rebelled against the limitations of the nation-state; with the emergence of a world economy the state could no longer exist as 'an independent economic arena'.[18] Because every capitalist state, by definition, was being driven into the compulsive competition for markets, it followed that: 'The future development of the world economy on capitalist foundations will mean an uninterrupted struggle for newer and newer divisions of the same world surface as an object of capitalist exploitation.'[19]

Viewed in this light the appeal to arms was ultimately futile. The war might enlarge the markets available to individual countries; but nothing could be done to salvage the capitalist system as a whole. Furthermore, colonial industrialization would quickly exacerbate the crisis. In an article entitled 'The Nation and the Economy' Trotsky summarized the argument as follows:

To the extent that capitalist development became constricted within the limits of the state, the latter was supplemented by annexations and colonial appendages. . . The competition for colonies led to the struggle of the capitalist states among themselves. The productive forces have finally become cramped within the limits of the state. . . The place of the shut-in national state must inevitably be taken by a broad democratic federation of the leading states, with the abolition of all tariff divisions.[20]

An international socialist economy would enlarge the purchasing power of the working class and resolve capitalism's leading contradiction. Imperialism was 'the capitalist-thievish expression of a progressive tendency in economic development; a tendency to build man's economy on a world scale, having liberated it from the confining fetters of the nation and the state'.[21] In February 1915 Trotsky urged that:

A democratic unification of Europe, the creation of a European United States, is the only political form in which the proletariat can resolve the implacable contradiction between the contemporary productive forces and the limitations of nation-state organization.[22]

All the countries of Europe had achieved a high degree of economic development and all were subject to the same dilemma. This being the case, Trotsky conjectured that they would all undergo socialist revolution at more or less the same time. In the improbable event of the revolution being confined temporarily within one country his main fear continued to be that socialism would be crushed by force of arms. As late as June 1917, three months after the fall of the Romanovs, he republished an earlier article in which he had said that the revolution could only develop and gain victory on a general European basis. 'Remaining isolated within national borders, it would be doomed to disaster.'[23] English, French and Italian militarism were no less dreadful enemies of the Russian workers than the German armies. If the European proletariat were defeated, the theory of imperialism suggested that Russia would be transformed into a colony of one or other of the victorious powers.

It was this growing fear of outright colonization which explained Trotsky's isolationism during War Communism. *Results and Prospects* had demonstrated the growth-inducing nature of trade and foreign investments; and the theory of imperialism had proclaimed the economic demise of the nation-state. Both approaches appeared to imply that a socialist economy in a single country would constitute an historical regression. The difficulty was that Trotsky's analysis of imperialism produced contradictory conclusions. Trade and capital imports might promote growth; however, they were now also seen as the main instruments of imperialist exploitation. A continuation of inter-capitalist rivalries suggested that Europe would be unable to provide for Russia's economic requirements in any case. Without a socialist revolution in the West, Europe was fated to decline in a state of 'permanent war'; the continent would become a graveyard.[24] If the nightmare of an imperialist hell resulted in the protracted suppression of the working class, civilization in the West would be doomed to decay, to degeneration, to a new barbarism.[25] Before they brought on their own destruction the bourgeois militarists might momentarily bury their differences, form a united front, and eliminate socialist Russia. Contact with the West would mean the end of socialist independence.

Lenin's view of imperialism was less abstract, more practical and more empirical than Trotsky's. While Trotsky concentrated on the universal problem of pre-war overproduction, Lenin believed the differences between the capitalist countries were more noteworthy than their similarities. Capitalism was characterized by the unevenness of its growth: 'The uneven and spasmodic development of individual enterprises, of individual branches of industry and individual countries is inevitable under the capitalist system.'[26] The problem of unevenness made Lenin unwilling to base the future of the Russian revolution upon the prospect of an immediate international solution. He concluded, although he too had used the slogan, that Trotsky's call for a United States of Europe might have an effect opposite to that which had been intended. By setting immediate objectives too high it might dampen revolutionary enthusiasm. It was perfectly conceivable that the revolution might advance in a more halting fashion; for a time it might even be limited to one country. In Lenin's words: 'the victory of socialism is possible first in several or even in one capitalist country alone'.[27]

Lenin thought in terms of the present and the immediate future; Trotsky was concerned with analyzing an entire historical epoch. Trotsky did not contend that the European countries would experience the revolution at precisely the same moment. But he was convinced that European capitalism had prepared the way for a socialist order which would embrace the entire continent. Replying to Lenin he argued that the problem of 'unevenness' would prove to be of passing importance:

That the capitalist development of various countries is uneven is quite incontestable. But this unevenness is itself extremely uneven. The capitalist levels of England, Austria, Germany or France are not the same. But as compared with Africa and Asia all these countries represent capitalist 'Europe', which has matured for the socialist revolution.[28]

The specific question of when and how the revolution would take place would, at least partially, solve itself with the passage of time. Inherent in Lenin's more thorough analysis of imperialism though were the sources of further conflicts. By implication Lenin's conclusions differed radically from Trotsky's in that they allowed for a limited capitalist recovery. Some of the imperialist powers might benefit from the war. The unevenness which already existed might be intensified and rearranged, resulting in a longer period of unstable post-war equilibrium than Trotsky expected. In that event Lenin's theory suggested that Russia could gain from a restoration of economic intercourse with the victors. Trade would be an obvious form for this relationship to assume. But Lenin also assigned an even greater importance than Trotsky to imperialism's dependence upon capital exports. In the final stage of capitalism, he wrote, 'the export of capital as disinguished from the export of commodities acquires exceptional importance'.[29] The triumphant powers could be expected to continue foreign investments in the effort to sustain a high rate of profit and to gain access to cheap material imports. From Lenin's standpoint it would be perfectly reasonable to exchange Russia's natural resources for capital and equipment. When Trotsky eventually came to disagree with these deductions, his break with Lenin was imminent.

The schism was rooted in Trotsky's uncertain image of Europe. Was the West a source of aid or a deadly enemy? *Results and Prospects* and the theory of imperialism produced conflicting answers; historical insight and Marxist theory were at odds. The ambivalence was not fully resolved until 1925, when a metamorphosis in the theory of imperialism, stimulated by the revolution's failures abroad and the evidence of capitalism's recovery, made it possible for Trotsky to complete the transition from isolationism to integrationism and to see Russia's own economy in terms of the inadequacies of the nation-state. By that time his political enemies had arrived at a position of forthright isolationism. In examining these parallel transitions, the following chapters will concentrate upon the most important events of the period. An exploration of the Bolshevik attempt to use theoretical Marxism as a basis for viable economic policies will make possible a reappraisal of the political tensions of the 1920s.

2

Isolation and the mobilization of labour

Early in the Great War Imperial Russia fell victim to an almost total economic blockade. German armies severed direct communications with Europe, leaving only the remote ports of Vladivostok on the Pacific and Archangel on the White sea as points of contact with the Allies. Unprepared for hostilities, the government failed to prevent a steady economic deterioration. Unprecedented demands for military transport caused frequent breakdowns; and scarce supplies, both military and civilian, were often impossible to move by 1916. Reductions in the movement of consumer goods to the countryside were matched by dwindling grain shipments to the cities. Hunger riots and industrial strikes followed. The replacement of the monarchy by the Provisional Government in March 1917 intensified the paralysis.

In November 1917 the Bolsheviks seized power. Lenin and his followers were moved by an unrealistic confidence both in the international proletariat and in their own ability to formulate successful policies as the need arose. Beginning with the simple faith that socialism would somehow arise of its own accord from the ruins of capitalism, the revolution shortly passed from a festival of anarchy to a period of authoritarian economic controls. The civil war brought with it a steadily widening gap between traditional socialist ideals and economic necessity. Within little more than two years a pattern of organization emerged which in many ways provided a prototype for Stalin's five-year plans of the 1930s. Ironically the main architect of this system was Trotsky.

The need for revolutionary discipline
The original naiveté of the party leaders was perfectly understandable. For the creation of the new order Marx had provided no specific guidelines. In the months immediately preceding the

revolution Lenin had sketched a limited number of proposals, but these were merely cursory suggestions, scarcely intended to constitute a thoroughgoing model for a socialist society. Among other possibilities Lenin included amalgamation and perhaps nationalization of the banks, nationalization of existing industrial syndicates, compulsory syndication of the larger independent enterprises, and compulsory organization of the population into consumer societies. The land question, one of the most serious problems of the revolution, was solved simply by adopting the programme of the Left Social-Revolutionaries; that is, by accepting *post facto* the results of an irreversible peasant jacquerie.

To some degree the difficulties of the new government must be attributed to the party's own propaganda. In August 1917 Lenin's pamphlet, *State and Revolution*, had proclaimed that the operation of a modern state and economy consisted of the simple tasks of 'registration, filing, and checking, that can easily be performed by every literate person'. 'We ourselves,' Lenin wrote, 'the workers, will organize large-scale production.'[1] Accordingly the workers seized the enterprises, believing that the popular slogan of workers' control meant workers' ownership. Independent industrial fiefdoms proliferated, and production continued to suffer.

Not until the spring of 1918 did Lenin even accept the need for general nationalization in industry. Instead he expected an intermediate period of what he termed 'state capitalism', a system which he loosely identified with the German war economy. Factory owners and their staffs were to be left in control of production subject to such general provisions as the eight-hour day and supervision of accounts by factory committees and commissars. Final administrative authority was to be vested in the Supreme Council of the National Economy (Vesenkha), an unwieldy organ created in December 1917. When the breakdown of negotiations with prominent industrialists convinced Lenin that responsibility could not be shared with private capital, on 28 June 1918 practically all industry was at last nationalized. However at least one major reason for the decision was entirely non-economic. Through the formal act of nationalization legal ownership of Russian properties would be prevented from falling into the hands of German citizens, whose rights were about to be guaranteed by a supplementary protocol to the peace treaty signed at Brest-Litovsk.

For much of this time Trotsky was preoccupied with the peace negotiations. In March 1918 he was appointed Commissar of War and President of the Supreme War Council. He inherited a perilous situation. In July, when the Left Social-Revolutionaries sought to overthrow the Bolsheviks, the government's defence rested upon a single rifle detachment. In Siberia the counter-revolution was already under way, forming around a nucleus of Czechoslovak war prisoners. The need to restore military discipline was apparent, and Trotsky called upon former tsarist officers for organizational guidance in creating the Red Army.

Trotsky's views on economic policy were a clear reflection of his military interests. In March 1918 he warned that anarchy constituted the greatest single threat to the survival of the revolution. Appealing for work, discipline, and order, he urged that 'in the political, revolutionary, and military sense the Soviet regime is not defeated – but it can stumble over its inability to deal with creative, organizational tasks'.[2] In line with his experiment in the army he proposed that bourgeois specialists be recruited, by force if necessary, to restore and maintain industrial operations. Factory committees and elected managerial collegiates must be replaced by qualified engineers and technicians. The revolution must not hesitate to appropriate the 'people's national capital', which had been invested in skilled bourgeois personnel.[3] The workers must think of themselves as soldiers, remembering their labour duty and their labour honour. If other means failed, labour courts should be created to discipline negligent proletarians. In a manner befitting a military commander he held out the vision of a perfectly functioning bureaucracy:

Now we must be accurate and economical, like good accountants. We must know exactly what property we possess, how much raw material and grain, what means of production, what work force, and precisely what their skills are. And all these must be arranged like the keys of a piano, so that every economic instrument acts properly . . . so that, for example, should it prove necessary it would be possible at any given moment to dispatch a number of metal workers from one place to another.[4]

The disciplinarian overtones in Trotsky's speeches coincided with a general retreat from collective decision-making and other forms of radical democracy in the course of 1918. Lenin began to stress the need for one-man management in industry and for more efficient accounting and control techniques. Although a number of self-designated Left-Communists, including Bukharin, Radek, Osinsky, V. Smirnov and others, protested that the attempt to restore labour discipline by such reactionary methods would alienate the workers, the concept of control by the masses soon fell into disrepute. Early in the year the official trade unions incorporated and restrained the factory committees. To discourage the unions from developing their own notions of independence Lenin declared: 'we can no longer confine ourselves to proclaiming the dictatorship of the proletariat. The trade unions have to be statified; they have to be fused with state bodies.'[5] But as an astute politician Lenin saw the need to avoid giving undue offence to the organized workers. The new party programme, adopted in the spring of 1919, provided that 'the trade unions must arrive at the factual concentration in their hands of the management of the entire national economy'.[6] The contradictory concession was a mere formality. By the end of 1919, in the midst of famine and civil war, the quasi-syndicalist visions of *State and Revolution* were all but forgotten by the party leaders. Nevertheless, egalitarian precedents had been established, which reasserted themselves when the prospect of greater normalcy returned.

The party's initial success on the labour front did nothing to mitigate the sense of external threat. As late as April 1918 Trotsky's views concerning socialist Russia's survival had altered very little from those he had expressed before the revolution. If capitalism were to remain in the West he suspected that a peace would ensue, 'ten times worse' than that achieved at Brest:

The Russian revolution cannot live side by side with imperialism for a long period of time. For the present we exist because the German bourgeoisie is carrying on a bloody litigation with the English and the French. Japan is in rivalry with America and . . . its hands are tied. That is why we remain above water. As soon as the plunderers conclude peace they will all turn against us. . . Then we are done for.[7]

The formation of a bourgeois 'united front' did not wait for the termination of hostilities. By August 1918 not only German, but British, French, Japanese and American forces as well were occupying Russian territory. Towards the end of the year, when peace approached in Europe, Trotsky believed that the only hope for thwarting the reactionary designs of the Entente lay in a German revolution, which would permit a military–political alliance with beleaguered Russia.[8] German railway equipment could then be exchanged for Russian grain, creating the basis for the future United States of Europe. In November though, when the Hohenzollern dynasty crumbled, Ebert and the moderate Social Democrats found themselves in power. Projections of the revolutionary timetable were dramatically revised. 'Several years might pass,' Trotsky reluctantly concluded, 'or months perhaps, if things go well.'[9]

Even this limited optimism was soon shown to be excessive. In January 1919 the radical German left was crushed in the wake of an abortive insurrection. The suppression of the Bavarian Soviet followed in April. By the end of the summer the Hungarian Soviet Republic met a similar fate. The Russian legation in Berlin was closed, and German troops still in Russia were committed to military intervention. American relief, shipped to the Central Powers during 1919, was deliberately calculated to prevent the fall of Ebert and the moderates, to fight the spread of Bolshevism. Otherwise, as the American representative Bullitt warned, 'the remainder of Europe will not long escape infection'.[10]

In the spring of 1919 an Allied cordon replaced the former German blockade. Trotsky dejectedly wrote that 'a genuine comprehensive socialist construction' would only be possible when the European working class came to Russia's assistance with its organization and its technology.[11] But Russia could wait no longer. The time for a fundamental reassessment had arrived. Both *Results and Prospects* and the theory of imperialism had erred in their estimate of events in Europe. On the other hand Trotsky's fears of a widespread peasant counter-revolution had proved to be equally unfounded. Placated by the land redistribution, the peasants preferred the Reds to a return of the landowners. Deprived of popular support, the White armies, despite the aid supplied by the Allies, were soon in retreat. Moscow and Petrograd both escaped capture. By the closing weeks of 1919 the decisive campaigns of the civil war had been won, largely because of Trotsky's capable generalship. Questions of economic organization now assumed greater importance.

The substitution of labour for capital
As his military duties grew less demanding Trotsky turned to the problem of reconstruction. Like Lenin he was certain that 'the so-called "war socialism" of Germany' provided an organizational

model suitable for Russian conditions.[12] Lenin had originally seen the relevance of the German patterns in its 'state capitalism'. Trotsky was more interested in the system of labour mobilization, whereby German industrialists and trade unionists were co-opted to work with state officials to ensure an orderly distribution of the labour force. Influenced by this example, in December 1919 he prepared a list of proposals for submission to the party's Central Committee. His intention was to create a system of universal labour mobilization by analogy with military conscription.

Before considering these suggestions it is important to recognize that the concept of compulsory labour service had several Russian precedents as well. The Provisional Government, under Kerensky, had attempted to devise a system similar to that in Germany. And a Bolshevik resolution providing for the introduction of obligatory labour service had been passed in Petrograd as early as June 1917. By the close of 1918 the first steps had been taken to put the resolution into effect. Technical personnel were declared mobilized; and labour was decreed to be compulsory for all citizens between the ages of sixteen and fifty years. In January 1919 agricultural specialists, together with railwaymen, workers in water transport, and employees of certain central institutions had similarly been declared mobilized.[13] In November 1919 compulsory labour service had been proclaimed for the peasantry in order to replenish fuel stocks and to provide horses, carts and sleighs for transporting essential materials.[14] In view of later developments it should be emphasized that Trotsky's proposals represented the logical culmination of a series of previously uncoordinated measures. The extension of his personal influence over decision-making by early 1920 was in large measure the consequence of his brilliant defence of Petrograd. To such an able lieutenant Lenin was prepared, for a time at least, to grant almost unlimited authority.

Trotsky realized that reconstruction must be preceded by orderly demobilization of the Red Army. However the military apparatus was the only efficient bureaucracy in the country, and he was reluctant to see its control over vast resources of manpower disappear with the coming of peace. As an alternative he recommended that the military department should assume increasing responsibility for administering the country's economic life. Civilian economic organs were to be made to correspond territorially to their military counterparts; military discipline and promptitude were to replace the over-centralized and haphazard controls hitherto exercised by Vesenkha.[15] The military authorities were to prepare and maintain a comprehensive file of labour records. Thus the entire able-bodied population of each region could be assigned to work suiting its qualifications. By projecting the army into this unique position of economic power the December theses carried the revolution into a new and extreme phase. The highpoint of War Communism was reached when the military danger had already subsided, and when plans were being initiated to replace the Red Army with a permanent militia.

The harsh features of the final stage of War Communism were directly linked with the economic ambitions expressed in Trotsky's theses. It was obvious that a systematic economic plan for socialist reconstruction was still a matter for the future; but the theses contended that a 'small' plan, providing for the labour requirements of a limited number of high priority industries, could be drafted immediately. Before the end of December 1919 projects were under way to assemble the necessary data. In the same month a Commission for Universal Labour Service was created with Trotsky at its head. Although the War Commissar was aware that recent military victories might be conducive to a mood of relaxation amongst the population, he had become accustomed to issuing commands. Labour conscription, he acknowledged, 'must inevitably be supported by measures of a compulsory character, that is, in the final analysis, by the armed force of the proletarian state'.[16] A decree issued by the Council of People's Commissars declared that workers who shunned the labour obligation should be summarily disciplined; penal labour detachments were to be created and in extreme cases labour deserters might be summoned before a revolutionary tribunal.[17] To indicate the solidarity of party opinion, on 5 February 1920 a statement appeared in *Pravda*, with Lenin's signature, explaining the significance of the reforms.

In practice the mobilization of labour presupposed careful attention to the differentiated skills and needs of the work force. Idle military units were to be converted into 'labour armies' with the job of gathering food supplies and fuel, building railways, and performing other easily supervised tasks. Peasants would periodically be conscripted for similar work under the control of local labour committees and the military authorities. One of the original labour armies was formed in the Ukraine under Stalin's supervision. A labour army formed from a military unit in effect constituted a postponement of demobilization. In the case of the peasants, organized and sustained resistance was not likely. To apply the concept of labour mobilization to the industrial proletariat represented a more serious and potentially explosive problem.

In theory the revolution had taken place to liberate the workers. Yet the December theses threatened to make a mockery of party proclamations: they provided no role whatever for the trade unions and promised only consultation concerning the details of the new policies. After discussion, the Central Committee sought to correct the omission in the final revised draft of the theses. The unions were required to bring their 'influence' to bear on skilled workers. New personnel were to be drafted into the labour bureaucracy to ensure 'iron labour discipline'. Labour books, which had been used on occasion since 1919, were to be made general. And a resolution at the end of January provided for labour courts. In cases where the unions failed to restore the required degree of discipline specific industries or critical sectors of the economy would be placed under economic martial law.[18]

Trotsky's insensitivity towards the unions was a foretoken of future complications. On 24 January 1920 he discussed their intended role as follows:

Where skilled workers are concerned . . . the task [of labour mobilization] will fall primarily to the trade unions. Only where trade union methods are inadequate will some other supplementary apparatus be required – particularly the method of compulsion; the labour obligation assumes that the state has a right to say to a skilled worker, who is sitting in a village and occupying himself with some mending work: 'You are obliged to pick up and leave for Sormovo, or the Kolomna factory, for you are needed there.'[19]

A similar lack of discretion could be seen in his notes of 25 February. In a workers' state, he claimed, there was no room for a 'trade-unionist' policy of disruptive bargaining and strikes; nor was there any need, for the state knew no other interests than those of the working people.[20] For the moment Lenin agreed with this view, declaring that the economy must be reconstructed 'by military methods, with absolute ruthlessness and by the sup-

pression of all other interests'.[21] The union leaders were predict-
ably less enthusiastic. Trotsky, they charged, was seeking to en-
force a new 'Arakcheyevshchina'. In their view the current
methods of labour organization resembled an attempt by Alexander I's War Minister to employ idle military units as agricultural colonists.[22]

Trotsky conceded that his designs were at odds with earlier
hopes. Nevertheless, he asserted that 'We ... are not suffering
from communism, but because the elements of communism are
interwoven with the remains of capitalism.'[23] The solution was
to strive for a consistently communist policy. This would require
a plan, and a plan depended on labour mobilization. As he explained in a speech on 6 January: 'This somewhat caricature-
like period in the development of our economy is unavoidable.
This is the transition from the destruction of capitalism to a
socialist economy under the most grave conditions.'[24]

Certainly one of the gravest conditions Russia faced was almost
total isolation from Europe. In more normal times the prospect
of isolation might not have seemed so overwhelming; but by 1920
the Russian economy had endured more than five years of warfare. Industry had experienced prolonged capital consumption;
the railways were at a halt; mines were flooding; the cities felt
the debilitating effects of famine. Large numbers of factories were
incapable of operating for want of spare parts, repairs to equipment, and sufficient raw materials. The scarce factor of production throughout the economy appeared to be capital. Inadequate
organization caused still more machinery to lie idle, giving the
impression that capital destruction had been even more extensive
than was really the case. The rationale behind Trotsky's counsels
therefore, was to substitute labour for capital. To organize Russia's vast human resources required rigid controls: labour ab-
senteeism in the cities was reaching appalling dimensions. Peasants, who had been attracted into industry during the war,
were now returning to the countryside in search of land and food.
Factory workers, many of whom had not yet completely severed
their ties with the villages, joined the exodus.

In the midst of this turmoil Trotsky courageously embarked
upon a personal campaign to dispel any lingering hopes of aid
from abroad. On 6 January he told the Moscow party committee
that accumulating shortages of vital technical equipment could

not be avoided. Labour mobilization was treated as the inevitable consequence of economic dislocation and capital scarcity: 'Possibly we will succeed in importing some locomotives from America . . . but we must not pin our hopes on them. We must speak of what we can do in the country during an epoch of nearly total blockade.'[25] In the final analysis, Trotsky declared, 'everything reduces to the living strength of the country. There is no other lever.'

From the party committee of the capital he turned to the party fraction of the All-Russia Central Council of Trade Unions. In a speech on 12 January he agreed that if machinery, master craftsmen, technicians, materials and fuel could be imported from England or Germany, 'a new factor would enter into our economic situation which would strikingly improve it'. But idle hopes had to yield to more factual appraisals: 'various gifts from abroad' would not be forthcoming. Russia had to rely upon 'the social factor', upon the organization of the work force.[26] In his summary Trotsky concluded: 'We must study the experiment of introducing labour service in the widest possible context; it is precisely because our technical equipment is worn out . . . that we must increasingly make up for all these shortages with living human energy.'[27]

Less than two weeks later he addressed the Third Congress of Soviets of the National Economy. Here the message was identical. Through revolution, war, and civil war, the country's mechanical equipment had suffered colossal physical destruction. Europe and America would provide only an insignificant number of machines. The basic lever of the economy would become 'doubly and triply labour power', including both the skilled industrial proletariat and the 'broad resources of raw labour power' which could be recruited in the rural areas.[28]

The final version of the December theses was accepted by the Central Committee on 22 January. Again the same themes were employed to justify the army's intrusion upon economic life and the policy of labour mobilization. In the words of the second thesis:

There is no basis for counting on the receipt of machines, coal, or qualified workers from the outside in any significant quantity in the near future – not only because of the blockade, whose future course cannot be predicted with any certainty, but also because of the extreme economic exhaustion of Western Europe.[29]

The third and ninth theses repeated the isolationist conclusion that Russia would have to rely primarily upon labour power in reconstructing her economy.

On 16 January 1920, at the very moment when Trotsky's plans were being accepted, the Allied Council formally lifted the blockade and decided to permit private trade with Russian co-operatives. A new element entered into the yet unsettled situation, and Lenin reacted with the hope that aid would soon arrive. He interpreted the decision to mean that normal international relations and machinery imports were about to resume.[30] Although his assessment was more an expression of wishful thinking than a serious appraisal of international events, it demonstrated one very important fact. While Lenin endorsed Trotsky's schemes, he did not share the reasoning which was their main justification.

Earlier differences over the theory of imperialism now reappeared in a new and unexpected context. In contrast with Lenin's optimism Trotsky worried that the imperialists would attempt to suffocate the revolution by economic means once intervention had failed. In February 1920 he wrote that if economic contact with Europe were restored at a time when Russia's own recovery was already in progress, the results might indeed be beneficial in terms of their effect on socialist construction. But he made a point of adding a second possibility:

Given our further economic deterioration, terms will be dictated to us by the world merchants who have commodity supplies at their disposal. In one manner or another they will reduce us to the position of an enslaved colonial country.[31]

England and France were said to be bent upon transforming the working people of Russia into colonial slaves; a starving country would not be able to stand up to the onslaught of Anglo-French capital.[32]

All the same Trotsky agreed with Lenin that an attempt must be made to purchase foreign machinery. With this object in mind he suggested that the country's remaining gold reserves might be used, assuming that the unofficial Allied gold blockade could be circumvented. France and England might be induced to accept Russian bullion in order to stabilize their tottering currencies. Russia, for its part, would shortly have no further monetary function for precious metals: 'We are making the transition to a communist structure; money in our country is more and more losing its importance.'[33]

The contradictory response was a measure of Trotsky's uncertainty. Unable to abandon completely the hope of surmounting the blockade, he was at the same time deeply sceptical of the possible benefits which might result. He believed that without a proletarian revolution Europe would founder in a state of postwar exhaustion punctuated by periodic crises. To all intents and purposes Russia's *de facto* isolation was likely to continue regardless of decisions being taken by the Allied Council. Crippled by their own economic difficulties, neither England nor France appeared to be in any position to provide the capital equipment Russia required. Rash hopes in this connection would be the 'purest utopia'; Russia must rely on her own forces.[34] False optimism might weaken the workers' resolve at a time when the greatest sacrifices still lay ahead. The Entente, he declared, must be treated as 'a force neither for good nor evil', in other words, with indifference. Until they could export the means of production their pronouncements were a matter of no consequence. Most important, the workers must understand the current capitalist strategy. Russia was hungry and poor. Trading upon human misery the capitalists would offer impossible conditions in exchange for 'a pound of tea and a tin of condensed milk'.[35]

Rhetoric aside, Trotsky appears to have suspected that Russia would be lured into a compromise over the twin questions of debt repudiation and nationalization. The fear was justifiable. The French government had every intention of making the resumption of commercial relations dependent upon settlement of the former state debts and indemnification for confiscated properties. If the price of alleviating the famine was to be the future of socialism, Trotsky was determined that Russia must resist the temptation until she might negotiate from a position of strength. His unyielding posture derived from a dangerous misinterpretation of party opinion. If he was unaware of this beforehand the debates of the Ninth Party Congress, in March 1920, left no room for further doubt.

The Ninth Party Congress
The congress assembled in an atmosphere of general uncertainty. The bravado of previous days, when Bukharin had called for a

revolutionary war against capitalism, or when Trotsky had summoned the proletariat to horse against the Whites, seemed a faint
memory. Words of praise, consolation, and a period of rest:
these were what the delegates expected to hear and discuss. But
Trotsky ignored obvious signs of discontent, refusing to believe
that the proletariat had lost its will. For each of the fallen he
professed to see new thousands, steeled with revolutionary class-
consciousness. 'These,' he had recently told a party meeting in
Moscow, 'are the most precious result of our October revolution
and the guarantee of its future successes.'[36] To date Russia had
accomplished the impossible. Trotsky looked for one more miracle.

Charged with delivering the Central Committee's official report on economic policy, he began his address by outlining a
concise, four-staged plan for the transition to socialism. For in-
genuous simplicity the plan was easily the rival of the economic
prerequisites enumerated in *Results and Prospects*. Briefly, it
provided for the sequential restoration of the transport, fuel and
engineering industries.[37] To the extent that foreign trade opened
up, imports were to be restricted to producers' goods and there
were to be no concessions to the current consumer psychology.
In *Terrorism and Communism*, written at this time, Trotsky
confirmed his indifference towards the consumer: 'We shall exchange part of our raw materials for locomotives or for necessary
machines, but under no circumstances for clothing, boots, or
colonial products; our first item is not articles of consumption,
but the implements of production.'[38]

On labour questions Trotsky explained the need for military
discipline in the factories. Skilled industrial workers were to be
moved abruptly from place to place in response to developing
crises. The proposed congress resolution called for 'a planned,
systematic, steady and stern struggle with labour desertion, in
particular by publishing a list of deserters, the creation of a penal
work command out of deserters, and their internment in concentration camps'.[39] The trade unions were to play the role of a
mobilization apparatus, adopting 'the same rights in relation to
their members as have previously been exercised only by a military
organization'.[40] In other words, the unions were 'to distribute, to
group, to fasten separate groups and separate categories of
workers and individual proletarians to the place where they are
needed by the state, by socialism'.[41]

Lenin's attitude closely resembled Trotsky's. While opening the congress he had endorsed the use of force to operate the programme of labour conscription, noting that no revolution had ever been effected without coercion. Iron discipline would be required for peaceful economic development just as it had been imperative in time of war.[42] For all their stress upon compulsion, however, Lenin and Trotsky were aware that punitive sanctions would have to be combined with positive incentives in the form of widely publicized bonus and premium schemes. Consumer goods, and particularly food supplies, were to be parcelled out with discrimination, giving preference to the most important branches of industry, to the best enterprises within the various branches, and to the most conscientious and productive workers as individuals. The name which had already come to be applied to this type of organized inequality was *udarnost'*, or shock work.

Because this was the first party congress to gather in time of peace, decisions taken here were likely to affect the entire future course of economic policy. Thus it was not surprising that the meeting brought to the fore several opposing strains of socialist thought. Many delegates who continued to look to the democratic experience of 1917–18 for inspiration were repelled by the dictatorial attitudes of Lenin and Trotsky. Speaking for the emerging Democratic-Centralist faction, Osinsky protested that the revolution was being imperilled by a clash between civilian and military cultures. The latter, he predicted, would soon extend into politics: 'Red governors' would complete the drift to reaction by assuming control of the local soviets.[43] New names could not mask a return to the old order.

Carrying on the tradition of the earlier Left Communists, Osinsky was especially critical of the system of *udarnost'*. The War Commissar, he cautioned the delegates, was attempting to convert the economy into a military machine. It was true that *udarnost'* might produce positive results, but only if it were used selectively. It was impossible to concentrate scarce resources on every weak point at the same time. Furthermore, success in a limited number of high priority shock points depended on creative initiative and independence elsewhere, which in turn must grow out of collegial management. Pointing to the absurdity of employing the army as an economic apparatus, he demanded that the labour armies be transferred to civilian control.[44] With regard to the trade unions the Democratic-Centralists deplored any attempt to accelerate the so-called 'statification' of organized labour by administrative decree. Sapronov, speaking for the same group, bitterly condemned Trotsky's use of political departments, modelled on the political commissariats in the army, to replace established party organs.[45]

Equally vigorous criticism came from the scholarly Ryazanov, who hotly repudiated Trotsky's presumed identity of interest between the unions and the state. A misguided emphasis on inequality, he submitted, would have the inevitable consequence of creating a new labour aristocracy of worker-heroes.[46] Lutovinov, representing the nascent Workers' Opposition, took a similarly reproachful line and demanded that the party adhere to its formal programme. The trade unions, he suggested, should assume sole responsibility for economic administration. Each union should be in charge of its own branch of industry with the central union council answering for industry as a whole.[47]

In a report devoted explicitly to the unions Bukharin answered the dissidents by asserting that the process of statification was already under way. True the unions did not directly control production; but they would gradually impregnate the machinery of economic management by sending their representatives to all discussions of policy and by putting forward candidates for the various economic organs. Conceding that managerial personnel should only be selected after consultation with union officers, Bukharin nevertheless insisted that the unions must be militarized in order to ensure 'order and discipline, accuracy and responsibility'.[48]Sharing Trotsky's assessment of Russia's position, in his major work of this period Bukharin wrote:

In the initial stages of development, when the proletariat inherits a badly damaged material, mechanical and technical framework, living labour power takes on a special significance. Hence the transition to a system of universal labour service . . . is an imperative need. The creation of a collectively functioning, living, mass productive force is the starting point for further work.[49]

The chief weakness of the party's more libertarian factions was their inability to establish a common cause with the second major group of Trotsky's critics. These were the new Soviet bureaucrats whose autonomy had been threatened by the ambitions of the War Department. A particular source of resentment had been

Trotsky's numerous attacks during recent months on the over-centralization and consequent ineffectuality of Vesenkha. In one instance Trotsky wrote that:

Centralism consists of the fact that the centre sends special plenipotentiaries here [to the Urals] with unlimited rights. But they have no connection with the centre. Only the creation of strong, permanent *oblast* (regional) centres with broad powers will be able to surmount the chaos.[50]

Reorganization at the local level was to be combined with reforms in the central administration. In January Trotsky had proposed that a new central planning agency be created by allotting many of Vesenkha's remaining responsibilities to the Council of Defence, the chief supply organ of the army. Two months later the proposal had been accepted. A new Council of Labour and Defence which formalized Vesenkha's decline had resulted. At the party congress Trotsky planned to consolidate these arrangements. The soviets of the six labour armies which were then functioning were to be transformed into *oblast* economic bureaux. Representatives of the central ministries were to have seats on these new councils, where they could be closely supervised by Trotsky's subordinates. Not unexpectedly a new chorus of opposition arose.

Before the congress Rykov, chairman of Vesenkha, and Milyutin, one of his deputies, had announced that they would dispute the proposal. In his speech to the party gathering Milyutin offered a compromise. 'I am convinced,' he declared, 'that the military character of our economy must be maintained despite the fact that the counter-revolution has been defeated and despite the peace we have achieved.'[51] More normal procedures could not prevail until after the socialist revolution had taken place in an international context. In the meantime he made a subtle attempt to gain trade union support by agreeing with earlier calls for collegial management. The strategy was doomed, however, for it was too obvious that the collegiate Milyutin had in mind was exclusively that of the central commissariats. When Lenin entered the debate he promptly denounced Vesenkha's attempt to form 'a separate bloc of the economic commissariats', which would be detached from the military department. With Lenin's approval the congress endorsed Trotsky's recommendations.

Leaving these administrative hurdles behind, Trotsky was convinced that the way was now clear for practical work. Since the transport industry was the main bottleneck he believed reconstruction should begin with the mass production of locomotive spare parts, in preparation for the eventual manufacture of complete units. The revolution had cleared away 'much that was routine and musty'. The country was making a clean beginning. Even so, the new Russia would resemble the old in at least one significant aspect: continuing to enjoy the benefits of economic backwardness it could base production from the outset on latest technological data. Only a single, final effort was needed to set the process in motion. The influence of *Results and Prospects* was not difficult to discern when Trotsky predicted: 'After we have gathered certain supplies and overcome our miserable poverty we will be able to leap over a whole series of intermediate stages.'[52]

To the rank-and-file party member it seemed that Trotsky's control over economic policy had become virtually complete. But this state of affairs could only last so long as the debate was not brought around to first principles; that is, to the fundamental problem of Russia's continuing isolation from the West. Rykov, a frequent victim of Trotsky's invective, was the first to perceive this critical connection and to understand that Trotsky's position depended on his central assumption of a prolonged separation from Europe. Confident that he had discovered a decisive weakness, the Vesenkha chairman vigorously denounced Trotsky's four stages of planning on the grounds that they had failed to consider the expansion of foreign trade that would soon result from international socialism; they had completely ignored the international revolution. As a result Trotsky was said to have produced a purely fictional theory of 'an isolated, segregated economy', which in turn led to the preposterous deduction that Russia should undertake to build her own machinery and equipment. In fact, Rykov claimed, Russia had always imported up to seventy per cent of her capital goods. The country possessed neither the machinery nor the skilled labour to meet its own heavy industrial requirements. To realize such a scheme would require decades, and it was apparent that the international revolution would take place before then.[53]

In its initial form Rykov's challenge suffered because his alternative to labour mobilization was merely hypothetical. It was not long, however, before Rykov recognized the need to modify the critique slightly. When the revolution did not take place in

Europe he began to urge that the only possible alternative was to restore Russia's ties with the capitalist world. His speech at the Ninth Party Congress was perhaps the most decisive event of the entire meeting. It was instrumental in reversing party assumptions and in setting in motion a new integrationist pattern of thought, which quickly undermined Trotsky's entire position.

Reserving this subject for more detailed discussion later, at this point we should note that Trotsky was swift to discern the implications of the threats. He responded by asserting that the capitalists would most probably soon restore the blockade: 'the possibility cannot be excluded that with the victory of the counter-revolution in Germany there will be a restoration of the blockade and new rabid efforts on the part of a dying imperialism. These efforts may last several years.'[54] Russia would perish in the interval unless locomotives could be manufactured domestically. Similarly, in *Terrorism and Communism* Trotsky denied that he had intended to create 'a narrow "national" communism'. If the blockade were raised the plan would be radically altered:

But we do not know when these events will take place; and we must act in such a way that we can hold out and become stronger under the most unfavourable circumstances – that is to say, in face of the slowest conceivable development of the European and world revolution.[55]

Trotsky's ambitious projects had seemed to be the very embodiment of revolutionary defiance. Rykov destroyed the image by pointing out that it was rooted in the deepest pessimism and based upon fixed assumptions in a changing world. As the hope of restoring trade grew it became increasingly obvious that Trotsky's persistence was the result of a closed mind. However, his opponents stood no chance of success, until they could discredit the War Commissar's policies in Lenin's eyes. For this purpose they needed a practical political issue, an issue which would unite the trade unionists, their sympathizers, and the economic administrators on a common platform. In the months following the congress they soon found one in Trotsky's management of the transport industry.

The crisis in the transport industry

Of all the trade unions those in the transport industry had consistently been the most unresponsive to party orders. A first attempt to mobilize the rail and water workers had taken place in January 1919. A year later a second decree had been issued with the same objective, but the unions continued to assert their independence. Since the Council of People's Commissars had already stated that the Commissar of Transport should exercise 'dictatorial powers', Lenin judged that Trotsky was suited for the office. In March 1920 he requested the War Commissar to put the industry in order.

Trotsky's first reaction was to attribute the industry's deterioration largely to the workers' attitude of 'shop narrowness'. To sharpen their political consciousness he created new directing organs. The first of these, Glavpolitput, was designed to distribute cadres of organizers throughout the country. This was done with such disregard for the unions that Osinsky asked whether Trotsky intended to dispense with the unions entirely, replacing them with political departments. In August Glavpolitput was joined by Tsektran, a new Central Committee of Rail and Water Workers. The union leaders who had obstructed Trotsky's designs were removed, and their more compliant colleagues accepted the Commissar of War as nominal head of the union. As a test case of 'statification' the experiment was unlikely to induce restraint. The slogan had normally been taken to mean that the unions would gradually absorb management. At the first opportunity Trotsky had inverted its meaning; the workers' organization had been swallowed by the state.

The general atmosphere of dissent on the railways reflected physical disintegration. On 9 April Trotsky declared that Russia's prime need was peace so that all efforts might be concentrated on the labour front. Two weeks later Poland invaded the Ukraine. Although Lenin and other party leaders looked upon victory over Poland as providing a bridge to Germany and Europe, Trotsky did not share their enthusiasm. The failure of an attempted Soviet counter-attack on Warsaw strengthened his conviction that a small, well equipped Allied force would shatter the Red Army on European territory. It was hopeless to try to spark the revolution abroad by military means. In desperation he threatened to appeal to the party rank-and-file if the Central Committee persisted in armed adventures.

The Polish war dealt the final blow to Russia's already shattered transportation network. Nine thousand six hundred locomotives out of a total stock of sixteen thousand were inoperative.

Working with Vesenkha, the Transport Department sought to cope with the emergency by drafting a repair plan known as Order No. 1042, and covering the period up to 1925. Even in this time-scale Trotsky refused to count upon outside aid. 'All this,' he remarked, 'is hypothetical, and in our plan all assumptions, conjectures, and hopes are excluded.'[56] Several party leaders did not agree. In their view the latest catastrophe had caused Trotsky's demands to become more erratic than ever.

Order No. 1042 was to be the first link in a systematic plan which would rapidly come to embrace all the central government departments. The locomotive repair plan was to be integrated with a food plan, a plan for the production of freight cars, another for track repairs, and still another for the utilization of rolling stock. These, in turn, would be accompanied by a plan for parts production. Industrial parts were to be restricted to a minimum assortment, guaranteeing long production runs and interchangeability.[57] Standardization, Trotsky believed, would shortly become the hallmark of socialist production. Locomotives would be constructed 'simply by way of assembling the component parts already prepared' in a selected group of shock-work industries. Through the interrelation and correlation of all these partial plans a general plan was to emerge. Bold organizational initiatives would overcome Vesenkha's bureaucratic incompetence.

In his zeal to salvage socialist Russia from an apparently hopeless situation Trotsky assumed too much. In particular he placed excessive confidence in the bonds of party loyalty and discipline. By the summer of 1920, through his preoccupation with abstractions and wilful indifference to elementary human relations, he had made countless political enemies. Disenchantment had spread from the party's peripheral factions into the main policy-making bodies. Rykov had recently been elected to the Central committee. A further threat came from Zinoviev, who as party chieftan in Petrograd was by this time seeking to undermine Trotsky's control over the Baltic fleet. When the Ninth Party Conference gathered late in September 1920 this personal vendetta suddenly took the form of a concerted attack.

Less than six months had passed since the War Commissar presented the party with his blueprint for socialism. Now Zinoviev dramatically reversed each of Trotsky's earlier recommendations. The exacting demands raised by the system of *udarnost'*

could not be continued; the principle of priority had to give way
to the principle of equality. Although the system of *udarnost'* had
hardly been Trotsky's personal invention, Zinoviev left no doubt
where the responsibility for recent hardships should be placed.
He spoke as if he had made a new discovery when he commented
that 'we still do not have full equality in the country or full
equality in the party'. The shock groups, the system of 'appointments' to theoretically elective positions, the suppression of criticism, the system of premia and bonuses: all of these, he declared,
had contributed to disaffection and sagging enthusiasm in the
ranks of the working class. Trotsky had repeatedly stressed that
the ability to effect rapid changes in the distribution of the labour
force was vitally important; Zinoviev proposed that 'each responsible worker should be attached to a definite cell'. It was no
longer possible to throw people 'today to one place, and tomorrow to another'.[58]

The protest found a receptive audience. A resolution passed
by the conference noted that the creation of 'shock-work (and
in fact privileged) departments and groups of workers' had been
necessary during the civil war. But conditions were changing,
giving rise to 'the necessity of directing the party's attention time
and again to the struggle for the realization of greater equality . . . within the party . . . within the proletariat, and . . .
amongst the entire labouring masses'. Special efforts were to be
devoted to the achievement of greater equality in the relation
between 'specialists' and the population at large. The conference
added that 'appointments' to elective posts should be discon-
tinued in favour of 'recommendations'.[59] The most sensational
case of appointments had occurred with the creation of Tsektran.
In effect the conference resolution directly repudiated the decisions of the previous congress. Once under way the challenge
rapidly gained momentum. In the same month a plenary meeting of the Central Committee decided on more specific measures.
The political departments in the transport industry were to be dismantled and absorbed into the regular trade union machinery.

A split had at last opened up in the party leadership. A.
Andreev, one of Trotsky's supporters in the trade unions, rushed
to the defence of *udarnost'*:

We are compelled to select the weakest and most important points of our
economic front and to direct our blows there. Today we have liquidated the

danger on one part of the front; tomorrow we will shift our forces to another part, and so forth. Today we are forcefully supplying one branch [of industry] with a labour force at the expense of another . . . tomorrow we will make a new distribution in accordance with the changing tasks.[60]

Andreev's article appeared in *Vestnik Truda*. The following issue of the same journal carried a systematic refutation by Lutovinov. Arguing that *udarnost'* ignored the connections between the various sectors of the economy, the spokesman for the Workers' Opposition demanded a simultaneous advance along a broad front. The goal must be 'equality of the unions' and 'equally distributed forces for the fulfilment of all tasks'. The basic difficulty, according to Lutovinov, was that the trade unions had been cut off from the healthy influence of the masses. In their frustration they had resorted to repression and Tsektranism: 'The old methods of educating the broad masses by way of agitation and propaganda are being replaced by circulars and orders.'[61]

The criticisms appeared even more timely when a provisional peace was signed with Poland on 12 October. With a national trade union conference scheduled to convene at the beginning of November, Lenin again prepared to make concessions. In a draft resolution he called for an end to the 'disproportionate growth' of Tsektran and a reversion to methods involving 'a broader application of democracy [and] the promotion of initiative'.[62] While the full conference adopted an innocuous set of theses prepared by Rudzutak, the party fraction took a tougher stand:

A most energetic and planned struggle is necessary against the degeneration of centralism and militarized forms of work into bureaucratism, petty tyranny, red-tapism, and small-minded tutelage over the trade unions . . . as for Tsektran, the time for special methods of management . . . is beginning to pass.[63]

Trotsky's reaction to these decisions was singularly indiscreet. Instead of following Lenin's lead he bitterly condemned Tomsky, head of the trade unions, and demanded a 'shake-up' of the union hierarchy. Since the inappropriate term 'shake-up' was subsequently misinterpreted to mean an attack on the unions as such, its implications should be clarified. Trotsky intended to complete the process of statification by patterning the entire trade union movement on Tsektran, with an interpenetration of personnel in the government departments and organized labour. When the charge that Tsektran was not democratic was raised, he facetiously suggested that the elective principle should be more consistently applied at the lower levels. Union officials, who in theory had been elected, were to be co-opted into the machinery of management. In a similar manner specialists and administrators were to be appointed to trade union offices. The two structures would thus be combined by placing the same individuals in charge of both labour and managerial functions.[64] At the same time the existing union officials were to be 'tested', for 'many of them were perfectly suited for the old organizational struggle, for leading strikes and battles on the barricades; but not all of them, by virtue of their qualifications, can be suitable for the organization of transport as such'.[65] What was true of transport applied equally to other industries. Trotsky's sense of self-righteousness was reinforced by a belief that he had been betrayed. As he commented a few weeks later:

With respect to ... Glavpolitput people say: look – they are making appointments, they are giving orders, they are frightening us. In response to a critical situation in the country's transport an exceptional temporary organ is created to salvage the industry. This exceptional organ proceeds with its work and then comrades come and announce that it is implementing the militarization of labour, that the exceptional organ is behaving exceptionally. But you see, it acts this way because it is an exceptional organ.[66]

At a Central Committee meeting on 9 November Lenin and Trotsky submitted rival theses. Trotsky generalized his proposals for Tsektran, arguing that organizers, specialists and administrators throughout the country should take over trade union offices. On the question of 'workers' democracy' he maintained that less militarized forms of work would have to be postponed. The psychology of the workers had to be remoulded; and if other means failed the transformation must be effected by administrative appointments.[67] Ignoring the decisions of the recent party conference, he pointed out that continued recourse to organs such as Glavpolitput might be necessary. In more general terms the need for *udarnost'* was said to flow inevitably from existing conditions. Lenin's call for 'equalization' was a political slogan, not an economic programme. In a subsequent address to Tsektran Trotsky renewed the demand for a 'surgical intervention' in the trade unions.[68]

Lenin reacted violently to the challenge, later admitting that he had made a number of exaggerated and even mistaken attacks. But because Lenin's own about-face had been so unexpected he failed to carry with him a majority of the party leadership. Ten members out of a total of twenty refused to take sides. The uncommitted faction, led by Bukharin and Preobrazhensky, formed a 'buffer group' in an attempt to reach an amicable settlement. Lenin's intended report on the meeting was cancelled. Instead Zinoviev was instructed to give the trade unionists a 'business-like and non-controversial' exposition of party policy, disguising the existing differences of opinion. Lenin was only partially mollified. A resolution taken on 9 November called upon Tsektran 'to strengthen and develop the normal methods of proletarian democracy'. *Udarnost'* was to be retained with respect to economic planning; but it was to be combined with an 'unwavering transition to equalization'.

To ensure that the issue was shelved a special committee was created under the direction of Zinoviev and charged with exploring the matter further. As far as Trotsky's projected role is concerned there is some confusion. His own account suggested that Lenin wished to exclude him entirely. Whatever the case, when later asked to serve he refused. With Zinoviev as the only member authorized to speak on the committee's behalf the manoeuvre was obviously designed to gag Lenin's opponents.[69]

In the immediate aftermath of the meeting the attempt to suffocate the debate gave the impression of succeeding. Trotsky was sent off to the Donbas as head of a special commission appointed to investigate a series of strikes caused by shortages of food and shoes. But the sojourn away from the capital did not have the desired result. Trotsky returned with the emphatic recommendation that the full panoply of shock-work techniques be applied, otherwise it would be impossible to forestall a complete cessation of coal and metal production. The mine and metal workers' unions should be strengthened by drawing upon labour and organizers from other parts of the country, especially from the military cadres; the Donbas labour army and political department should be reconstituted; the area should be accorded a privileged status in terms of food and equipment supplies.

The disagreement reached a climax when the extent of the divisions in the Central Committee became public knowledge. Trotsky's opponents in the transport industry decided that this was an opportune moment to renew their struggle. Late in November a bitter dispute broke out between Tsektran and the water workers. Anticipating further complications, on 30 November Trotsky wrote to the Politburo that 'under no circumstances' could the political department in charge of water transportation be dissolved during the coming two to three months.[70] Nevertheless, when the Central Committee convened early in December a resolution was carried demanding that the hated supervisory organs be immediately dismantled. The two sides were almost evenly balanced. In addition seven members of the Central Committee, headed by Rykov and Zinoviev, prescribed either personnel changes in Tsektran, or even better, its complete abolition. By aligning himself with the remaining seven members present Trotsky was able to secure what appeared to be a dubious compromise: new elections were to be held for Tsektran in February of the coming year.

From the standpoint of labour policy the transition to the New Economic Policy began with these decisions. The human and organizational consequences of Trotsky's policies had finally been repudiated. More important, as will be discussed in the following chapter, his isolationist assumptions had been discredited too. In large measure the NEP was a derivative of this fact, an outgrowth of the integrationist alternative to which Rykov had vaguely alluded at the Ninth Party Congress.

The reversals of policy and the underlying changes of attitude which had brought them about should have indicated to Trotsky the need to assume a less exposed position. By the end of December 1920 that option was closed: the possibility Lenin had dreaded at last materialized. The debate could no longer be confined within the higher echelons of the party but burst into the open in the form of an abusive public wrangle. In the face of mounting accusations Trotsky had no choice but to defend himself. At first he sought to simplify the conflict, suggesting that it might be resolved by a concise arithmetical formula. From one-third to one-half of the members of Vesenkha should be given seats on the Central Trade Union Council and *vice-versa*, a policy which he summarized by the term 'coalescence' (*srashchivanie*).[71] Hoping that this new term would prove more acceptable than 'statification', he believed that through coalescence at all levels of administration the existing enmities would evaporate. Engaged in the continuing search for an organizational panacea he failed to understand the enormity of the issues at stake.

He infuriated Lenin when he continued to make provocative comments in the press and at public meetings while still refusing to serve on the Zinoviev committee. Such behaviour, Lenin charged, was 'bureaucratic, un-soviet, un-socialist, incorrect, and politically harmful'. The last concern was the most significant one, and Lenin warned that 'the best thing to do about "coalescence" right now is to keep quiet. Speech is silver, but silence is golden. Why so? It is because we have got down to coalescing in practice.'[72]

Lenin hoped to maintain many of the stringent features of Trotsky's programme but to do so surreptitiously. As late as January 1921 he personally engineered a Central Committee resolution condemning agitation against the remaining political commissars on the railways. On another occasion he admitted that his personal dispute with Trotsky had 'nothing to do with general principles'.[73] His real worry was not Trotsky's authoritarianism, but the clamour being raised by the Workers' Opposition under Shlyapnikov. Every statement made by Trotsky served to incite a more violent demand from the left until the inflationary spiral of ultimata culminated in the proposition that exclusive control over the selection of economic managers should be vested in the trade unions. Even worse, in their endeavour to build a bridge between the two extremes Bukharin, Preobrazhensky and the buffer group temporarily found themselves tugged in the same direction. A full-scale return to the anarchy of 1917–18 appeared to be in the offing. Lenin contemplated the outcome of such a disaster with horror. 'All this syndicalist nonsense,' he insisted, '. . . must go into the wastepaper basket.'[74] The unions were being presumptuous in seeing themselves as anything more than 'a school of communism'.

The latter suggestion provoked a sneer of astonishment from Alexandra Kollontai, Shlyapnikov's mistress and the most articulate leader of the Workers' Opposition. Ridiculing Lenin's unexpected manifestation of pedagogic proclivities she presented a resounding case for doing away with Vesenkha altogether. Its departments, she claimed, were anti-proletarian, subversive nests of former capitalist directors. Her solution was 'freedom for the manifestation of class-creative abilities, not restricted and crippled by the bureaucratic machine, which is saturated with the routine spirit of the bourgeois system of production and control'.[75] Trotsky was at least given credit for his frankness; he openly avowed that he planned to educate the workers with a club.

Notwithstanding a deluge of pamphlets and speeches the respective positions did not substantially alter until the eve of the Tenth Party Congress, in March 1921. Shortly before the meeting the buffer group gave its support to Trotsky and abandoned the hopeless attempt at mediation. For all the shrillness of the preceding encounters, however, the debates at the congress constituted a vacuous anticlimax. The attention of the entire party was suddenly diverted from labour issues by a staggering disaster. At Kronstadt, Petrograd's fortress of the revolution, the sailors rebelled against the Bolshevik regime. A further call from Trotsky for discipline would have been fatuous. With his attention riveted on the resurgent threat of anarchism he delivered his speech in a perfunctory manner. The local party delegates endorsed Lenin's position and the controversy which had lasted for more than a year terminated in a murmur.

Immediately after Trotsky's defeat the futility of his actions became apparent. Through Lenin's caution, not to say duplicity, the prestige of the Central Committee was rescued at Trotsky's expense. Collective responsibility for past decisions was evaded by tacitly attributing to one man policies previously endorsed by the entire party leadership. Tsektran was fully restored, and by October 1921 the controversial political departments were reconstituted as well. The trade unions were brought under control by means of administrative appointments, and the Workers' Opposition were dispersed and rendered politically harmless through transfers.

The whole affair was brought to a final ironical conclusion with the introduction of the NEP in the spring and summer of 1921. One of the major causes of the change was completely extraneous to the question of labour mobilization or *udarnost'*. Since 1913 cultivated acreage had been declining. In February 1920 Trotsky had proposed that the trend might be reversed by means of a system of economic incentives analogous to those used in industry. Instead of compulsory grain requisitions the peasants were to be supplied with consumer goods in return for delivery of a tax in kind to the state.[76] Because adequate supplies of manu-

factured goods could not be provided, the measure had been rejected by the Central Committee. At the end of the year special
sowing committees were created to force the peasant to provide
for more than his own needs. When this last palliative failed,
Lenin revived the idea of a tax in kind and decided that industrial production should be concentrated on commodities for the
rural market.

During the summer of 1921 numerous small enterprises were
leased to co-operatives and private entrepreneurs, who might
sustain operations by drawing upon local supplies of food, fuel,
and materials. In July Lenin was worried that from one-half to
four-fifths of industry might be unable to continue functioning
under government control. When the tax in kind yielded even less
grain than forced requisitioning, subsidies were limited to the so-
called 'commanding heights' of the economy. The larger enterprises were removed from the direct supervision of Vesenkha and
grouped into trusts. Collective wage agreements were restored,
and the trusts were transferred to a commercial footing, buying
and selling on the market in place of the abandoned system of
centralized supply. Subsequent attempts to rationalize production
resulted in a reduced work force and unemployment. The *raison
d'être* for labour mobilization vanished. On at least two occasions in 1921 peasant labour was conscripted. But by the end of
the year the concepts of labour armies and labour service passed
into history. With them went the last vestiges of War Communism as an economic system.

The significance of Isolationism in Trotsky's thought

According to Lenin, Trotsky's conduct during this period (as
well as his later insistence upon economic planning) was caused
by 'excessive self-confidence' and a 'disposition to be too much
attracted to the administrative aspect of affairs'.[77] As a personality
assessment this appraisal was accurate. An insight into the rationale behind many of Trotsky's decisions can be found in his
basically nineteenth-century philosophy of administration:

I consider that in all areas of life and creative work certain common
methods are applied . . . in the area of administration a good administrator of a factory or plant will also be a good military administrator. The
methods of administration, in general and on the whole are identical.
Human logic is applied in much the same way in the military field as in

others: accuracy, persistence, these are qualities necessary to any field where people wish to build, to create, to learn.[78]

But if the evidence presented in these pages is considered as a whole, it will be clear that the most decisive factor influencing Trotsky's judgement was Russia's isolation from Europe. The strategy of *udarnost'* was an attempt to concentrate scarce resources in a series of bottlenecks which could not be widened through imports of commodities, materials, and equipment. Trotsky's theoretical interpretation of imperialism convinced him that aid from Europe would not be forthcoming. He hoped that an economic plan, conceived first in terms of labour inputs and later in more complex forms, would facilitate a more stable pattern of growth. By the end of 1920 one of the key words in his discussions of planning policy became 'proportionality', meaning the ability of industry to satisfy its own needs and those of agriculture (and the reverse). The object of the plan would be to establish the necessary proportionality in the different departments and different branches of the economy.[79] *Udarnost'* was necessary because: 'We cannot establish this proportionality by way of competition, by way of supply and demand on the free market.'[80] In practice proportionality meant an approach to self-sufficiency. In 1930 Trotsky denied that this was the case. In his *History of the Russian Revolution* he limited discussion of War Communism to the following comment: 'The policy of so-called "War Communism" . . . was not based upon the idea of building a socialist society within the national boundaries. Only the Mensheviks, making fun of the Soviet power, attributed such plans to it.'[81]

Despite Trotsky's later disavowal of his policies they were by no means irrational. Once protracted isolation was assumed the idea of substituting labour for capital followed with a degree of inevitability. Like his contemporaries Trotsky exaggerated the physical destruction of Russia's capital equipment. But until idle industrial plant could be brought back into operation it was perfectly sensible to treat labour as a 'free' factor of production and to apply it on the most extensive possible basis. Soviet industrialization during the 1930s was founded on lavish expenditures of labour power, possible because surplus rural population could be taken from the land without substantially altering potential agricultural productivity.

The system of *udarnost'* was no less logical, at least in theory. The bottleneck approach to economic development, emphasizing the importance of promoting forward and backward linkages with the key growth sectors, finds persuasive advocates to the present day. For Trotsky these linkages meant 'proportionality'. If he erred it was because scarcities were too pervasive for the speed of recovery he anticipated. In Russia's unusual condition *udarnost'* was likely to perpetuate a crisis situation by underrating the importance of industries producing inputs for the priority sectors and processing their final products. On the other hand, *udarnost'* was a matter of degree. There could be greater and lesser priorities. Stalin's later concentration on heavy industry was a strategy of *udarnost'* on a grand scale. By the mid-1920s however, Trotsky recognized the need for a more balanced pattern of development in order to preserve economic relations with the peasantry. Similarly, he eventually became aware of the incompatibility of a 'command economy' with local initiative. In exile he called for a more flexible variety of socialism, based upon interaction between the plan and the market. Stalin ignored the plea, and Soviet planners are still attempting to achieve a satisfactory balance between vertical and horizontal controls and decision-making.

Finally, the influence of *Results and Prospects* should not be neglected. In 1905–6 Trotsky believed that he had established Russia's 'ripeness' for socialism. War Communism constituted a logical endeavour to unify thought with action, to rush headlong into an experiment in social engineering of unprecedented dimensions. By analogy with tsarist Russia's 'leap' into capitalism Trotsky was convinced that socialist Russia would similarly 'leap' into the future. The main impediment, he thought, was not technical backwardness, but traditional socialist commitments to democracy. If these commitments could be overcome a supreme manifestation of human will would launch Russia into a new phase of history.

3
Integrationism and the New Economic Policy

Writing of War Communism a contemporary historian aptly referred to the period as the 'heroic' phase of the Russian revolution.[1] With the advent of the NEP the reckless experimentalism of 1920 quickly gave way to less bizarre if no less imaginative visions of the Soviet future. The military threat receded further into the past, and the pre-eminence of the War Department ended. The search for an escape from Russia's cul-de-sac resulted in a far-reaching reappraisal of the country's domestic as well as its international position.

Adjusting slowly to the changed intellectual and political climate Trotsky found himself out of his element. The decline in his personal influence began even before the crisis in the transport industry and thereafter became steadily more pronounced. The various projected alternatives to labour mobilization all implied the need to reintegrate Russia into the world economy. Pressured by issues and events, Trotsky modified his theory of imperialism. But even his revised estimate of developments in Europe precluded the likelihood of external aid. His reluctance to endorse the new integrationist panaceas subsequently gave rise to an unexpected political rivalry which strongly influenced the entire history of the early 1920s.

The substitution of capital for labour
Besides the immediate political objections to labour mobilization Trotsky's policies were fundamentally at odds with long-established Marxist traditions. In *Capital*, his major economic treatise, Marx had invariably attributed economic growth to capital accumulation and technological innovation. To many party members it seemed that labour mobilization was an anachronistic throwback to pre-modern economic methods. The socialist revolution was to mark man's progress to a higher social order; yet

militarized labour bore a suspicious resemblance to nineteenth-century serfdom. Few denied that extraordinary circumstances required extraordinary measures; but early in 1920 many began to look beyond the current crisis and to suggest more orthodox roads to the socialist future.

The most illustrative expression of this tendency was the excitement engendered by proposals for electrification. In March 1920, only weeks before Trotsky's triumph at the Ninth Party Congress, Krzhizhanovsky published a pamphlet entitled *The Main Tasks of the Electrification of Russia*. In contrast to the programme of labour armies the pamphlet outlined an engineer's dream of a modern industrial country, surging ahead as a result of massive expenditures on power stations. Although Lenin was giving undivided support to Trotsky at the time, he hastened to endorse Krzhizhanovsky's work as well.

In his theses for the Ninth Congress Trotsky appears to have compromised with Lenin's wishes by including a section on electrification. In his oral report, however, he touched on the subject only in passing, revealing his preoccupation with more immediate problems. Compared with the technological mystique of electrification Trotsky's proposals appeared increasingly uninspired and amateur. Lenin's confidence waned. In November 1920 Lenin sent a memorandum to Trotsky urging that a reconstruction plan 'without electrification would amount to nothing; and to discuss "basic tasks" without reference to this plan would not even be serious'.[2]

This initial disagreement was reinforced when Trotsky continued to demand increased authority for the Council of Labour and Defence. In the spring of the year Lenin had clashed with Rykov on this point; but in December he foresook his previous position and assigned the Council 'a very modest role'.[3] Arguing that electrification had become the party's 'second programme', by February 1921 Lenin decided that Krzhizhanovsky's electrification commission (GOELRO) should become the main planning agency.[4] In July Lenin's Politburo notes observed that Trotsky was 'against GOELRO' and wanted 'liberation from the idea of electrification'.[5]

Krzhizhanovsky's ideas were indicative of a general aversion to the notion of substituting labour for capital. No less influential in promoting the new capital-orientation in Soviet thought was

Rykov. Seeing that electrification might require decades to complete, the Vesenkha chairman limited himself to elaborating the benefits of a more modest programme of short-run mechanization. In November 1920 he listed three possible ways in which to expand Russia's productive forces: (1) the number of employed workers might be enlarged; (2) the present work force might be used more productively; or (3) more capital might be put at the disposal of each worker. The first two possibilities, although theoretically feasible, were ruled out because the country was unable to provide even for the numbers of workers already mobilized. Mechanization remained the only possible solution.[6]

The whole question of the relationship between labour and capital was reviewed in December 1920 at a congress of soviets. Here Rykov commented that 'one of the military comrades' had made the 'undoubted error' of confusing the economy with military detachments. Disregarding Trotsky's recent suggestion to militarize the Donbas, he saw no way to restore production in the area except through the import of foreign machinery:

The investigation which we conducted in the Donets region revealed the terrible destruction of all the technical equipment in the coal mines. . . This state of affairs has resulted from the fact that . . . the equipment has traditionally come from abroad. . . We have never made either lamps for the miners, pumps, or electrical installations – all of these items came from Western Europe.[7]

Comparing Trotsky's use of martial law in the Urals to serfdom, Rykov insisted that peasant labour must be replaced by machinery. At the same meeting Lenin stressed the need to introduce more machinery everywhere, and to resort to machine technology as widely as possible.[8]

Krzhizhanovsky took up the same theme, elaborating the dangers of excessive reliance upon manpower. Mobilization was described as a temporary expedient. Sheer numbers were nothing when the capitalists could multiply the productivity of their workers by several horsepower thanks to electrical machinery. 'It would be extremely dangerous,' he warned, 'to overestimate the element of the so-called living force, to count on the fact that the mass of the labouring population in our enormous country might triumph, relying only on its numbers.'[9]

Already emerging as one of Trotsky's most stubborn antagonists, Stalin too noticed the shift in party opinion. In a note to

Lenin he praised Krzhizhanovsky's pamphlet fulsomely as 'a masterly draft of a really unified and truly statesmanlike economic plan'. Turning to Trotsky he abusively added:

You remember . . . [the] 'plan' proposed by Trotsky for the 'economic ressurection' of Russia on the basis of applying the labour of the masses of unskilled peasants and industrial workers to the fragments of pre-war industry. How pitiable! How backward in comparison with the GOELRO plan! A medieval handicraftsman, who considers himself an Ibsen hero, called upon to 'save' Russia.[10]

However attractive the capital-oriented proposals of Rykov and Krzhizhanovsky were, they did not lead to any immediate tangible results. The reason for this was simple; in their attempt to reverse Trotsky's system his critics readily assumed that Russia's return to the world economy would happen as a matter of course. Exports were to be restored, providing the wherewithal to purchase foreign equipment. And capital imports were to be resumed as foreign investors again looked upon Russian investments as a justifiable economic risk. So dramatic was the resurgence in confidence that many actually believed that capitalist countries might be induced to finance Soviet reconstruction. The result was a major revision of the official party line.

Throughout 1920 the prevailing belief had been that capitalism stood on the brink of total and irreversible collapse. The onset of the international revolution was a question of time alone. By the spring of 1921 Lenin offered an entirely different assessment. It would be 'madness', he told the Tenth Party Congress, to assume that the revolution would succeed in the near future in any of the more important countries.[11] A year earlier Trotsky had made a similar forecast. But in the belief that Europe's economic stagnation and decline was imminent he had concluded that Britain and France would be unable to provide the capital equipment Russia required. Now he and Lenin were again led in opposite directions by their respective theories of imperialism. According to Lenin, America and the other capitalist countries were 'growing in economic and military might at a tremendous speed'.[12] Capitalism had proved more durable than originally expected; machinery imports were again possible.

Seeking to bolster their case the integrationists went on to enunciate a plainly contradictory proposition; recovery in the West, although admitted to be under way, could not proceed without Russia's participation. An element of wishful self-deception was evident when Rykov declared that 'the quantity of raw materials which Western Europe [traditionally] received from Russia is so great that without these materials, without Soviet Russia's participation in the restoration of the European economy, the restoration . . . will be impossible'.[13] Lenin concurred:

For the world economy to be restored Russian raw materials must be utilized. You cannot get along without them – that is economically true. It is admitted even by . . . a student of economics who regards things from a purely bourgeois standpoint. That man is Keynes. . .[14]

Thus in view of the apparent interdependence of Russia and the West Lenin proclaimed that 'it would be absolutely ridiculous, fantastic, and utopian to hope that we can achieve complete economic independence'.[15] Only through the import of machinery and other goods would it be possible 'to ensure the continued existence of an isolated socialist republic, surrounded by capitalist enemies'.[16] The same reasoning suggested that the capitalists, in order to acquire access to Russian raw materials, would perceive the need for an economic reconciliation. It seemed obvious that both parties would benefit if foreign investors were permitted to come to Russia, bringing their capital equipment with them to assist in the exploitation of natural resources. Because foreign investments, for doctrinal reasons, could not be allowed to assume the form of private property, leasehold arrangements, or concessions, were to be employed instead.

The idea of concessions had originated with discussions of the Brest Treaty in 1918. After Germany's defeat similar overtures had also been made to the Entente. In February 1919 Chicherin, the Commissar of Foreign Affairs, had even agreed to recognize the tsarist debts if concessions could be arranged in a number of extractive industries. Now Krzhizhanovsky hoped that imports for electrification might be financed by foreign investments in Russia. Similar hopes guided Rykov's mechanization plans:

A real concessions policy [will] attract resources from other countries into the development of Soviet Russia's productive forces and will make it possible to advance in the exploitation of the vast empty spaces of the north and east . . . for which the application of highly developed European and American technology is required.[17]

Rykov saw no contradiction between co-operation with the capitalists and revolutionary principles. When the proletariat came to power in Europe Russia would continue to export mainly raw materials and food, thereby confirming the trade patterns which would have been operating in the meantime.[18] Domestic attempts to restore market relations with the peasantry would also benefit. Lenin urged that prospective concessionaires should be obliged to provide the Soviet government with large quantities of consumer goods.[19] The idea of reintegrating Russia into the world economy inspired fantastic visions of windfall gains. A typical expression of totally unrealistic expectations came from Krasin, the Foreign Trade Commissar:

Foreign concessionaires, having had certain large undertakings in the Urals, Siberia, the Donets area and the northern caucasus put at their disposal, will be able to plunge quickly into these areas with hundreds of train loads of grain, food, clothing, shoes, instruments, and of the necessary supplies of parts and scarce equipment, and will be able to supply the required administrative and technical personnel.[20]

On 23 November 1920 a decree issued by the Council of People's Commissars outlined a tentative juridical framework. A more detailed policy declaration, issued by Vesenkha, cited numerous projects which might be of interest to foreign capital and casually dismissed the idea of a 'self-sufficient' economy.[21]

Irrational enthusiasm was further encouraged by the spectacular conclusion of a trade agreement with Britain in March 1921. When the Tenth Party Congress met in the same month, the belief was widespread that the problem of isolation was at last on the way to solution. In a report dealing with the fate of the Soviet republic in the capitalist encirclement Kamenev explained that Russia faced 'a struggle for the consolidation of communism in one country, and [politically] isolated at that... We never set ourselves the task of building a communist society in one isolated country.' Political isolation, however, did not imply economic isolation:

The division of labour in the world economy developed not by accident, but as a result of a long historical process. The fact cannot be altered that the Russian workers and peasants were the suppliers of raw materials and food for Germany, for England, and for a whole series of other states. For the last three years Europe has tried to manage without these supplies, on its own resources. Now we are arriving at the point where we see that with their own labour, and without the labour of the Russian workers and peasants, without the supplies of raw material, without an alliance with the Soviet republic, they cannot develop their own economy in Europe any further.[22]

The central premise of integrationism, the West's assumed dependence upon Russia, became an official item of party doctrine. Trotsky sat in silence as Kamenev denied that any responsible communist had ever intended to build up socialist Russia, 'without relying on the world economy as a whole, on its inventions, on its materials'.[23]

Immediately after the congress Lenin undertook to fortify the ideological legitimacy of the new programme, claiming that it represented a return to the state capitalist policies of late 1917 and early 1918. Concessions were to become one of many state capitalist elements in a new mixed economy. The argument was tenuously based on the fact that the first months of the revolution had witnessed an attempt to co-operate with private capital through the system of workers' control. The current task, Lenin explained, was 'to find the correct methods of directing the development of capitalism (which is to some extent and for some time inevitable) into the channels of state capitalism, and to determine how we are to hedge it about with restrictions to ensure its transformation into socialism in the near future'.[24] To all but a handful of party theoreticians, most notably Bukharin and Preobrazhensky, these arguments seemed unobjectionable.[25] The circumstances in which the term state capitalism was revived, however, are worth remembering; in 1925 the same slogan played an important part in the dispute over Socialism in One Country.

Although Trotsky made no immediate comment on Lenin's theoretical rationalizations it was clear that he did not share the party's new-found optimism. Socialism had no meaning apart from industry, and he believed that Krzhizhanovsky's dreams of technological revolution were diverting attention from the need for a genuine economic plan. Gosplan, a new state planning agency, was created in February 1921, but its chairmanship went to Krzhizhanovsky. In May Trotsky complained to Lenin that 'the planning commission is more or less a planned negation of the necessity for a practical and business-like plan dealing with the immediate future'.[26] If Krzhizhanovsky were given the chairmanship of Vesenkha as well the needs of industry might be more sympathetically appreciated. Three months later Trotsky again urged that the main task must be 'the restoration and strengthening of large-scale industry'.[27] The current retreat would not have been necessary if a revolution had come in Germany: Russia would have received 'enormous technical, productive, and administrative help'.[28] Retreat was in the air though, and in August Trotsky disavowed the concept of statification for the trade unions. Later he resisted attempts to employ the army for economic work on the grounds that military training would suffer.[29]

On the question of concessions his feelings were less clearly defined. He shared the desire to break out of the blockade and he agreed that areas such as Kamchatka or the far north might safely be leased to foreigners. To trade space for capital in the country's geographic extremities would involve little political risk. Furthermore, foreign investments were preferable to armed intervention: if American capital could be attracted to the Far East, a counter-balance could be created to Japanese militarism.

As in February 1920, however, when the Allies first raised the embargo, he was uneasy. He worried that concessions might be carried too far, that the party might forget that the effect of foreign capital would depend upon the pace of Russia's domestic recovery. If the pressure of European capital were brought to bear at a time of 'protracted collapse' it would be impossible to 'escape the fate of the European colonies'. Ideally concessions had been conceived as a substitute for labour mobilization. But if Russia were reduced to a colonial status a second 'militarization' would take place 'under the Japanese or someone else. We will have nothing to say in the matter. The negroes under the domination of the French do not negotiate: they bleed and they submit.'[30] Occupied Germany had already become a 'concession' of the Entente. Poland was about to suffer the same fate through the more indirect route of financial entanglements.[31] At the very least Trotsky seems to have believed that concessions must be limited to the joint development of natural resources, leaving industry firmly in Soviet hands. The railways were a case in point. As he told the congress of soviets at the end of 1920, temporary leases might be given 'in one place or another which happens to be beyond the reach of our own [economic] abilities; but we shall give our Russian worker–peasant railway network to no-one as a concession'.[32]

Whereas Lenin told the same meeting that economic independence was a fantastic and utopian delusion, Trotsky exclaimed: 'If there is now a single country out of all those not belonging to the gang of victors, which is genuinely independent, which determines its own present and future, that country is worker–peasant Russia.' Answering the familiar complaint that he had minimized the possibility of locomotive imports he protested that he supported the orders being placed abroad and he hoped they would be filled. But it would not be prudent to rely upon them: 'We might not receive [the locomotives] because of new international complications, because of a new onset of madness, which might find expression in a new period of blockade. . . Comrades, none of us possesses the gift of prophecy.'[33] In subsequent months this uniquely negative view of capitalist intentions was strengthened by an important adaptation of Trotsky's theory of imperialism.

The cyclical theory of capitalism's decline

Separated from Lenin by his refusal to believe that Europe would seriously promote Russia's recovery, Trotsky obliquely explained the source of his doubts in a report to the Communist International. Given in June 1921, the report specifically addressed itself to the question of whether capitalism had achieved a new state of equilibrium. The answer to this problem would permit a proper reading of the enemy's behaviour as well as his motives, and would help to determine Russia's most advisable response. Before any conclusion could be reached Trotsky suggested that the concept of equilibrium must be defined more clearly. There were three possible connotations: first, international equilibrium in the world economy; secondly, the rural–urban equilibrium of each country; and finally, equilibrium between light and heavy industry, or between consumption and investment.

Looking first at the rual–urban equilibrium, he pointed to current shortages of meat and grain in Europe. In his theses he attributed the problem to scarcity of labour; depletion of herds; lack of fertilizers; the dearness of manufactured goods; and the peasant's deliberate curtailment of production in response to wartime requisitioning. The resulting rural–urban imbalance was the first obstacle to Europe's complete recovery.

A more consequential inequality was said to prevail between production and consumption and it was leading to a deterioration of capital. Real capital, Trotsky explained, had been displaced during the war by fictitious capital in the form of monetary instruments. Treasury notes, bonds and currency issues had been employed to finance hostilities. The ruthless destruction of commodities resulted in a failure to match real values with paper values and a postponement in investments: 'the war and post-war regimes alike survived and continue to survive at the expense of Europe's productive capital.'[34]

But the most important of the three disequilibria existed on the international level. Before 1913 'the world market . . . had already become inadequate for the development of German, English, and North American capitalism'. Returning to his pre-revolutionary analysis of imperialism Trotsky argued that the productive forces of capitalism were no longer compatible with markets artificially divided into nation-states. A catastrophe had only been averted because the war, through its massive destruction, had cleared the flooded markets of unsaleable goods.

Although complicated by the difficulties of post-war readjustments, the present crisis could only be understood within its international context. Capitalism was a world system: the various countries were economically interdependent; their mutual interconnections found expression in the 'world division of labour and a world exchange of products'. Nevertheless, a momentous change had occurred since 1918. Before the war imperialist expansion tended to free economic forces from the state. But this progressive historical tendency had led to an explosive contradiction, and the world division of labour had now been 'severed at its roots'. Wilsonian involvement in Europe had been replaced by a new onsurge of isolationism: an impassable economic gulf had opened up between Europe and America. As Trotsky observed: 'Europe's purchasing power has shrunk. She has nothing to offer in exchange for American goods. . . While Europe is suffering from anemia, the United States suffers no less today from plethora.'[36]

International balance of payments difficulties had been compounded by the proliferation of tariff barriers within Europe caused by the Versailles Treaty. 'Richer in boundaries and tariff walls than ever before', the continent had been Balkanized. The decline in trade would inevitably riddle the West with needless economic bottlenecks: 'Europe . . . will have to level herself out in accordance with the most backward, i.e. the most ruined areas and branches of industry. This will mean a prolonged levelling out in reverse.'[37] Capitalism's secular decline was a certainty.

Neither the evidence of secular decline, however, nor the cumulative effects of the three disequilibria, guaranteed that the immediate disintegration of the capitalist system was at hand. Recalling Parvus's earlier dispute with Bernstein, Trotsky now superimposed an entirely novel approach upon his previous theory of unilinear collapse. Capitalism, he proclaimed, lived by cycles of booms and crises. Europe's current distress therefore, should not be exaggerated. Cyclical fluctuations would continue to take place; and analysis of the business cycle implied that the West was due for a limited recovery. That much could be conceded to Lenin.

The integrationists were mistaken though when they linked the West's recovery with Russian raw materials. The forthcoming cyclical upturn would be generated not by a restoration of trade, but by purely autonomous factors implicit within the cycle itself. With or without Russia Europe did not face final ruin:

Things are not yet so terrible as to cause European or American imperialism to throw itself at Soviet Russia in seeking salvation from the plight into which capitalism has fallen . . . The situation is still far from being so terrible, and our country . . . is still far too ruined to attract foreign capital on a [sizeable] scale.[38]

Whereas the integrationists had now pre-empted the theory of unilinear colapse (unless Europe was saved by Russia), Trotsky's concern with cyclical phenomena produced less optimistic conclusions. The capitalist countries would be indifferent to Russia's plight until Soviet domestic conditions improved. But Russia's revival, without a large-scale influx of foreign capital and given the NEP retreat, was bound to be languid. On the other hand Europe's own capital shortages would militate against large foreign investments even if the capitalists were so motivated. The integrationists sought to avoid this conundrum by portraying Russia as an enormous natural market for European surpluses of manufactured products. As Krasin wrote in September 1921:

There are now in France, England and America hundreds of thousands of automobiles, hundreds of thousands of tractors, and all sorts of transportation machinery, locomotives, tools, scientific instruments, supplies of iron, steel, etc., for which there is not outlet at all . . . the idea has begun to work itself into the minds of the most far-sighted capitalist leaders that without an economic reconstruction of Russia, there is no possibility of attaining a healthy circulation of the blood of this great world economic organization.[39]

To this argument Trotsky replied that 'the reappearance of Russia on the world market cannot produce any appreciable changes in it in the period immediately ahead.'[40] Krasin had fallen into a *non sequitur*. Russia could not buy for a very obvious reason: the country had been pauperized by civil war and famine. Herbert Hoover, the American Secretary of Commerce, believed that Russia was nothing but a gigantic vacuum. And it was a fact that neither exports nor imports were likely to be of any consequence for several years.[41] Integrationism was founded on spurious premises.

Satisfied that this was the case Trotsky resisted any temptation to convert concessions into another *cause célèbre*. In fact he went out of his way at the Comintern meeting to deny reports in the Social–Democratic press to the effect that the question had divided the Bolshevik leadership. A year later, however, when improved domestic circumstances mitigated the party's self-doubts and permitted a more objective approach, he frankly confessed the reasons for his initial caution:

> If our concessions policy were to grow boundlessly, multiplying and accumulating; if we began leasing ever newer and newer groups of nationalized industrial enterprises; if we began creating concessions in the most important branches of the mining industry or railway transport; if our policy were to continue sliding downwards on the gravity chute of concessions for a number of years, then a time would inevitably arrive, when the degeneration of the economic foundation would bring with it the collapse of the political superstructure.[42]

Having unburdened himself of an imposed silence he went on to reaffirm his belief that collaboration with Russia could not yield the imperialists any immediate economic gains. Russia's return to the world economy would have to be a gradual process: and the country would become an important international factor only over a period of years. Large-scale capital imports were unlikely because the bourgeoisie had been paralyzed by its fear of revolution and was no longer capable of long-range policies. If matters had been otherwise, 'One would then imagine that the English capitalists would try with might and main to invest their funds in Russia; one would then imagine that the French bourgeoisie would orient German technology in this same direction [to ensure reparation payments]... But we see nothing of the sort.'[43]

If Europe had no genuine economic interest in Soviet welfare it followed that recent events must be explained in more sinister terms. Conspiracy was the meaning of attempts being mounted in the West to alleviate the famine. In August 1921 Trotsky alleged that the real objective of the American Relief Administration was to create a counter-revolutionary apparatus.[44] Similarly he linked the All-Russian Committee for Help to the Starving (founded under Prokopovich, a former minister of the Provisional Government) with alleged émigré intrigues. While other Soviet leaders turned to the West for salvation he warned of the danger of new military interventions. In October 1921 he described the coming period as one of surprises and about-turns:

> The ring will contract, there will be new interventions, new military interference, new attacks and new attempts to smother us. And the ring will expand, there will be trade agreements. We are entering upon a long period of struggle.[45]

For the proletariat in the West he foresaw 'rising waves and falling waves. How long this will last is difficult to predict.' Only one thing was certain: the changed conditions in Europe meant that the workers should give up playing at revolution, enter into 'united fronts' with the Social Democrats, and go about the more serious business of forming coalition governments. At least the moderates of the democratic left would not initiate military adventures against Russia.

By reawakening Trotsky's interest in international phenomena the Comintern report made a significant break with the tradition of War Communism. Russia's isolation was now seen within the larger framework of an entire world divided and compartmentalized by regressive forces. Ultimately capitalism's decline would permit more progressive secular tendencies to reassert themselves, restoring the shattered world economy in a new unity. But until that time prophecy was futile: the world had entered a period of anarchy in which the ideals of Versailles conflicted with the march of history. In these circumstances the Soviet state had no option but to wait cautiously until events at home and abroad assumed a more definite pattern. To plead naively for foreign aid might be disastrous. Concessions might become a Trojan horse.

The Trotsky–Sokol'nikov conflict

The emergence of an integrationist consensus within the party did not prevent others from sharing Trotsky's doubts and misgivings. Lenin's notes refer to Bukharin's initial scepticism.[46] Karl

Radek feared that Russia might fall prey to international finance capital, that the proletariat might become little more than 'white negroes'. In his view Lloyd George and the other Entente chieftans were counting on concessionaires to assume leadership of the Russian bourgeoisie.[47] Preobrazhensky feared that the 'unnatural alliance' of a socialist state with foreign capital might break and be replaced by 'a natural alliance between the latter and all the bourgeois forces of Russia'.[48] The criticisms of the minority, however, went unheeded.

Late in 1921 Lenin found a new protégé in the person of Gregory Sokol'nikov, who rapidly distinguished himself as a most outspoken advocate of integrationism. Several years Trotsky's junior, and possessing a doctoral degree in economics, Sokol'nikov was appointed Commissar of Finance early in 1922. In that office he was to succeed in translating the new international outlook into specific policy objectives designed to reinforce the domestic NEP and to establish firm market relations with the peasantry. With unbounded confidence in the future Sokol'nikov maintained that capitalism was 'a giant with feet of clay'. The destruction of Europe was inevitable 'if it is not saved by Russian raw materials'. A perfect spokesman for the new optimism, he assured the party leadership that 'in Germany . . . the common wail of the bourgeois politicians is "Our salvation lies in Russia" '.[49]

To Trotsky such unwarranted enthusiasm was both absurd and hazardous. At the Eleventh Party Conference, in late December 1921, he told the delegates that capitalism would experience limited reconstruction. Europe could look forward to 'real signs of a commercial-industrial upsurge'. Recent events had altered nothing of substance: 'in essence the blockade of Russia is continuing'.[50]

Sokol'nikov, secure in the knowledge of Lenin's complete support, reacted violently to such pessimistic views. Trotsky, he charged, had become so fascinated with data and statistics that he had failed to see the obvious. Europe was in the throes of a universal crisis:

If it is said that an industrial upturn is beginning now, that would mean it is beginning without you and me, that is, without Soviet Russia, without the capitalist world being forced to arrive at an agreement with us. But if the industrial recovery begins without capitalist America and Europe being compelled to establish some kind of agreement with us, that would mean that we are beaten; we are not needed to put the capitalist machine into motion.[51]

Of course, in Sokol'nikov's mind such a possibility was unthinkable. The revolution's funeral oration was premature. His conclusion therefore, was the exact opposite of Trotsky's:

Our point of view is as follows: capitalism is not experiencing any kind of industrial recovery and cannot manage without us. All Europe is crying out about this, and anyone who follows the European press . . . says that France, Germany and England are wailing about the fact that they cannot escape from the economic crisis unless Russia plays a part. . . That is why they are forced to come to an agreement with us.[52]

Behind this outward pomposity Trotsky thought there lurked a capitulationist blank cheque. He reminded the delegates that Sokol'nikov had been the Soviet signatory to the Brest Treaty of 1918. With such an odious training in international affairs, 'he [Sokol'nikov] is an excellent diplomat'. Trotsky then queried the price to be extracted from Russia in return for normalized relations – the Entente would demand the removal of the Comintern, the forfeiture of the Caucasus oil-bearing regions, the disbandment of the Red Army. If these 'small demands' were not met, renewed military intervention could not be ruled out.[53]

This heated exchange in December 1921 was the first of many such arguments between Trotsky and Sokol'nikov. In *Pravda* on 25 December Trotsky claimed that 'the upswing in the industrial *Kon'yunktura* (state of business) signifies that the decay of the capitalist economy and the course of the revolutionary epoch are far more complex than certain simplifiers imagine'. Sokol'nikov was no less obstinate. At the Eleventh Party Congress, in March 1922, he argued that Europe's crisis was continuing; the idea that capitalism might achieve a new equilibrium on its own was preposterous; it ignored reality. In fact 'There is no stabilization, no stability for capitalism in post-war Europe. It would be the purest illusion to claim that there is.'[54] It was clear which prognosis the party wished to hear. Sokol'nikov's ascendancy was formalized by his election to the Central Committee. Trotsky was kept away from economic topics, left to supervise the peacetime operations of the War Department and to nurse his resentment.

Convinced that War Communism had been a perversion of history, Sokol'nikov began to put his views into practice. 'Puritannical isolation' could have only one result: 'a communism of poverty'.[55] Unlike Rykov and Krzhizhanovsky, however, the Finance Commissar was only marginally interested in the import of machinery for industry or technical equipment for electrification. The role he attributed to foreign trade was determined by circumstances which had not been anticipated in 1920. A drought in 1921 had brought with it a catastrophic harvest failure, putting the survival of the regime in jeopardy unless the peasant could be encouraged to produce by a supply of consumer goods. To satisfy the countryside by the circuitous route of restoring domestic industry seemed impossible. Time was of the essence, and Sokol'nikov emphatically demanded that manufactured commodities be acquired from abroad.

The main impediment to trade, he thought, lay in the cumbersome machinery of Vneshtorg, the Foreign Trade Commissariat under Krasin. To improve the dismal record of exports and obtain foreign exchange he proposed to dismantle the bureaucratic monopoly and to replace it with a system of 'mixed companies'. These would be financed by foreign capitalists, working together with the Soviet government, and would be regulated by a system of customs duties. Less direct controls appeared to conform with the dual nature of state capitalism. At the end of 1921 both the Eleventh Party Conference and the Ninth Congress of Soviets approved the measure, calling upon industries and the co-operatives to re-establish their own direct commercial contacts with the West on this basis. The reform stopped halfway in that it allowed Vneshtorg to continue trading operations as well. Nevertheless, the authority of Krasin's department was further reduced in March 1922. In the same month a decree sanctioning mixed companies was issued, thus implementing the recommendations of a committee headed by Sokol'nikov. The policy showed its first signs of success when two such companies enlisted the aid of Dutch and British capital in the timber industry.

Besides financing imports the foreign currency earned through customs revenues was intended to support Russia's own return to a modified gold standard. The switch from grain seizures to a tax in kind had enabled the peasants to dispose of their produce on the market once taxes were paid. It was originally hoped that this process might be confined to 'commodity exchange' on a local scale, barter being less ideologically reprehensible than normal commercial transactions. But the return of itinerant traders (NEP-men) meant the consolidation of traditional capitalist practices. In consequence, the circulation of goods between town and country could not take place without a reliable monetary unit. The peasant would not expand production of grain and industrial materials when the money he received lost its value through rampant inflation before he could spend it. Similarly the system of *khozraschet*, or economic accounting in industry, could only lead to rationalized production if there were a stable unit of account.

Sokol'nikov did not expect that it would be necessary for Russia's currency to be internally convertible into gold or foreign exchange. The psychological effect of a hard currency hoard at the disposal of the state would be adequate for the restoration of domestic confidence. The real rationale for a metallic guarantee sprang from more venturesome objectives and underlined the unity of the Finance Commissar's programme. The capitalists would obviously have nothing to do with the Soviet paper ruble (*sovznak*); and foreign trade would not grow on the basis of barter.[56] Sokol'nikov's supreme ambition therefore, in the tradition of his tsarist predecessors, was to symbolize Russia's renewed stability and credit-worthiness with a currency acceptable on the European bourses. This goal was his personal equivalent of Trotsky's earlier plans for locomotive construction. While it inspired the Finance Commissar to reveries it provoked dismay amongst his critics. Strumilin and Preobrazhensky, who shared neither his integrationist aspirations nor his vision of a hard ruble, treated the fetishism for gold as a luxurious and totally irrational eccentricity.[57]

Sokol'nikov's position on concessions was potentially even more incendiary than his plans for monetary reform. When the programme produced meagre results in 1921, he planned to achieve two major ends at a stroke. By leasing manufacturing industries as well as natural resource deposits he would both reactivate idle factories and reduce the need for inflationary subsidies to support faltering trusts. The suggestion was cleverly framed in order to disarm any opposition. The industries involved were not to be denationalized; they would simply be converted into joint-stock ventures similar to mixed companies. Former owners would be allowed to purchase 'participations', thereby removing one of the final obstacles to an amicable international settlement.[58]

Once the Allied governments were relieved of pressure from their own expropriated citizens Sokol'nikov believed they would pursue self-interest and provide Russia with a substantial loan. In December 1921 a short-lived project had already been broached in the West. This was for the creation of a multi-national consortium, one of whose purposes would be investments in Russia. The plan was later vetoed by Poincaré, but not before it had provided additional 'proof' of the main integrationist thesis that Europe and Russia were interdependent. Assured that the magnitude of the reward would amply justify the risk, the Eleventh Party Congress guardedly accepted the need to admit foreign capital into state enterprises. On the eve of the Genoa Conference, called by the Powers to chart Europe's reconstruction, the energetic Commissar of Finance thus completed Russia's preparations. With the exception of one sensational outburst from Larin, party discipline suppressed domestic disagreements.[59]

Shortly before the meeting at Genoa convened, Lenin declared that the country was about to undergo a new test, 'the test set by the Russian and international market, to which we are subordinated, with which we are connected, and from which we cannot isolate ourselves'.[60] The nature of the test became clearer in April 1922. Having travelled to Italy to explain Russia's conciliatory position, Chicherin agreed to recognize responsibility for the tsarist debts. But a settlement would have to be based on a mutually satisfactory formula: the Soviet government would consider debt recognition only if the Allies granted government credits in return. In a note to Lloyd George, Chicherin stated that Russia was prepared either to restore nationalized property, or where this was impossible to reach a 'mutual agreement' with the former owners – provided financial help was given. In private conversations Litvinov, Chicherin's deputy, appears to have established an acceptable *quid pro quo*. The British would find mutual agreements satisfactory if they could also secure an oil concession for the Royal Dutch group. For a fleeting moment Soviet hopes that Sokol'nikov's forecasts would be substantiated rose. The Belgians and the French, however, with more at risk than the British, would agree to nothing less than complete restitution of nationalized properties. The talks were at an impasse. The Powers refused to grant a loan, and a Russian declaration on 11 May effectively brought the proceedings to an end.

In June a second round of discussions took place at The Hague. Here Litinov presented a precise list of oil fields, mines, chemical and electrical industries and other prospective fields for foreign investments. He even went so far as to drop previous demands and agreed to accept unofficial private credits with government guarantees. In the weeks between the two meetings though, American pressure had persuaded the British to give up their attempt to secure exclusive oil privileges. They too now endorsed the Franco-Belgian position. The Russians' only achievement after both meetings was the Treaty of Rapollo, signed with Germany at Genoa. Apart from aid to the armaments industry Germany was in no position to provide either the kind or the degree of assistance that had been sought.

With the disappointment of the Genoa conference Russia was suddenly thrust once more into a position of exclusive reliance on the domestic economy. Apart from Trotsky none of the most prominent party leaders had even considered the possibility that the conference might terminate in such an utter failure. Overnight the inflated predictions of Rykov, Lenin, Krasin and Sokol'nikov were incontestably refuted. The theoretical fulcrum of a co-ordinated system of domestic and international policies devised by Sokol'nikov vanished. Having oscillated violently between the isolationist extremes of War Communism and the Finance Commissar's single-minded integrationism, the Bolsheviks were now left with only one course. Elements of both orientations would have to be combined in the quest for a viable compromise.

Part two

The politics of economic isolation

4

The search for a new faith

The first three chapters of this book have examined the isolationism of War Communism and the integrationism of the early NEP. These two international outlooks, together with their corresponding systems of policies, provided the economic background for more than half a decade of ensuing political conflict. Although a number of excellent works have been devoted to the political history of the 1920s none have analyzed the material in terms of this economic dichotomy. For that reason none have managed to explain satisfactorily either the origins or the meaning of Trotsky's conflict with Stalin. The justification for interpreting political events in these terms is readily at hand in the Bolsheviks' own belief that 'politics is concentrated economics'. Perhaps the famous dictum would have been more accurate if reversed; that is, if economics had been described as concentrated politics. But the fact remains that the intimate connection between the two spheres of action was never more evident than in the years 1922–8.

The party's age of innocence ended in the spring of 1922. Shortly thereafter Lenin's terminal illness initiated a vicious and protracted contest among his potential successors for total political power. Economic policy emerged almost immediately as one of the main issues in dispute. Lenin had led his followers into the wilderness only to die before he could lead them out. The road to socialism had still to be defined. Confusion bred the desire first for certainty and ultimately for a faith supplemented by force. The confusion originated with Sokol'nikov's failure in 1922 and was only partially reduced by the end of 1924, when Stalin proclaimed the new orthodoxy of Socialism in One Country.

Post-Genoa reassessments
When Sokol'nikov finalized the early NEP he studiously linked integrationism with the restoration of Russia's agricultural

economy. Domestic imbalance was to be redressed by importing consumer goods for the peasant. For a time Soviet industry was to be given an unprecedentedly low priority. Once the Finance Commissar's programme collapsed the government had virtually nothing to offer the rural areas other than official promises of good will. All the preconditions for a return to the internal tensions of War Communism were present: none of the party leaders was immediately prepared to offer an easy solution.

For the moment Sokol'nikov was forced to acknowledge that his plans had suffered a setback and that 'the emphasis now is on our growing stronger internally'.[1] By that he meant continuing with the plan for currency stabilization. In November 1922 he at last succeeded in introducing the first issue of the *chervonets*, a new currency with a gold guarantee. He hoped that foreign confidence in Russia's future might eventually be restored, permitting capital imports through security sales on European markets.[2] Until then, he promised, there would be no capitulation for the sake of foreign credits.[3]

Lenin's disillusionment was more pronounced. In mid-September 1922 he told the Fifth All-Russia Congress of Trade Unions that 'the only road open to us is the long and extremely arduous one of slowly accumulating our savings, of raising taxes in order to be able gradually to repair our destroyed railways, machinery, buildings, *etc.*'[4] In a speech to the Fourth Comintern Congress he claimed that the uproar over concessions was 'not worth much more than the paper it is written on'.[5] Russia, he believed, would now have to recover through her own 'single-handed' efforts.[6] In October 1922 he overruled a Central Committee decision to accept a concession agreement with Leslie Urquhart and the Russo-Asiatic Consolidated Company. Urquhart had demanded compensation for minerals removed during the civil war from the mining sites he had once owned. Lenin refused to accept the precedent.

Trotsky on the other hand, along with Zinoviev and Kamenev, thought Urquhart's offer should be seized. Genoa had established that Russia would not surrender on the questions of debt and nationalization. Trotsky was anxious to demonstrate that in these circumstances he was perfectly prepared to be reasonable. Even before the talks at Genoa ended he agreed that 'separate deals' and 'practical combinations' with individual capitalist interests were quite acceptable.[7] When a preliminary oil concession was granted to an American company in North Sakhalin (currently under the control of Japan), he welcomed the decision as he had said he would. Britain's behaviour at the recent conference suggested that inter-capitalist animosities would discourage a united front. Hoping to exploit these divisions Trotsky considered that Lloyd George might be given the oil concessions he demanded if he would first agree to a 'military-political' settlement.[8]

Although he had become less negative in his approach, the War Commissar still thought of Russia as a 'besieged fortress'; concessionaires could only be admitted if they were realistic enough to accept the prevailing order. If not, the best policy was 'to await a change of humour on the part of the capitalists without becoming unduly nervous'.[9] With or without assistance the construction of socialism would proceed:

When we speak of concessions [and] loans we have in mind accelerating the tempo of our growth and recovery. An influx of foreign capital, of foreign technology, would permit us to surmount the chaos and the poverty more rapidly. To do without them means greater suffering, poverty, and a slower development – that is all! It is within this framework that we conduct negotiations. This is why we did not and will not . . . accept bondage to world capital after it has demonstrated its inability to crush us with its mailed fist.[10]

The concessions programme had failed thus far because 'there is not and will not be any capitulation to capitalism on our part'.[11]

Anxious to complete his reconciliation with the party majority Trotsky also began to realize that the domestic NEP might have some redeeming features. A successful harvest in the autumn of 1922 presented an opportunity to follow Lenin's advice, raising taxes and implementing a programme of 'primitive socialist accumulation'. The incipient capitalists within the country, in particular the *kulaks* (wealthy peasants) and the NEP-men, might be forced to subsidize socialist industry. If the market were properly directed and controlled it might even provide a rational guide for investment decisions. *Udarnost'* could only effect violent adjustments determined by bottlenecks and military necessity. But the data resulting from uniform industrial accounting would make it possible to ascertain the most efficient enterprises and to concentrate production there. Cost reductions could be achieved through standardization; the principle of priority could be projected into the market context.[12]

The NEP could only be transformed into a path toward socialism, however, if it were subordinated to a plan. In February 1922 Trotsky wrote to Lenin insisting that the system of *khozraschet* must be completed by means of centrally organized book-keeping.[13] Early in May his complaints again provoked Lenin to deny that Gosplan, through its non-involvement in day-to-day industrial administration, suffered from 'academic methods'.[14]

Trotsky's stubborn devotion to the needs of industry inevitably boded ill for his relations with Sokol'nikov. In the spring of 1922 industry had experienced a period of severe capital consumption known as the *razbazarivanie*, or 'auctioning off'. As a result of the previous year's crop failure the majority of the peasants were unable to purchase manufactured goods. Seeking to preserve a market, the trusts depleted their assets in a series of price reductions. Later in 1922 marketing was concentrated in the hands of syndicates and prices were stabilized. The successful harvest of 1922 reversed the situation, creating a seller's market or 'goods famine', and enabling the syndicates to drive up industrial prices. But because factories were working at substantially less than full capacity, costs were abnormally high and the losses continued. Sokol'nikov remained almost oblivious to the crisis, sparing no effort to reduce industrial subsidies in the interests of a stable currency.

There is no doubt that Trotsky understood the importance of monetary restraint if the market were to serve socialism in the manner he proposed. In a little-known speech to a trade union audience in October 1921 he had presented the anti-inflationary case in a tone worthy of the Finance Commissar himself.[15] In the autumn of 1922 he again stressed that 'a market must have a universal equivalent. In our case . . . this universal equivalent [the currency] is in a rather sorry condition'.[16] Even so, the currency question had to be kept in a socialist perspective. Believing that the needs of industry came first, Trotsky protested that Narkomfin (the Finance Commissariat) was wrecking the economy. Gosplan was being denied any control over financial policy. Sokol'nikov was balancing the budget at the cost of 'disorganization, destruction and a further collapse'. Gosplan, not Narkomfin, should be 'directly controlling, connecting, regulating, and directing the economy'.[17] Only the central planning agency could possess the breadth of vision required for such a task.

The Finance Commissar's own vision was said to be so ob-

scured by purely monetary considerations that he was insensitive
to the real factors at work in the economy. Already the harvest
had reached seventy-five per cent of the pre-war norm; the comparable figure for industrial production was twenty-five per cent.
If more suitable proportions were not restored excess peasant purchasing power, in the form of marketable grain, would provide
fertile soil for private enterprise, for 'primitive capitalist accumulation'.

Every economy can exist and grow only provided a certain proportionality
exists between its various sectors. Different branches of industry enter into
specific quantitative and qualitative relations with one another. There must
be a certain proportionality ... a certain correlation of agriculture and
industry.[18]

In reality both Trotsky and Sokol'nikov possessed half of the
truth. The Finance Commissar understood that continued inflation would discourage the peasant from coming to market. He
hoped that real incentives for agriculture could be achieved
through grain exports in exchange for foreign commodities.
Trotsky took the opposite approach, resisting imports of consumer
goods in the interests of industrial protectionism and assuming
that the peasant would tolerate shortages until Soviet industry
expanded production. At the end of 1922 these differences of
opinion led to a decisive altercation concerning the still undecided
fate of the trade monopoly.

Protectionism and planning

The new debate over the trade monopoly began as a purely
economic question, inherited from the past and sparked by the
contrast between War Communism and the integrationism of
the early NEP. It ended by defining the political alignments
which would prevail throughout the initial phase of the struggle
for Lenin's succession. The incompatibility of the two contradictory world views produced its first lastingly important political
consequences.

Among the monopoly's most prominent defenders were two
key groups of industrial protectionists. First there were trade
unionists such as Holtzman, who voiced the fears of a growing
number of unemployed workers. In May and June of 1922
Holtzman alleged that foreign trade was a capitalist plot, that
Europe was posing as Russia's 'friend' in the conviction that an

uncontrolled influx of foreign goods into the Soviet republic would eliminate any chance of independent industrial growth.[19] Shlyapnikov took a similar position, pointing to the folly of importing locomotives, rails, pipes, and other items at a time when Vesenkha was ordering reductions in Soviet production.[20] During 1922 the pathetic disarray of the trusts incited countless appeals on behalf of industry from Larin, Pyatakov, Milyutin, Bogdanov (the new chairman of Vesenkha) and Preobrazhensky. Pyatakov and Preobrazhensky represented the nucleus of a second group which soon emerged as the Trotskyist Opposition.

Trotsky's appreciation of the mechanics of protectionism dated from his analysis of tsarist policy in *Results and Prospects*. If the monopoly were weakened he believed that neither 'proportionality' nor planning would be possible. The planners would be helplessly buffeted by the changing whims of the consumer. 'It is imperative,' he wrote, 'that someone should know and decide what may be imported, what must be exported, and what must be preserved for our own use.'[21] Decisions of this magnitude could not be entrusted to private merchants, to mixed companies, or even to state enterprises; they had to be centrally determined and centrally implemented. The peasant could be provided with inexpensive foreign goods 'only within limits deemed desirable . . . by the workers' state'.[22] Assessing the role of Vneshtorg from the standpoint of planning and production rather than consumption, he was anxious to overcome integrationist prejudice and to institutionalize the distinction between capitalism and socialism with a clear economic frontier.

The original purpose of the trade monopoly, however, had not been to protect Soviet industry, but to concentrate the country's buying power in order to break the blockade and to secure the best possible terms of trade. Sokol'nikov thought Russia would be better served by a system of duties and mixed companies. He explained his position in his book, *State Capitalism and the New Financial Policy*:

The proletarian state represents an economic line which separates the small commodity producer in the depths of Russia from the world market. It stands between him and . . . world capital. It would be . . . incorrect [however] to transform this 'line' into a Chinese Wall, into an impassable barrier in order to prevent the 'overflow' of capitalist relations from the banks of the Atlantic and Pacific Oceans into the peasant ocean of Russian fields.[23]

A clash between these two points of view became unavoidable when Sokol'nikov persisted in his endeavour to undermine Krasin's department. Shortly after the Genoa Conference Krasin complained in a letter to his wife of the difficult 'fuss' that was being raised in Moscow.[24] Encouraged by the Finance Commissar industrial managers and department heads organized a sustained criticism of the remaining quantitative controls over imports. In October 1922 a decree was published by the Council of Peoples' Commissars limiting Vneshtorg to a veto over the independent transactions of a number of central and local organs. The inspiration for the changes clearly came from Sokol'nikov's latest report on the subject to the Central Committee. In his new recommendations the Finance Commissar included 'temporary' permission for traffic in several commodities, across certain frontiers, without any direct regulation. The ports of Petrograd and Novorossiisk were to be freed entirely of Vneshtorg's supervision. The reforms were accepted by a Central Committee resolution of 6 October.

A stroke prevented Lenin's attendance at the meeting. In recent months unemployment and protectionist pressures had caused Lenin to worry that state industry was being dangerously neglected.[25] When he learned of the decision he immediately drafted a letter of protest to Stalin, the party secretary, arguing that customs duties could never provide revenues comparable to those which would come from the monopoly. It was true that Sokol'nikov had described his projects as temporary; but Lenin considered them tantamount to wrecking the monopoly. 'Comrade Sokol'nikov has been trying to get this done and he has succeeded. He has always been for it; he likes paradoxes and has always undertaken to prove that the monopoly is not to our advantage.'[26]

Deserting the Finance Commissar as suddenly as he had once abandoned Trotsky, Lenin circulated his letter among the members of the Central Committee together with Krasin's rebuttal of Sokol'nikov's proposals. This move had little effect: in Lenin's absence lesser men saw an opportunity to assert themselves. Stalin commented that 'Comrade Lenin's letter has not persuaded me that the decision of the Central Committee . . . was wrong.'[27] Zinoviev, Kamenev and Bukharin similarly supported the Finance Commissar. The cabal soon gave birth to an enduring political coalition.

Following Lenin's objection a final decision was postponed until the Central Committee meeting scheduled for mid-December. On 12 December 1922 Trotsky wrote to Lenin offering an alliance. The letter suggested that trade plans should be prepared by Gosplan and executed by Vneshtorg.[28] Lenin replied that apart from minor differences over Gosplan 'You and I are in maximum accord.'[29] He agreed that Trotsky should defend their mutual position. To Krasin's deputy, Frumkin, Lenin wrote that 'the question of the work of Gosplan must be taken separately, although I dare say that it is possible Trotsky and I will have no disagreements if he will limit his demand to the proposal that the work of Gosplan, standing under the banner of state industry, should be to give its opinions on all aspects of the work'.[30]

To avoid the imminent confrontation Lenin wrote to Stalin a second time, taking issue with the various arguments Bukharin had adduced in support of Sokolnikov. Not only would weakening of the monopoly, as suggested, allow private capital to acquire profits which should accrue to state industry; but even worse, Lenin feared industrial recovery would prove to be impossible.[31] Surprised by Lenin's intransigence, the anti-monopoly faction sought to delay the critical meeting until the party leader could attend. Lenin would not hear of the idea. In the final analysis there was no doubt that his will would prevail. Resistance crumbled, and Lenin dictated a letter to Trotsky congratulating him on their victory 'without firing a shot'.[32]

The real significance of the victory was that it had been Lenin's – not Trotsky's. And paradoxically its effect was not to strengthen Trotsky's position in the party leadership, but to weaken it disastrously. The irritating spectacle of the War Commissar plotting to thwart a decision legitimately arrived at by the Central Committee could only confirm suspicions regarding his probable ambitions in the forthcoming struggle for succession. The party's leading collective had been polarized. On the one side stood Trotsky; against him were ranged Bukharin, Sokol'nikov, Zinoviev, Kamenev, and Stalin.

This initial political division took the form of more definite commitments when Lenin suffered a second stroke (soon followed by a third) at the end of 1922. Fearful and envious of Trotsky, Zinoviev and Kamenev joined with Stalin to form a mutual defence pact. On their own, with three votes, the triumvirate could deadlock the Politburo. Supported by Tomsky and Rykov, Trotsky's enemies from an earlier era, they could isolate the War Commissar completely.

If Trotsky had been a more adept politician he might yet either have secured the succession, or at least have delayed his personal eclipse. Even at this early date Stalin was the power behind the triumvirate. Zinoviev was flamboyant and well-known but obtuse. Kamenev, a man of more subtle mind, lacked both will and ambition. From his sick bed Lenin provided Trotsky with the issues which might easily have led to Stalin's ruin. In February 1923 he prepared a devastating critique of the party machinery as it had developed under Stalin's supervision. At Trotsky's insistence the document was published despite an attempt by the other members of the Politburo to suppress it. A shrewder politician would have taken the opportunity to pose as Lenin's faithful disciple, loudly and indignantly condemning such treacherous disloyalty. Trotsky let the chance slip by. On 5 March Lenin again requested that Trotsky serve as his mouthpiece, attacking Stalin's nationality policy. Trotsky remained idle.

Trotsky's ineptitude at this time has produced considerable speculation amongst historians. A false sense of security and disdain for his intellectual inferiors have figured prominently among the explanations offered. It seems more probable, however, that Trotsky's interest in building socialism outweighed his desire for personal power as such. Once the problem of the monopoly had been settled he was anxious to redefine the NEP in larger terms, to reformulate internal policy in the light of long-run socialist objectives. Seeing this weakness the triumvirs deliberately encouraged their rival to think that he would be given a free hand in economic policy in exchange for a political truce. The strategy resulted from a complicated process of bargaining early in 1923. The memory of 1920 was still vivid: then too Trotsky had ignored obvious signs of political difficulty in order to implement measures which he believed were the only ones with any validity.

Now in league with Sokol'nikov, Stalin made the first move by proposing to reshuffle the economic organs thereby enhancing the influence of the Finance Department. The Council of Labour and Defence was to be merged with the collegiate of deputy premiers and representatives from Narkomfin, creating a new, supreme decision-making centre. Both Gosplan and Vesenkha, the two bodies which might logically be expected to favour industrial interests, were excluded from the proposed arrangement. If the plan succeeded Stalin would have the Finance Commissar politically in his pocket; if it failed he had an alternative.

Trotsky immediately protested that the project constituted an organizational expression of the prevailing 'incorrect relationship between finance and industry'. A 'financial dictatorship' would mean a continuing disregard of Soviet industry's capital requirements. The ruble was too unstable to regulate the market in the manner Sokol'nikov intended; Gosplan should stand at the centre of administration. To ensure that its work was practical rather than 'academic', the planning agency should have a joint chairman with Vesenkha.[33] Its decisions should have the force of law.[34] As for the relations between the planners and the Council of Labour and Defence, they should be similar to those between the general staff and the Supreme War Council: when questions of principle were resolved operational decisions should be left to Gosplan.

Confronted with these counter-recommendations Stalin advanced the plot to its second stage. Trotsky had recently been advocating that Gosplan be placed under the aegis of one of the party's political leaders. Since the aim was to give the planners and industry a direct voice in the highest councils, it was not difficult to imagine whom Trotsky would like to see take on this responsibility. At the time each of the deputy premiers assumed nominal control over one or more government departments. Stalin suggested therefore that Trotsky accept the deputy premiership he had twice rejected during 1922. Then he might either exercise trusteeship over or even become chairman of Gosplan or Vesenkha.[35]

Trotsky was left with no acceptable course of action. If he declined the offer he would abandon control of the economy to Sokol'nikov, lose the moral right to criticize, and appear to be nothing more than a loquacious chatterer. The chance to regain some of the influence he had exercised with such apparent zeal during War Communism might be permanently lost. But if he accepted he was certain to earn Lenin's wrath and to jeopardize his recent rapprochement with the stricken party leader. It was well known that Lenin considered Krzhizhanovsky the most appropriate person to administer Gosplan. It was also common knowledge that Lenin thought Trotsky unfit for such a post, fearing that he was too much inclined towards *administratorstvo* (literally, administrator-ism).[36] A more suitable portfolio would be a less controversial one such as Education.[37] In effect Stalin was suggesting that Trotsky gamble on Lenin's death, make the first visible move to divide the spoils, and earn all the opprobrium of a premature pretender. Moreover it was questionable whether a positive response would in any case bring real authority; the triumvirate still controlled the Politburo. In the hope (or fear) that Lenin might yet recover, Trotsky dismissed Stalin's offer.

Had he known the current directions of Lenin's thought Trotsky's decision might not have been so difficult. Disillusioned with Sokol'nikov's interpretation of 'state capitalism' Lenin had already acknowledged that the term must not be interpreted in a 'literal sense'.[38] In a series of notes dating from the end of December 1922 Lenin also expressed the desire to 'move in the direction of comrade Trotsky' by strengthening Gosplan's authority.[39] The planners' decisions were to be binding unless overruled by the highest government bodies. Armed with these documents Trotsky might have confounded his opponents without incurring any personal risk. These notes, however, did not become known until June 1923. Because Lenin had requested (probably to avoid an even more pronounced image of personal inconstancy) that they not be published, Stalin succeeded in having them quietly suppressed.

Following Trotsky's aggressive reaction at the beginning of 1923 Stalin was anxious for a time to avoid exciting too much suspicion. As a 'conciliatory' gesture he apparently encouraged Trotsky to serve as chairman of a committee formed in February to plan industrial policy. Trotsky was to be appeased and hence diverted. Trotsky accepted this offer. He failed to see that his decision would marshall the party into a rigid economic division corresponding exactly to the current political configuration.

Already two schools of thought were crystallizing over whether or not agriculture or industry should play the leading role in the country's recovery. Proceeding from the ambiguous heritage of his earlier integrationism Sokol'nikov took the general position that a rapid increase in industrial production would not be possible until there had first been a sufficient expansion of rural purchasing power. In this view he presently came to be supported by Zinoviev and Kamenev, and later by all Trotsky's enemies. The supporters of industry began with the opposing assumption that a return to War Communism could only be averted if industry could provide the peasant with an increased volume of consumer goods. If the goods famine were allowed to continue, grain and raw material production would again decline despite the favourable harvest of 1922. Ruling out significant imports on protectionist grounds, they believed that Sokol'nikov's plan to stabilize the currency by eliminating subsidies to the trusts would be suicidal. But in their impatience to make good the capital depletion caused by the *razbazarivanie* they failed to notice that the syndicates were now driving prices so high that even the modest volume of goods being produced could not be sold. Rural resistance to soaring industrial prices was causing the market to collapse. If Genoa meant that the country's growth must be predominantly self-contained, in one manner or another these tensions had to be resolved. Hence the appointment of the ill-fated industrial committee.

Once he accepted chairmanship of the committee Trotsky suggested that the trusts be permitted to pledge their fixed assets in exchange for loans of working capital. Credits would be extended to each other, and in default of repayment the weaker trusts would fall into the hands of the stronger, creating more effective vertical combinations.[40] With Stalin casting the deciding vote the measure was rejected. Late in February 1923 the committee was enlarged to include Pyatakov, the deputy chairman of Gosplan and one of Trotsky's loyal supporters. But the balance was overwhelmingly uneven: Rykov, Sokol'nikov, Kamenev, Smilga and Dzerzhinsky, among others, were simultaneously co-opted.[41] None of the latter were at all disposed to support their figurehead chairman. The inevitable result was deadlock.

The committee submitted a final draft of its theses in March. Compromise and indecision were evident throughout. Approval of Sokol'nikov's financial programme was offset by a call for the 'energetic development' of industry. A warning that industry must not lag behind agriculture sat uneasily beside the observation that production was 'in the closest way dependent upon the development of the agricultural economy'. A carefully worded section on Gosplan employed the formulation 'general staff' and promised 'a more defined position, a more stable organization, more clear and incontestable rights, and especially responsibilities'. But the decisions of the planners were to be denied legal force. Solid endorsement of 'socialist protectionism' was to be balanced by 'further systematic measures' to create concessions and mixed companies.[42] In short, the committee achieved one thing only: it intensified existing differences of opinion. Each of the opposing sides determined to take its arguments to the Twelfth Party Congress in April 1923.

The Twelfth Party Congress
In his opening speech to the Congress Zinoviev set out the triumvirate's position concerning each of the main points in dispute. Supporting Sokol'nikov he declared: 'Lenin was perfectly correct in saying that the NEP was and remains a system of state capitalism, introduced above all in order to establish the present *smychka* (union) between the proletariat and the peasantry'.[43] 'Our Vladimire Ilich taught . . . that it is necessary to begin with the peasant economy.'[44] The peasant question was 'the basic question of our revolution'.[45] It was obvious that the peasant could not be sacrificed to industry by means of heavy taxes and socialist accumulation. Moreover, the concessions programme had already brought thirty million gold rubles. The hope of accumulating capital from foreign sources must not be repudiated yet.

In the meantime the party was to avoid the risky ventures into planning being advocated by Trotsky. Lenin himself had 'scoffed at a number of comrades who were too excited about "paper" plans. We know from our daily work with Vladimir Ilich that no-one jeered as much as he at "new", "great", hypertrophic "plans".'[46] There were only two plans worthy of the name: electrification and Sokol'nikov's budget. A 'dictatorship of industry' would destabilize the currency and imperil the *smychka*. Current talk of overcoming the NEP was foolhardy. There was no need to abandon a sound policy, only to develop it, to make it more precise.

Trotsky's report on industry answered Zinoviev's banalities with the gripping charge that thus far the NEP had been moving towards a capitalist restoration. Large-scale industry had proved unable to compete with small producers. Industrial prices were soaring while agricultural prices were declining because of the

1922 harvest. The resulting 'price scissors' had to be closed by lowering industrial costs, by rationalizing and concentrating production, and by means of proper accounting techniques. The budget should be treated as a subordinate component of a general plan. Budget subsidies to heavy industry would have to be continued, and the criterion governing bank credit should be long-run profitability. Sokol'nikov had introduced the first issues of the *chervonets* in the form of loans to light industry, expecting rapid repayment. Trotsky sardonically noted that 'Financing [must] take place from the point of view of foresight over a number of years rather than deciding that a sausage factory is making a profit and therefore has a right to credits'.[47] There were industries more essential to the dictatorship of the proletariat; notably transport and metallurgy, which provided for the needs of the military.

Zinoviev's discussion of the NEP, Trotsky added, had admitted 'an incorrect formulation which could lead to misunderstandings'.[48] The construction of socialism required not merely that the market be modified, but that it be overcome:

> In the final analysis we will spread the planning principle to the entire market, thus swallowing and eliminating it. In other words, our successes on the basis of the New Economic Policy automatically move towards its liquidation, to its replacement by a newer economic policy, which will be a socialist policy.[49]

Sokol'nikov's reply to Trotsky strained the frail façade of political truce still further. Hoping to sustain market incentives and to expand rural incomes, the Finance Commisar argued that minimal peasant taxation was 'in our own interest, in the interest of the Soviet power, in the interest of the Communist Party, and in the interest of the proletariat'.[50] In the circumstances an advance towards socialism required that industry be deprived of subsidies:

> I stand for complete clarity on this question... If we choose not to take one hundred thousand poods of grain from the peasant, this means that next year we will deprive our metallurgy, our oil, our industry, our transport... of sixty thousand rubles' worth of support from state resources.[51]

Reporting on agriculture Kamenev too contended that the regime's stability rested on the *smychka*, not on some fictitious 'dictatorship of industry'.[52] If steps were not taken immediately to reinforce peasant buying power an industrial sales crisis would be inevitable, whatever plans were written up on paper. The independent handicraft producer was not the real enemy in any case. Increased availability of manufactured goods, whatever their source, helped to lower industrial prices. The exploiting money-lender, fattened by inflation, was a more fitting object for hostility.

Kamenev rightly saw an inherent contradiction in Trotsky's position. If socialism were to be financed by taxes levied on domestic capitalist elements it seemed the latter should be encouraged within certain limits to grow. Similarly the threat of a sales crisis could not be averted without the services of the NEP-men. Capitalism and socialism, from this viewpoint, were not mutually exclusive but complementary. Furthermore, Trotsky appeared to have misunderstood the logical priority of currency stabilization over industrial expansion. If accounting and rationalization were to lower production costs it was imperative first to have a stable unit of account. To prepare an imaginary plan, as Rykov later remarked, was a simple task: 'When I worked in Vesenkha there was nothing easier than to acquire a plan. Every department and every centre had its own *literateur*. You called him on the telephone and literally within three hours a plan was ready.' A real plan, which depended on funds, organization and credits, was something quite different.[53]

On almost every point in dispute the rival leaders could only agree to disagree. The inconsistencies of the industrial committee's theses were allowed to reappear in the congress resolutions, and party policy continued to drift. Only one proposal evoked a general consensus: whatever path recovery took it would be necessary to mobilize the country's grain reserves for export. Believing that indications of a second good harvest signalled Russia's own stability, Trotsky was now less reluctant to contemplate closer relations with the West. Grain sales would raise the agricultural price index and help to close the scissors. At the same time Russia could take the first cautious step towards returning to the trade Pattern discussed in *Results and Prospects*. Europe's continuing recovery meant that machinery imports could be renewed. A 'grain blockade' was impossible because Europe was unable to pay for a North American alternative to pre-war Russian supplies. Soviet grain could be paid for with machinery and manufactured goods, the latter being purchased in 'the smallest amount possible'.[54]

By restricting imports of consumer goods Trotsky hoped to avoid a *smychka* between the Russian peasant and the European capitalist. The need to lower industrial prices was therefore doubly important. A marked differential between foreign and domestic prices would result in contraband and the subversion of socialism. In later years Trotsky's fear of contraband became an obsession. At the party congress he outlined the danger as follows:

Contraband is inevitable if the difference between internal and external prices goes beyond a certain limit . . . contraband, comrades . . . under-mines and washes away the monopoly. . . . If Vesenkha were to become con-taminated by a fatalistic frame of mind, and if it were to tolerate for too long the monstrous cost prices, the peasant would not share this fatalism and . . . would say: 'Open up the frontier', 'Down with the monopoly of foreign trade'; he wants to have cheap commodities. . . Well if the peasant says: 'Down with the monopoly of foreign trade' – that will be a lot worse than our waverings and hesitations in Moscow on this question.[55]

Despite this anxious reference to the monopoly Trotsky's com-ments on Russo-European trade potential at the Twelfth Congress marked a further substantial movement away from his earlier isolationist outlook. In this respect the industrial report was a significant transitional document, anticipating a subsequent development in the direction of resolute integrationism. The evolution was not completed however for another two years. In 1923 Trotsky was convinced that the restoration of trade must not be allowed to obscure the military threat from abroad.

As imperialism regained its strength capitalist antagonism toward the socialist republic would grow. The French invasion of the Ruhr in January 1923 had demonstrated that militarism still stalked Europe. On 15 February Trotsky had warned that 'the epoch of imperialist wars and revolutionary shocks will last not months, not years, but decades, enveloping the world after short breathing-spaces with new, increasingly severe and painful spasms'.[56] A few days later he observed that Russia was building its armed forces 'in the conscious knowledge of the profound in-evitability of wars so long as class society exists. And the present epoch of unstable equilibrium teaches us that the time between armed conflicts turns out, as a general rule, to be shorter than we would like to expect.'[57] A proletarian revolution in the West did not yet appear likely; the European workers were currently passing through a phase comparable to the Stolypin period in

Russia. At best the Soviet government could expect to take advantage of the interim situation through trade. Foreign investments remained impossible because Europe would be unable to surmount the currency crisis.[58]

Trotsky's approval of grain exports corresponded to Sokolnikov's interest in higher peasant incomes and might have been expected to remove one source of animosity. But Sokol'nikov had recently been conducting his own reassessment of trade. Following his unsuccessful confrontation with the protectionists at the end of 1922 he had been forced to give up the idea of importing foreign manufactures. By the spring of 1923 he had found a way to counter his critics' argument that trade would intensify industrial unemployment. Russia could bring her own idle factories back into operation by purchasing raw materials and semifabricates. During War Communism agricultural specialization had vanished. Land once used for industrial crops had been converted to grain or left uncultivated. By importing materials the peasant could be provided with consumer goods and ultimately agriculture would return to normal. As Sokol'nikov told the congress:

> How is it possible to provide cotton for our industry and industrial materials for our central region, for our manufacturing industry? It is only possible in the following manner: . . . until Turkestan's cotton production is restored we must export grain and use the currency we receive to purchase cotton abroad. Thus we will ensure the production of the textile industry and these products will return to the peasant. To be sure this is a . . . complex cycle. But in my view, even though the cycle between industry and agriculture must pass through the world market it does not constitute a *smychka* between the peasant and Western European or American capital. . . the idea that we might exist in isolation from the world market – this idea, if it is an idea at all, is a reactionary utopia.[59]

Certainly this use of Russia's import capacity was more justifiable at the time than Trotsky's call for machinery purchases. The rationale for industrial concentration was to employ at least some of the country's existing plant more fully. Trotsky's position can only be explained by assuming that he had in mind a long-range programme of industrial re-equipment and expansion. Sokol'nikov was more concerned with the immediate future. By the time new industrial equipment was necessary he believed the gold currency would provide a solution. It would be the key to both long- and short-term loans, 'the condition which in the eyes of the capitalist countries is the main indicator of the improvement in our economic *kon'yunktura* (conjuncture)'.[60] Prospective concessionaires would become more flexible when they saw Russia's revival symbolized in gold. The *chervonets* would act as 'a monetary intermediary . . . between our external and internal markets'.[61] In the Finance Commissar's words:

> Only the existence of a stable currency will make possible a significant revival in relations between the internal and external markets. . . Our inclusion in the world turnover will assume increasing dimensions and this means that our . . . currency will go out into international circulation. . . . That is why, having in mind this great perspective of our inclusion in the world economy . . . it was necessary from the very beginning . . . to issue . . . gold banknotes.[62]

Contrasting visions, irreconcileable personalities and political hatreds produced a stalemate; the Twelfth Congress compounded the disarray in the party leadership. The road to socialism was yet to be found. Later attempts to rationalize industry provoked a wave of strikes, and the price scissors widened. In the autumn of 1923 Trotsky continued with his futile demand that 'the dictatorship must be in the hands of industry, not finance . . . the restoration of a stable currency must be rigorously subordinated to the interests of state industry'.[63] But events were passing him by. With the harvest the major economic difficulty of the early NEP, that of establishing a workable relation between industry and agriculture, was sharply defined. Before decisive measures could at last be taken the political feud had to be resolved.

The sales crisis and Trotsky's defeat
The gratifying physical yield of the 1923 grain harvest (about seventy per cent of the pre-war average) was a disaster in disguise. In terms of relative degrees of recovery agriculture and industry stood in much the same ratio as Trotsky had mentioned a year earlier when discussing the question of 'proportionality'; that is, approximately 3 : 1. Relative prices on the other hand were in precisely the opposite ratio. Compared with the pre-war period industrial goods retailed at prices three times higher than those prevailing for agricultural products. For his efforts to provide the country with foodstuffs the peasant was rewarded with terms of exchange he was totally unwilling to accept.

By attempting to carry through the currency reform Sokol'ni-kov inadvertently provided the means whereby this resistance could be expressed. To effect a tranisition from the tax in kind and to reintroduce a monetary economy in agriculture he had given the peasant the option of making payments to the state in cash. Because monetary taxes were calculated on the basis of agricultural prices, which were plummeting downwards, the wealthier peasants simply hoarded their grain. Industrial market-ing power precluded price reductions on manufactured goods and the flow of trade between town and country halted. In a desperate attempt to acquire grain the government was forced to have recourse once more to the printing presses. An inflation of avalanche dimensions ensued, culminating in the final ruin of the *sovznak* (the paper ruble) and threatening even the *cher-vonets.*

At its plenary meeting in September the Central Committee appointed a further economic commission. As in 1920 Trotsky refused to participate. In his mind the issues were simple; the fault lay entirely in his rivals' failure to implement the recommen-dations of the previous report of the industrial committee. Al-ready piqued by a recent attempt to include Stalin in the War Commissariat, on 8 October he put his complaints in writing. The crisis, he declared, was the result of 'clear fundamental mis-takes in economic policy'. Lenin's advice regarding Gosplan had been disregarded and financial policy had been prepared with no reference to a plan. Further *ad hoc* measures would be equiva-lent to a restoration of War Communism. Jolted by the scheme to weaken his organizational position he decried 'appointments', condemned the secretariat's use of transfers to remove critics, and issued an appeal for workers' democracy.[64] Forgetting about Tsektran, martial law and the trade union debate, Trotsky had second thoughts when his own commissariat was threatened with a 'shake up'. At the beginning of the year the succession had been within his grasp. Now he sought frantically to reverse the conse-quences of past negligence. The triumvirs calmly replied that after the experience of War Communism they had no intention of accepting 'a dictatorship of Trotsky in economic affairs'.[65] The imaginary 'truce' was at an end.

Trotsky's letter of 8 October was an act of ill-considered im-petuosity. There is no evidence to suggest that he even took time to forewarn his own supporters. Nevertheless repercussions followed quickly. On 15 October the opposition gathered its forces and submitted the Declaration of the Forty-Six to the Politburo. Endorsing Trotsky's attack on the current party regime the declaration bore the signatures of Preobrazhensky, Pyatakov, Sapronov, V. Smirnov, and numerous others. By a curious twist of fate it succeeded in bringing Trotsky's supporters into an alliance with the former leaders of the Democratic-Centralists. The sympathetic relationship between the two groups would endure until the beginning of 1927.

A further letter from Trotsky on 24 October made menacing references to Lenin's dissatisfaction with Stalin.[66] Had the issues of nationality policy and Stalin's control of the party machinery been raised earlier they might have had a decisive impact. By October it was too late. As if tempers were not already tried by these exchanges, at the end of the month the Comintern suffered its most grievous disaster to date. In Hamburg the German Communist Party was routed. The uprising failed in conditions which from Moscow appeared to be tailor-made for revolution. Trotsky had no doubt that his enemies had mismanaged the entire affair.

From this point events paralleled those of 1920. When the widening splits in the leadership spread to the party's lower ranks an open 'discussion' was announced, the first in three years. The proclaimed purpose of the public controversy was to discover more effective ways to guarantee workers' democracy. The real intention was to encourage oppositionists to betray their location. In order to disable Trotsky politically his colleagues in the Politburo also suggested that he append his name to a compromise resolution purporting to initiate a 'new course' in party affairs. On 5 December Trotsky signed. Three days later he wrote to local party meetings that there was hesitation among 'conservative-minded bureaucrats' about putting the new policy into practice.[67] Against the 'degeneration of the "old guard" ' he set the need for 'collective initiative' and 'the collective will'.[68] Coming from one who had threatened labour deserters with penal servitude the letter appeared incongruous. It was difficult to visualize the Commissar of War as a champion of democracy. The implausibility of Trotsky's conversion and the manipulations of the secretariat jointly ensured solid majorities against the opposition in elections to the forthcoming Thirteenth Party Conference.

At the height of the mêlée Trotsky was stricken with a recurring fever, leaving the burden of defending the opposition case to Preobrazhensky, Pyatakov, Smirnov and Osinsky. The debate was almost invariably on the level of petty and indiscriminate personal abuse. Bukharin made his original contribution by inventing the famous charge that Trotsky had underestimated the peasantry.[69] Stalin recalled the War Commissar's Menshevik past.[70] Rykov vindictively cited Order No. 1042 as an example of Trotsky's style of planning.[71] Trotsky answered that if Rykov had not been in charge of Vesenkha during 1920 the transport repair plan would have been an unqualified success.[72]

Out of the welter of allegations and innuendoes only one new idea of consequence emerged – the concept of 'commodity intervention'. In a *Pravda* article on 20 October Larin proposed that the syndicates be permitted to import foreign commodities which they would then sell in combination with the particular domestic product they manufactured. Profits from sales of the low-cost imports were to be used to subsidize reductions on the Russian product, establishing a median price and helping to lower the industrial index. Recognizing that the current sales crisis made Trotsky's appeal for machinery purchases seem ludicrous his supporters saw in commodity intervention an opportunity to reconcile industry with agriculture. Imports would have to be channelled through Vneshtorg; but if such a policy were properly regulated it might conciliate the peasant and rescue the hope for grain exports.[73]

Sokol'nikov's traditional attitude to the import of finished goods gave every reason to think that the proposal would be accepted. On 10 November the Finance Commissar openly implied that the domestic market would benefit from such a policy.[74] But by this time the dispute was in the hands of the professional politicians. Opposition approval was sufficient reason to cause commodity intervention to be universally condemned. Larin repudiated his own idea as a *kulak* deviation, a concession to the rich peasant and a conspiracy to ruin Russian industry.[75] Rykov exclaimed that importing consumer goods during a sales crisis was as senseless as flushing city streets at the height of a flood.[76] The official party line held that commodity intervention ran counter to the need for an active trade balance. A surplus in the balance of payments was necessary to preserve the *chervonets*. Not until

1925, in completely different circumstances, was Larin's concept revived.

The political farce reached its climax at the Thirteenth Party Conference in January 1924. In Trotsky's absence the opposition received three votes. Nothing indicated more clearly the magnitude of Trotsky's personal defeat. Having served as the main source of ideas for the triumvirate throughout the preceding year, Sokol'nikov was now free to shape policy in accordance with his own designs. The conference resolution provided that the odious concept of 'primitive socialist accumulation' would henceforth be replaced by industry's pursuit of 'the minimum necessary profit'. During the early months of 1924 the Finance Commissar's position seemed to be fully vindicated by events. The market was gradually brought back under control as grain exports (although still modest in total volume) helped to raise peasant incomes. The industrial index was lowered when bank credits became less readily accessible, causing the process of inventory accumulation to be reversed. The import bill concentrated on raw materials. And finally, the monetary reform was completed giving Russia a stable currency for the first time since the war. After the setback at Genoa the Finance Commissar again appeared to have matters in hand, justifying the responsibility entrusted to him by his more politically oriented allies. His programme was not seriously challenged again for another two years.

Summarizing the essentials of that programme, it can be said that its chief characteristic was the new element of realism which had appeared since the highpoint of integrationist expectations early in 1922. Concessions and foreign loans were still among Sokol'nikov's primary goals, but these were to be the result of domestic consolidation and a sound currency. The illusory hope for windfall gains from abroad had been displaced by a more prosaic awareness of the need to restore international trade in a normal manner. In this connection too the currency was assigned a key role since a grain strike might result from continued inflation. In short, Sokol'nikov's integrationism had been shorn of its excesses and was now reduced to the essential unifying monetary premises he had developed before Genoa.

The year 1923 can properly be viewed therefore as one of practical and theoretical consolidation on the part of the Finance Commissar. Much the same could be said of Trotsky, although his ideas were not yet so coherently formulated. In particular Trotsky had not yet succeeded in determining a satisfactory method for utilizing Soviet import potential. The idea of importing foreign machinery did not regain the topicality it had assumed during War Communism until 1925, when domestic industry approached pre-war levels of production. Nevertheless, Trotsky had come to appreciate the relationship between foreign trade and socialist construction. Europe's unfavourable balance of payments with America, first mentioned in the 1921 Comintern report, had indicated the possibility of an economic symbiosis between Russia and the capitalist West. By 1925 Trotsky would explore this question much more comprehensively. In doing so, however, he would encounter a new upsurge of isolationist sentiment in the party leadership, deriving mainly from the views of Stalin and Bukharin.

We can complete this survey of the ways in which the isolationist–integrationist conflict re-emerged by considering now the three major events of 1924: the failure of a project to secure financial aid from Britain; the appearance of a theory of capitalist stabilization; and the debate over Permanent Revolution. From these three sources sprang the doctrine of Socialism in One Country.

The British loan negotiations

At the beginning of 1924 the internal improvements sponsored by Sokol'nikov were accompanied by a series of diplomatic triumphs. On 3 February *Pravda* jubilantly announced the receipt of *de jure* recognition from Great Britain. Similar reconciliations followed with Italy, Greece, Norway, Sweden and eventually France. Although Lenin died in January his successors boastfully, and with apparent justification, assured the party that the revolution was secure. Flaunting their own confidence they pilloried the opposition as abject defeatists.

Because Trotsky had maintained that Soviet industry could not compete with small-scale manufacturers Zinoviev conceived of a propaganda *tour de force*. At the party conference in January he alleged that the opposition had proposed the acquisition of investment capital by making 'greater concessions to the international bourgeoisie'.[77] Acknowledging that an inflow of foreign capital would accelerate Russia's growth he now warned that the 'socialist fatherland' would be surrendered to international capitalism if the opposition were to succeed. In this context Zinoviev took the liberty of dramatically altering the party's whole official view of concessions. Greater caution, he declared, was now required in negotiations with foreigners. He reminded his listeners of Lenin's opinion of Urquhart: 'better that our Soviet Russia should be ignorant, still poor, and covered with wounds, but *our own* . . . than to admit into its kitchen garden a wild beast such as Urquhart.'[78] If the capitalists were preparing to recognize Russia it was not because they liked 'the colour of our eyes', but because they knew that recovery had begun in any case. 'We can see,' Zinoviev continued, 'that slowly, with our own forces we are beginning to raise the country from the position into which it fell. Our point of view is that Russia . . . will find its own way.'[79]

This new attitude was announced just as Ramsey MacDonald and the first Labour government were elected in England. A high level of British unemployment prompted speculation that in order to acquire markets the British might consider granting Russia a long-term loan. Under pressure from his own left wing MacDonald acted in accordance with Sokol'nikov's predictions. Negotiations for a settlement of mutual financial claims were scheduled to begin on 14 April 1924. According to the Soviet interpretation MacDonald and the Labour Party were merely expressing the wishes of their capitalist masters, who had finally realized that England and Europe depended on Russia.

Satisfied that objective economic factors had turned in Russia's favour Zinoviev called for a tough bargaining position. British claims against the Soviet government were to be balanced against damages incurred during the civil war and foreign intervention. England claimed that the Russians owed British citizens eleven milliard rubles because of nationalization and debt repudiation. Zinoviev contended that the discussions must begin with a clean slate: 'We believe that there can be no talk of our paying eleven milliard, or one milliard, or even half a milliard.' The English capitalists would have to realize that their money would only be acceptable on Soviet terms. 'They are not giving to just anyone,' Zinoviev fulminated, 'but to the Soviet government – to the most stable government in the world.'[80] If the British would not accept Russia's conditions Russia would rely on its 'own efforts'.

The City of London, unaware of capitalism's impending doom, was equally unbending. On 4 April the directors of Lloyds, Barclays, the Westminster and Midland banks and other financial firms sent a memorandum to the Cabinet. Confidence in Russia, they submitted, could only be restored if the Soviet government assumed rightful responsibility for state and private debts, restored private property to its legitimate owners, guaranteed the sanctity of contract within the USSR, gave assurances against further confiscations, dismantled the trade monopoly, and ceased all propaganda directed against the institutions of other countries. Even if Russia complied with these demands the financiers would not commit themselves to a loan.

The London papers published the statement on 14 April. Undaunted, on 20 April Zinoviev replied that time was on the Soviet side. Repeating another statement attributed to Lenin he warned that 'The longer you wait to conclude an agreement with Soviet Russia, the less profitable it will be for you.'[81] On 8 May Kamenev concurred, arguing that 'Our strength lies in the growth of our internal power.' Dutifully following the example set by his political alter ego he affirmed that a loan would be acceptable on a mutually profitable basis:

But if the English bankers want to give us money on terms which amount to enslavement or to the enserfment of proletarian labour in the USSR, then we have no need of their money. We will get along without it. Let the gentlemen who are entering into negotiations with us be aware of this.[82]

The conquest of foreign markets by Russian exports was 'a link with the international market which is very likely stronger than all the negotiations being conducted'. Dismayed by this unforseeable transformation of his colleagues' position Sokol'nikov avoided direct mention of the subject and concentrated on monetary reform.

The unaccustomed belligerence of the Soviet leaders plainly mirrored their restored faith in Russia's economy. At the same time they were intent upon creating a satisfactory political image both at home and abroad. In so doing they would communicate to London that they expected better terms than those preferred at Genoa when Russia had been starving. Their approach to the actual negotiations was more realistic. On 20 May, only days before the opening of the Thirteenth Party Congress, they made a concerted effort to reach an agreement. The Russian delegation – which included Preobrazhensky, thus conveniently removing him from the domestic scene – offered to set aside a lump sum to cover pre-war obligations to British citizens. In exchange the British government was to guarantee a loan. The mistrust of the City had convinced the Russians that without a guarantee the project would not succeed. These initiatives failed, however, to secure more than an offer of official support for Soviet efforts to secure a loan privately. Heading the Russian negotiators Rakovsky again dangled the prospect of concessions without drawing a response.

In these circumstances the tone of the party congress was predetermined. Unable to present the delegates with the hoped-for victory, Zinoviev renewed his warning against a one-sided understanding of Lenin's views on concessions. Like Trotsky in 1920 he summarized the international situation as representing 'neither a direct threat nor direct help'.[83] Five days later, on 29 May, *Pravda* reported that the Soviet delegation had once more attempted to break the impasse by offering concessions. But in the interval the congress had called for 'maximum care' in negotiating leases with foreigners.[84] A second resolution, claiming industrial protection as its justification, had important isolationist overtones. In view of the failure to consummate the London discussions the congress demanded 'the production of means of production inside the [Soviet] Union'.[85]

From the end of May until the end of July 1924 the Anglo-Soviet talks foundered. When Rakovsky offered to redeem sixteen per cent of the nominal value of tsarist bonds held by British citizens the creditors rejected the proposal. In the absence of a final decision official party statements monotonously asserted the need for Russian self-reliance. The original tactical motives behind Zinoviev's platitudes were gradually forgotten. The psychological atmosphere of the country began to change. Having intended to convince others of their strength the party leaders in fact convinced themselves. Rykov, who had been one of the first to recommend capital imports during War Communism, now agreed that 'questions of concessions must be considered more strictly and more carefully than they would be if our economic position were worse than it is currently. The attraction of bourgeois forces must be restricted to limits which are strictly necessary.'[86] Two weeks later he addressed the Communist International in a similar vein:

[Our] accumulation is sufficiently rapid; it is progressing, increasing from year to year, and has made it possible for us at the last [party] congress to pass a resolution to the effect that we must now be more cautious in giving concessions. For this reason we will parley more carefully with Macdonald ... than we did earlier with Urquhart. ... We will do so because now, given the development of our internal strength, we are moving forward with sufficient speed. ... We will now assess [the] advantages and disadvantages of concessions more strictly than we once did. Our demands have grown.[87]

On 26 July Sokol'nikov belatedly joined the refrain. Flushed with the current success of the *chervonets* he lauded Russia's developing capacity for internal savings:

with a proper mobilization of the financial and economic resources of the country it is possible to ensure the continued development of the productive forces right up to the moment when we are strong enough to receive credits on conditions sufficiently advantageous to us. This support will come because the time will arrive when it will become profitable to those circles who are capable of extending a foreign loan.[88]

On 10 August the startling news arrived that Rakovsky had concluded a preliminary agreement with the British. The proposed treaty made provision for a guaranteed loan if certain remaining difficulties concerning nationalization could be solved. The obligations which the Soviet government agreed to recognize were to be met by supplementary interest payments on the loan and through concessions. After the sustained propaganda barrage of recent months it was no surprise that many Russian workers greeted the announcement with some hostility. Ryazanov publicly condemned the agreement, arguing that better terms could have been secured through waiting.[89] As it happened the Soviet government did not have long to wait before the treaty was irretrievably lost.

On 8 October the British Labour Party was defeated in Parliament. The infamous Zinoviev Letter, wherein the head of the Comintern allegedly called on the British Communist Party to subvert the royal armed forces, caused a monumental scandal in Britain. In the subsequent elections the Conservatives won a phenomenal victory. Riding a tide of popular anti-Soviet outrage the Baldwin–Chamberlain cabinet would have nothing to do with the sinister Kremlin conspirators. On 21 November the

Foreign Office informed Rakovsky that Parliament refused to ratify MacDonald's terms.

The Bolsheviks had only one response. At a meeting of textile workers Rykov outlined his own attitude and that of the leadership as a whole:

The basis for the stability of our international relations is the stability of our internal conditions. There is no doubt that recognition of the USSR by a large number of states was the result of our successes in the reconstruction of our economy. It is incorrect to think that loans are given to the poor. Loans are given to the wealthy. Europe refuses us loans now; but if we continue the process of economic reconstruction over the coming years ... they will give us a loan. We will receive one. For this reason ... the centre of gravity lies in our internal policy.[90]

The reaction was reminiscent of that which had followed the Genoa conference. In a renewed attack on the supporters of heavy industry Sokol'nikov took the same position he had adopted in the summer of 1922. The party, he promised, had no intention of grovelling for a loan or of selling Russia to the politicians and bankers of Europe and America.[91]

Despite their publicly negative approach to the London negotiations the Soviet leaders were genuinely troubled by Britain's behaviour. The fact that Europe was capable of providing financial aid two years after Genoa exploded the integrationist theory of pending capitalist collapse. A conclusion Bukharin had reached in the spring of 1924 now assumed new significance. Speaking to the Thirteenth Congress Bukharin had asserted that capitalism was achieving 'a certain stabilization'. Unemployment had declined in a number of countries, and on the whole the financial condition of the West was improving. The basic factors working towards the system's decline were still operative. But by impoverishing the masses the capitalists had converted inevitable disaster into a 'creeping crisis'.[92]

Uneasy over his earlier statements, in June 1924 Zinoviev also professed to see 'certain symptoms of capitalism's consolidation'.[93] By the end of the year Sokol'nikov, still stressing imperialist contradictions, agreed that Germany and Central Europe had achieved a limited stabilization or 'breathing space'.[94] Stalin's appraisal echoed Trotsky's forecasts for capitalism two years previously. The party secretary believed that 'Stabilization is not stagnation; it is a strengthening of the present position and a further development.'[95]

The theory of stabilization fundamentally changed the basic premises of the party line, just as Lenin had done when he disavowed Trotsky's theory of unilinear collapse in 1921. The revised estimate of capitalism's future was put forth at a time when Russia's continuing isolation could no longer be denied. Anglo-American co-operation in providing Dawes Plan aid to Germany made Moscow's recent rebuff particularly poignant. Moreover, greater stability in Central Europe appeared to minimize any remaining chance for a successful European revolution. When MacDonald fell one of Russia's most influential sympathizers in the West disappeared. The confidence of the first months of 1924 was now overlaid with a growing apprehension, not unlike that Trotsky had experienced when the blockade was nominally lifted in 1920. Many party spokesmen concluded that Chamberlain, the arch-imperialist, would co-ordinate Europe in fresh interventionist plots. The blockade might even be restored. Kamenev spoke of the Dawes Plan as a direct threat to Soviet security and the precondition for a 'united front against us'.[96]

Stalin carried the reasoning one step further, proclaiming the division of the world into two hostile camps: the camp of socialism and the camp of capitalism. With new insight into the original disagreements between Lenin and Trotsky over the theory of imperialism he rightly observed that 'It is not true [to say] that capitalism cannot develop, that Lenin's theory of the decay of capitalism excludes . . . development.'[97] The question, however, was whether the two systems would develop in mutual partnership, as Lenin had once predicted, or whether they would find themselves locked in deadly combat until one or the other succumbed. A major dispute with Trotsky at the end of 1924 clarified the implications of capitalist stabilization.

From Permanent Revolution to Socialism in One Country
Throughout 1924 Trotsky's adversaries had worked relentlessly to sap his political strength. Control over the War Commissariat was divided with the appointment of Frunze, one of Zinoviev's satellites, as Deputy Commissar. Stalin's manipulation of the party machinery resulted in not a single oppositionist being elected to the Thirteenth Congress as a voting delegate. The same meeting enlarged the membership of the Central Committee and included a long list of Stalin's otherwise undistin-

guished creatures. When Lenin's Testament was read to the congress, calling for Stalin's removal from the secretariat, Zinoviev rushed to his ally's defence and the issue was buried. Bukharin was promoted to full membership of the Politburo and Sokol'nikov gained candidate status. For Trotsky's adherents there was an unbroken torrent of abuse.

Trotsky determined to repay the calumny in kind. He made a tragic mistake though when he selected Zinoviev and Kamenev as his targets rather than Stalin. In an essay entitled 'The Lessons of October' he reminded the party of the irresoluteness the two triumvirs had once displayed. In 1917, when Lenin had first called for a seizure of power, the men who now posed as his successors had shrunk in despair at the enormity of such an adventure. Zinoviev's charge of defeatism and lack of faith was thus flung back at its originator. The same character defect was said to have been revealed again in 1923. By analogy with 1917 Trotsky attributed the defeat of the German Communist Party exclusively to Zinoviev's irresolute leadership of the Comintern. Under the weight of Trotsky's pen Zinoviev's painstakingly constructed image of self-assuredness crumbled. Neither he nor Kamenev ever recovered their previous public stature.

The immediate result of the attack was to provoke a storm of reproach and slander. The entire gamut of Trotsky's alleged disagreements with Lenin was covered and re-covered. Of the many issues raised the most consequential was the claim that Trotsky's 'pessimism' derived from the theory of Permanent Revolution. His enemies declared that the War Commissar's major theoretical achievement spelled disaster for Russia if the revolution were to remain isolated.

The charges had sufficiently remote foundation in fact to make them appear plausible. Sometime in 1922 (the date is uncertain although the autumn appears likely) Trotsky had written a postscript to 'Programma Mira', one of his pre-revolutionary pamphlets. Adhering to the analysis contained in *Results and Prospects*, the original essay had predicted Russia's military defeat should the revolution not be transmitted abroad. Trotsky's reputation as a Marxist theorist depended on the concept of Permanent Revolution, and he rationalized the forecast of defeat by pointing to Russia's post-Genoa economic difficulties. Socialism had not been overthrown; but Trotsky implied that the theory

was valid in its stress on international revolution because Russia
had experienced 'an extraordinary lowering of the productive
forces'.[98] Had the United States of Europe emerged (as predicted
in 'Programma Mira') Russia would not have suffered the humiliation of Genoa. During the period of capitalist encirclement concessions and other agreements with the bourgeoisie were thought
likely to be minimal in their effects. In 1922 Trotsky wrote:

So long as the bourgeoisie remains in power in other European states we
are forced, in the struggle against economic isolation, to look for agreements with the capitalist world; at the same time it can be said with
certainty that these agreements in the best instance can help us to heal
one or another economic wound, to make this or that step forward, but a
genuine upsurge of the socialist economy in Russia will become possible
only after the victory of the proletariat in the most important countries
of Europe.[99]

In January 1922 Trotsky had inadvertently provided additional evidence to support the contention that he lacked faith in
the Russian revolution. A new foreword to the book *1905* gave a
summary of the theory of Permanent Revolution and included
the following remark: 'The contradictions in the position of a
workers' government in a backward country, with an overwhelming peasant population, will be resolved only in an international
context in the arena of the world proletarian revolution.'[100] Although the foreword was written at a time when agriculture was
outpacing industry it was a précis and nothing more. Trotsky
made no attempt to relate it to the prevailing circumstances. Had
it not been for his antagonists' assiduity in uncovering these obscure quotations history would have forgotten both of them. Instead, as a result of the debate inspired by 'The Lessons of
October', their importance has been inflated beyond the bounds
of reason. They have become the authoritative definition of
'Trotskyism'.

The ridiculous quarrel over who was more irresolute and pessimistic assumed a new dimension when Kamenev interpreted the
theory of Permanent Revolution to mean that 'Soviet power
would long ago have ceased to exist in Russia'. Trotsky had ignored the *smychka* between the proletariat and the peasantry:

In conditions such as these a delay or protraction of the world revolution
would mean the rapid collapse of the government of workers' dictatorship
in Russia. This is why the 'permanentists' inevitably experience convulsive
transitions from fits of despair and profound pessimism to the attempt

to cope with the economic backwardness of the country forcefully, by military orders.[101]

On 30 November Zinoviev's article 'Bolshevism or Trotskyism?' proferred a similar indictment. *Results and Prospects* had seen a need for state support from Europe. Zinoviev protested that Russia survived seven years after the revolution when all that was being received from the West were insulting pronouncements from Baldwin and Chamberlain. Zinoviev also noted that Trotsky had recently characterized the Dawes plan as an American attempt to establish a 'rotten equilibrium' in the West. Here he saw evidence that Trotsky had over-estimated 'the miraculous peace-making characteristics of American ultra-imperialism'.[102] It followed that Trotsky's pessimism had not one, but two sources: his conviction of Russia's inevitable defeat and his supposed belief that America had resolved capitalism's contradictions.

The most closely reasoned and shrewdly calculated attack on Permanent Revolution came from Stalin. Trotsky's theory was said to leave only two alternatives: 'either to rot or to degenerate into a bourgeois state'.[103] Surpassing Kamenev's insight, in December Stalin hit upon the idea of linking Trotsky's despair with Lenin's views regarding 'unevenness'. Lenin, he suggested, had detected the hidden menace of 'Trotskyism' when he had rejected the theory of a universal revolution and had announced that for a time a single socialist state would 'stand up against the rest of the world'. The Russian workers need not be despondent; they had only to follow the sure and certain path charted by Lenin. The Soviet Union would build Socialism in One Country.

As late as the spring of 1924 Stalin had subscribed to a different view:

For the final victory of socialism, for the organization of socialist production the efforts of a single country, and particularly of a peasant country like Russia, are inadequate – for this the efforts of the proletarians of several of the leading countries are necessary.[104]

Correcting this careless lapse into 'Trotskyism' Stalin redefined his position by quoting from Lenin's 1923 article 'On Co-operation'. Russia, he now believed, possessed 'all that is necessary and sufficient' for a socialist society.[105]

No-one had realized previously that Lenin's answer to 'Trotskyism' had been the theory of Socialism in One Country. The utter nonsense of Stalin's interpretation is perfectly obvious if one considers how much better a case for Socialism in One Country could have been constructed out of Trotsky's remarks during and after War Communism. But in 1924 the party wished to be deceived. Carefully searching through Lenin's writings Stalin had discovered an ideal formula. His clever marshalling of quotations allowed him to impart a degree of forensic sophistication to an argument which otherwise would have been dismissed as a contemptible fraud. The possible consequences of Stalin's foray into the realm of theory were difficult to foresee. Certainly the current campaign to discredit Trotsky, as Rykov candidly admitted, bore no direct relation to questions of policy.[106] Out of Lenin's literary remains, however, a Frankenstein had been created.

As the first party leader to reflect upon the new theory's practical meaning Bukharin immediately underscored its implicit isolationism. In January 1925 he published an article concerning the economic proposals of the opposition. Taking Pyatakov to task for the view that Russia would benefit from inclusion in a world socialist economy, Bukharin suggested that foreign help would not materialize either before or immediately after the revolution in Europe. For the moment Europe was preoccupied with restoring its own fixed capital. After the revolution came in the West civil war would follow, involving serious economic dislocations similar to those suffered in Russia after 1917.[107]

Bukharin concluded that Sokol'nikov's domestic policies had to be modified. An even greater emphasis must now be placed upon the peasant. He explained that in the aftermath of the socialist revolution, when the political power of the workers had been consolidated, the class contradictions within society would progressively diminish in scope and intensity. Despite Trotsky's warnings with regard to the *kulak* and the NEP-men, Bukharin thought a 'peaceful-economic-limited' class struggle was to be expected. Victory in this type of class struggle would constitute 'the final victory of socialism'.[108] The party would build the new society if the lessons of the NEP and the sales crisis were consistently followed. In the years 1922–4 an expansion of internal trade had led to a general increase in national income. The period of capital turnover in industry (that is, the period of production plus the period of distribution) had been simultaneously reduced. The effect was as if the total capital available had been increased.[109] On these grounds Bukharin believed that major new industrial investments might be postponed for some considerable time. The whole problem of Russian industry had been misinterpreted: the country's capital stock was for most purposes quite adequate. The real need was to curtail monopoly prices more strictly, to expand production and lower costs, and thus to fortify the *smychka* with the peasant.

Sokol'nikov had been justified in making this kind of analysis in 1923, given the short-run problems and crisis atmosphere of the time. But Bukharin now held forth low prices and a low rate of industrial profits as a prescription for long-term growth. The policy of expanding trade with the countryside was to be amplified in every way possible. Peasants were to be encouraged to accumulate whether they were *kulaks* or *bednyaks*, rich or poor. A rise in rural incomes and savings would mean greater purchases of both consumer goods and agricultural machinery. A larger volume of rural purchases, even if industry earned only a modest rate of profit, would mean greater total earnings than if industrial prices were maintained at high levels. Thus higher rural incomes would have a salutary impact on the cities. Moreover, by encouraging the peasants to concentrate their resources in co-operative and other savings institutions, it would be possible to put the savings of the *kulak* to work for the benefit of the *bednyak*. Further income transfers would eventually become possible through taxation. Thus, according to Bukharin industry and agriculture, like Russia's different classes, would gradually draw together in a peaceful manner. This policy pre-supposed, however, that the savings process must begin in the agricultural sector. Bukharin rationalized the role assigned to co-operative (mainly *kulak*) savings by reinterpreting the history of the NEP.

In the beginning, he argued, Lenin had treated co-operatives as elements of state capitalism, a system which was to be founded mainly on concessions. However, in 1923 Lenin wrote 'On Co-operation' and portrayed co-operatives as being 'identical . . . with the growth of socialism'. And why had Lenin's attitude changed? Bukharin answered that the programme for capital imports from the West had been a fantasy. Lenin had turned to socialist co-operation as the only conceivable alternative means by which to generate a pool of new capital:

[By 1923] it had become clear that foreign capital . . . is not very inclined

to locate itself within the limits of our [Soviet] Union. We have extraordinarily few concessions agreements...The second fact was that we
proved to be in the position to develop our internal resources ourselves...
We are climbing out of the rot, out of the stench, out of famine and cold
quickly enough without outside help and without paying interest.[110]

In the spring of 1925 Bukharin explained the connection
between his domestic policy suggestions, the doctrine of Socialism
in One Country, and the theory of stabilization. The change
taking place in the West, he noted, 'to a certain degree influences
the way we consider the question of our internal economic position'. It was necessary to speed the turnover of capital because
'We know that we can scarcely expect much from foreign capital
now.'[111] 'A certain stabilization of Western European capital'
meant that Russia was 'almost totally isolated'. The capitalists
had overcome their worst difficulties, notwithstanding their apparent indifference to the Russian market. The seemingly
irreversible fact of Russia's isolation called for a declaration of
faith in the revolution's future:

if it is admitted that capitalism in Western Europe is recovering does it
not follow that this implies an end to our hope of building socialism?
In other words, can we succeed without the direct help of a victorious
European proletariat? This reduces to a question of the possibility of
building socialism in one country.[112]

Scorning the fatalism of the 'permanentists' Bukharin was no less
impatient in his reference to the party's earlier integrationism:

It won't fall from the skies; foreigners will not give us...capital. [But]
we do not conclude that without any foreign help (either proletarian or
bourgeois) we will perish. No! We will build socialism. We have the
resources, or more accurately, we will have them. What do they consist
of?...These resources are being acquired thanks to a more vigorous
application of labour which is a consequence of speeding up the turnover.[113]

Bukharin's arguments were persuasive but dangerously anachronistic. To implement a progressive reduction of industrial selling prices, even assuming costs might in some cases be lowered,
would be to eliminate or restrict one of the primary sources of
potential capital accumulation in the state sector. More intensive
use of existing capital would also lead, in most industries, to more
rapid deterioration of equipment, more frequent production
breakdowns, and thence to rising production costs. The irony was

that Bukharin began to develop this strategy only a year before light industry attained pre-war levels of production.[114] Thereafter no further buffer in the form of idle equipment remained against capital consumption, and Bukharin was forced to reconsider the country's need for industrial investments. In the meantime, attempts to lower industrial selling prices by decree helped to increase the profits accruing to a dwindling number of private merchants.

Despite these oversights, to many it seemed that Bukharin had opened up the prospect for a peaceful transition to socialism, free of major social or political struggles. In 1925 Bukharin's views exerted a strong influence on party decisions, and the process of reinterpreting the NEP was thus completed. Whereas Lenin had equated state capitalism with integrationism, hereafter the NEP would be identified with isolationism. But traditional patterns of thought were less easily reversed than Bukharin imagined. Trotsky's problem of 'proportionality' was yet to be answered. Sokol'nikov's integrationist convictions had not been taken into account. And Stalin would shortly realize that the construction of socialism in an isolated country required more than statements of confidence such as those being circulated by Bukharin.

5

Socialism in One Country

Co-authoring the doctrine of Socialism in One Country, by the spring of 1925 Bukharin converted Stalin's contentious essay on the fictitious perils of 'Trotskyism' into a coherent view of Russia and the world. Among those struggling for Lenin's mantle, theory had become an instrument of power. Lenin's own authority had been based as much upon his polemical skills as upon organizational and manipulative insight. And his successor would likewise require recognition as both organizer and thinker. By imparting a wider, practical significance to Stalin's originally limited and purely abstract formulations, Bukharin significantly advanced the party secretary's plans for total personal power. As early as June 1924 Stalin had already begun to 'correct' the occasional theoretical error of Zinoviev and Kamenev. Now, with Bukharin's help, he seemed to be taking creative initiatives of his own.

Socialism in One Country was more than a slogan or even an economic programme: it was a psychological watershed in the history of the revolution. The party had reached the point where many longed for a reconfirmation of purpose. For three years, during the holding operation designed by Sokol'nikov, a sense of drift, aimlessness and confusion had been taking hold. The new doctrine helped to restore the sense of mission which had been lost in 1921. During the first months of 1925 an awareness of change became steadily more pronounced. With industry completing its recovery many of the old fears seemed less enormous than in the past. Throwing Sokol'nikov's caution to the winds Stalin proclaimed the beginning of a new and heroic battle – the battle for socialism through industrialization. The urge for personal survival impelled his rivals to view these initiatives with apprehension.

The 'debate' over Permanent Revolution had effectively destroyed Trotsky's reputation as a theoretician amongst the party

masses. Infuriated and vengeful after 'The Lessons of October',
Zinoviev demanded that Trotsky be expelled from the party and
permanently removed as a political threat. Stalin, already antici-
pating the day when he might require Trotsky's support against
Zinoviev, agreed only to deprive Trotsky of the War Commis-
sariat. With a show of calculated magnanimity he ensured that
Trotsky retained his seat on both the Central Committee and the
Politburo.

Refusing to sanction Trotsky's total humiliation, Stalin had
recently given his former colleagues in the triumvirate even more
substantive grounds for suspicion. In the autumn of 1924 he had
weakened Kamenev's control of the Moscow party organization
by installing one of his own supporters as local party secretary.
Early in 1925 he moved to undermine Zinoviev in the latter's two
main power bases, the Leningrad party organization and the
Comintern. Later in the same year he sought to repeat his Moscow
success by penetrating the Leningrad secretariat. Although Zinoviev successfully resisted the move, he and Kamenev had been
badly shaken by Trotsky's sensational revelations. Unable to risk
a direct confrontation, they decided to counter Stalin's moves by
deflating his pretensions as a theoretician. The result was an
abrupt end to the unanimity which the party leadership had
maintained in 1924, when all but Trotsky spoke with one voice.

Having repudiated Trotsky's sceptical view of the NEP in
1923, Zinoviev now indirectly criticized Stalin by implying that
Bukharin's was the voice of degeneration: that, while the new
interpretation of party policy might correspond with Socialism in
One Country, it was an unwarranted surrender to the *kulak* and
the petty bourgeoisie. For reasons of his own Sokol'nikov sympathized with and eventually joined the emerging Zinoviev opposition. As these political realignments paralleled the current shifts
in theoretical perspectives, the struggle for the succession entered
its second phase and the triumvirate visibly dissolved. Born of
fear, the alliance could not survive Trotsky's defeat. Watching
the changing distribution of power, Trotsky held aloof until he
could determine the significance of the competing factions.

Divisions in the triumvirate
On 10 January 1925 Kamenev made the first experimental probe
of Stalin's position. Employing the same tactics of textual criticism

recently used against Trotsky, he told a Moscow audience that Lenin had seen the seizure of power in a 'backward country' only as a means to call forth the international revolution: 'We must begin, Lenin said, but we can only continue and finish altogether, or at least in combination with several of the leading industrial countries . . . For this reason it is true when people say that the teaching of Ilich is not . . . a theory of the victory of socialism in a separate country.'[1] The speech was intended to serve notice on Stalin that he too was vulnerable, that his deliberate misconstruction of Lenin's writings was both unique and dubious.

While running the risk of being charged with 'Trotskyism' Kamenev had no success in deterring Stalin. Preparations for the Fourteenth Party Conference accentuated mistrust within the Politburo. Late in April 1925 Zinoviev enlarged upon the thoughts Kamenev had expressed in January:

The experience of the Russian revolution has shown not only that . . . a preliminary victory is possible, but also that under favourable circumstances this first country . . . can (with a certain degree of support from the international proletariat) maintain and stabilize itself over a long period, even if this support does not come in the form of direct proletarian revolutions in other countries.

But at the same time Leninism teaches that a *final* victory of socialism, in the sense of a full guarantee against the restoration of bourgeois relations, is possible only in the international context (or in several of the leading countries).[2]

On 29 April Zinoviev told the party conference that Lenin had believed the 'full victory' of socialism was possible in 'a country such as ours' so long as there was no military interference from abroad. 'But . . . as an international revolutionary . . . [Lenin] never ceased to underline the fact that without an international revolution our victory is unstable and incomplete.'[3] To have a 'full' victory which was 'incomplete' was a subtlety only Zinoviev could understand.

At various times during the following months Zinoviev predicted that Russia faced a long period of isolation, that stabilization would probably last several years, leaving no apparent alternative but to build socialism in one country. But he contradicted himself by clinging to the hope of foreign aid and by insisting that 'a general revolutionary situation' still existed throughout the world.[4] As head of the Communist International he warned the party to beware an attitude, already 'in the air', which he described as a 'national limitation'.[5] Then he proceeded to emphasize Russia's *de facto* isolation by denying that the country could be thought of as part of the world economy.[6] The attempt to cast doubt on Stalin only strengthened the impression that it was really Zinoviev who was inconsistent and uncertain, perhaps even 'pessimistic'. Unwittingly the titular party leader now confirmed Trotsky's charge of indecisiveness.

An effort to clarify his position in the summer of 1925 compounded the confusion. In his book *Leninism* Zinoviev drew a careful distinction between the act of building socialism and the finished product. 'The possibility of building socialism' was conceivable within the limits of one country; 'the definitive establishment of a socialist regime, or a socialist society' was not.[7] Essentially, Zinoviev believed that Russia's backwardness was an impediment to socialism because it complicated the maintenance of the *smychka* with the peasant. 'If we were victorious in the leading countries,' he wrote, '. . . we would immediately be able to avail ourselves of both their enormous industry and of our own, which would permit us to realize our union with the peasantry in a more satisfactory manner, in circumstances considerably more favourable.'[8] The natural reply was that Russia must begin the process of industrialization with its own forces. This was the position Zinoviev himself had taken only a year previously. To industrialize, however, was to build socialism. And Zinoviev now thought that socialism could not be built in one country. He had talked himself into a trap.

The futility of these declarations stood out all the more clearly when compared with the first practical measures for industrial expansion discussed at the Fourteenth Conference. In January 1925 the Central Committee had raised production targets for the metallurgical industry. The conference revised the figures upwards once again. Dzerzhinsky, currently chairman of Vesenkha, projected an increase in the machine-building programme for 1924–5 of no less than eighty-three per cent. To co-ordinate the expansion he outlined a three-year industrial plan, the forerunner of the later five-year plans, and emphasized the need to begin with additional factories and equipment for the metallurgical sector.

Disregarding Bukharin's attempts to minimize the need for

new investment in industry Rykov similarly concentrated on the theme of industrialization. He told the conference that Soviet light industry was now approaching full production capacity: 'the rapid tempo of the reconstruction process has brought us to the point where we have exhausted the possibilities of further expansion within the limits imposed by the old technical equipment inherited from bourgeois Russia. Before us stands in all its magnitude the task of expanded reproduction of basic capital.'[9] On 13 May Rykov boasted that Russia was the only country in history to undertake large-scale industrial construction without external aid. Such a country would not beg 'on her knees' for help from Europe. Although 'enormous investments of capital' were required, past Soviet victories were a sure guarantee of success in meeting the new challenge of industrialization. 'To raise ourselves from such poverty to the level we have presently achieved is much more difficult than to base ourselves on these achievements and to go forward.' In 1923 Rykov had been scornful of Trotsky's demand for economic planning. Now he remarked that industrialization would require 'a single co-ordinated plan for the reconstruction of all branches of our economy'.[10] Special commissions were created by both Gosplan and Vesenkha to study the question of planned industrial growth.

Stalin agreed wholeheartedly with Rykov and Dzerzhinsky. Endorsing increased budget support for heavy industry he quoted Lenin to the effect that without her own metallurgy and machine building Russia would perish as an 'independent' country.[11] Industrialization was to be the party's answer to pessimism, in whatever quarter it arose, and the country's answer to the capitalist world. Expectations of another good harvest in 1925 highlighted the need to begin to plan now for future industrial growth. A partial crop failure in 1924 had restricted peasant demand for consumer goods; but sooner or later light industry would have to be expanded. After the disappointing experience with MacDonald Stalin believed that Russia must rise to this task with her own resources. The required budget subsidies were not long in coming. During the early months of 1925 bank credits also flowed freely into both light and heavy industry. In May Rykov noted with satisfaction that the market was a picture of order. Increased financial liberality had not generated inflation and the price scissors of 1923 remained firmly closed.[12]

A predictable note of discord arose, however, from Sokol'nikov. As late as December 1924 the Finance Commissar had persisted in the belief that it was unnecessary for the present even to restore fixed capital to its pre-war levels, much less to expand beyond them. The basic capital of Soviet industry, he had claimed, was fully adequate. 'Our economy suffers not from an insufficiency of basic capital, but more from . . . [industry's] lack of correspondence with a weakly recovered market.'[13] Like Bukharin, Sokol'nikov was looking backward to the 1923 sales crisis rather than forward to new endeavours. Accordingly he interpreted the stress placed by Stalin and Rykov on investments in heavy industry to be a political move involving needless economic risks. If such luxuries were to be indulged, he believed the Finance Commissariat should not be held responsible for them. Russia should again try to secure a foreign loan.

Sokol'nikov had not yet realized that according to Stalin's vision foreign capital no longer had any role in Russia. On 22 March 1925 Stalin described Germany's dependence upon capital imports as 'financial enslavement'.[14] Two days later the Finance Commissar disputed the belief that Russia could build socialism without foreign assistance. 'In order to acquire loans from abroad,' he declared, 'it is permissible to give some ground provided [the loans] guarantee sufficient benefits for our economy and do not affect the political and economic independence of the Soviet state.'[15] On 1 May he explicitly cautioned against the passive acceptance of isolation: 'If it is basically true that we can pull ourselves up by our own resources this does not mean that we must develop in isolation.'[16] The more quickly Russia approached pre-war levels of production the more important foreign investments would become. Every means must be employed to remove the threat of a financial blockade. Soviet industry could only be re-equipped if a *smychka* were established with the world economy.[17] Isolationism was as repugnant coming from Stalin and Bukharin as it had been when embraced by Trotsky. To Sokol'nikov it was self-evident that: 'We cannot isolate ourselves from the remaining five-sixths of the globe. It exists around us.'[18] In 1924 the Finance Commissar had answered Britain's perfidy by pointing to Russia's own future capacity to accumulate savings. Fearful that his remarks had been misconstrued he clarified his position: 'My comments concerning internal credit are by no means intended to suggest that now we can in fact go without foreign credit, or particularly that we will be able to do so in the future.'[19]

By the middle of 1925, however, the political position in the party was too uncertain to justify premature risks. In June plans were initiated to finance both industry and agriculture with a long-term reconstruction loan supervised by the Treasury. Sokol'nikov reluctantly agreed to oversee the project. Two months later Gosplan issued its first skeletal plan in the form of annual control figures. To Sokol'nikov's horror they included a total estimated expenditure on industry of nine hundred million rubles. A dangerous expansion in the money supply was inevitable if Gosplan's projections were accepted. Sokol'nikov protested that the planners were encroaching upon the established prerogatives of the financial authorities. Recalling past conflicts with Trotsky he warned that industry's need for credit must not interfere with the stability of the currency. Gosplan's position was 'utterly wrong'; the control figures were an unabashed prescription for inflation.[2] Sokol'nikov was now totally at odds with the party mood. Missing the political significance of Socialism in One Country he vainly sought to counteract a vision by appealing to the gold standard:

Why are we unable to depart from a gold basis? The general answer ... is that gold still remains the decisive factor on the world market; and we are not strong enough to be able to detach ourselves from the economic laws of the world market.[21]

Stalin was understandably indifferent to his former associate's complaints. It was obvious that the Finance Commissar lacked faith.

Stalin's relationship with Bukharin was less tense, although here too there existed the potential for future conflict. The two men were united on the theoretical question of Socialism in One Country; but they interpreted the concept differently. Stalin believed that socialism meant industry, especially heavy industry. Bukharin assigned first importance to light industry and the peasant. Rural marketing of grain, flax, hemp, and food products in general remained in 1925 at levels far below those characteristic of the pre-war years. As the land redistribution had divided the large estates which had produced the marketed surplus,

Bukharin hoped to reunite small peasant plots into larger individual and eventually co-operative holdings. Stalin would agree
to these policies only as long as it was reasonable to suppose they
would provide more food and materials for industry. In April
1925 Bukharin secured a number of vital concessions to the
country's most efficient farmers, the *kulaks*. Hired labour was
sanctioned; rights of land leasing were extended; and the Fourteenth Conference announced a reduction in agricultural taxes.
Sokol'nikov had originally supported the proposal for a reduction.
But he abhorred the *kulak*, subscribed to a populist ideal of
peasant equality, and pleaded for a class-oriented policy of more
progressive taxation. Bukharin invited the entire peasantry, including the *kulaks*, to 'enrich' themselves, to save, and to provide
a market for industry.

Traditionally the *kulak* had been thought of as the arch-
enemy in the villages. Now Bukharin claimed to discover the
means for rehabilitation. Co-operatives would permit the *kulak*
to grow into socialism.[22] He and Stalin both assumed that the
kulak was willing to 'co-operate' with the state. They also assumed
that the party would tolerate their pro-peasant excesses. However, the proposed amnesty to the *kulak* provided Zinoviev with
the tangible issue he had so far been unable to find. By attacking
Bukharin he could covertly impugn Stalin's claims to leadership
and at the same time avoid a final, open breach in the triumvirate.
Branding Bukharin's policies a 'retreat' from socialism he attributed them to the delay in the international revolution and to
Russia's failure to conclude a foreign loan.[23] Lenin was said to
have anticipated Bukharin's unreliability several years earlier,
when Bukharin had first failed to understand the nature of state
capitalism. According to Lenin the NEP, although a form of state
capitalism, would lead to socialism. 'Certain young comrades' had
been confused by this dialectical insight and were now converting
socialist co-operatives into capitalist instruments by including
the *kulak*.[24] Zinoviev's attack succeeded in forcing Bukharin to
withdraw the controversial suggestion that the *kulak* enrich himself. But Stalin explained that the dispute with Lenin over state
capitalism had been merely a misunderstanding.

The year 1925 abounded with misunderstandings. Sokol'nikov
sympathized with Zinoviev and Kamenev. He hesitated to commit himself publicly, however, for fear of losing the Finance Com-

missariat. Rykov and Bukharin emerged as Stalin's new allies, yet Bukharin and Stalin were noticeably uneasy partners. Zinoviev and Kamenev endorsed legitimate co-operatives as a path to socialism, but both claimed that socialism could not be built in one country. Trying to make sense out of this plethora of contradictions Trotsky was understandably bewildered.

Trotsky's assessment of the competing factions

In previous years Trotsky had been among the first to warn of the *kulak* menace and to elucidate the danger of a capitalist restoration. On these grounds it would have been reasonable to expect that he would support Zinoviev's condemnation of Bukharin. In his 1923 report on industry, however, Trotsky had also foreseen the need to undertake industrial expansion by means of machinery purchases in the West. Since imports presupposed exports, Trotsky now agreed with Bukharin that Zinoviev's diatribes constituted a serious threat to further economic growth.

Like Bukharin Trotsky recognized that 'the liquidation of the landlords . . . has brought about the liquidation of the big estates, among which were [included] some of the most up-to-date farms. This [is] one of the reasons . . . for the temporary decline of agriculture.'[25] Bukharin's remedies therefore seemed quite reasonable. If grain production could be increased exports would multiply and industrial machinery could be acquired. As Trotsky wrote in *Izvestiya*:

Was it possible to avoid expanding the opportunities for more freely developing the market economy in the village? No, because then the peasant economy would fall into decay, the market would narrow down, industry would be slowed down. . . Without the growth of the area sown with . . . wheat . . . there can be no exports; and without exports . . . there can be no imports either; and without imports we cannot acquire industrial equipment.[26]

In contrast to Zinoviev he condemned the idea of 'de-kulakizing' the *kulak*, for 'the next day this would strike the middle peasant, kill [his] . . . personal interest . . . and lead the countryside to the level of 1920–1'.

Although Trotsky would have preferred to see agriculture developing in a collective, socialist pattern, he did not believe this was possible until the Soviet state was capable of providing adequate supplies of mechanical equipment.[27] As for the limited number of collective farms currently in existence, he considered them incompatible with personal incentives.[28] There appeared to be no obvious solution to the dilemma apart from the one Bukharin recommended, particularly as the major share of new agricultural machinery would also have to be imported for several years to come.[29]

In a speech on 1 September Trotsky concluded that it was imperative to encourage the development of the productive forces in agriculture 'even with the help of capitalist methods. This is the essence of our policy in the present period.' The proposed gamble on the *kulak* had to be tested in practice:

> We require a development of the productive forces in the village. The *kulak*, the rich peasant, who sells grain by way of the state, enables the state to acquire foreign currency with which it can import machines for our factories. This is a positive factor. It promotes movement toward socialism.[30]

Trotsky believed that Zinoviev and his allies were over-stressing the dangers of class differentiation in the countryside; the new stimulus to agriculture would result in a general improvement, embracing all strata of the peasantry and causing the share of *kulak* marketings in the total volume to decline.[31] In his book *Towards Socialism or Capitalism?* he expressed confidence that 'the growth of capitalist or semi-capitalist tendencies in agriculture cannot possibly at any conceivable time in the near future pass beyond our control'.[32] This overriding concern to expand exports and to purchase foreign machinery was the main reason why Trotsky initially refused to become involved with Zinoviev and the new opposition.

A serious intensification of the goods famine in the autumn of 1925 emphasized even more strikingly the need to regain access to European capital equipment. Plans had been made sometime in advance for a significant increase in grain shipments to foreign markets. But the plans were one-sided; inadequate preparations had been made to stock the market with manufactured commodities. Once again, as in 1923, the wealthier peasants clung to their grain. Sokol'nikov's attempts to restrain the planners failed; lavish expenditure by the procurement agencies and new inflationary convulsions followed. The year had opened with Rykov's calm assurance that 'never before in our entire seven years have we faced a better perspective for the restoration of our economy.[33] It ended in stunning disappointment.

For the Zinoviev opposition the chaos could not have been more timely. Kamenev leapt at the opportunity to blame the *kulak*, claiming that a mere twelve per cent of the peasants controlled sixty per cent of the nation's grain supply, holding the government to ransom for the sake of speculative gain.[34] Smilga, who had headed Gosplan's commission on the control figures, seconded the charge and lent his prestige to the opposition. Zinoviev delighted in remorselessly sounding the alarm against the *kulak*. Later Kamenev diversified the critique, arguing that inadequate provisions had been made to accelerate industrial production and that the crisis highlighted the need for 'an expansion of our economy's links with the world market'.[35] From a theoretical rejection of Socialism in One Country the new opposition turned to an all-inclusive attack on virtually every aspect of economic policy.

The very pervasiveness of their charges gave the Zinoviev alliance a certain formlessness. If the opposition were to succeed Trotsky judged that Sokol'nikov would shape its complaints into a more systematic programme of his own making. And Sokol'nikov still denied that a goods famine even existed, explaining the crisis in terms of excess purchasing power and interference by the planners.[36] Holding Gosplan to blame he scorned what he believed to be an overestimation of the country's socialist 'ripeness' and ridiculed plans in general.[37] Zinoviev used the phrase state capitalism as a perjorative description of the retreat Bukharin had initiated; Sokol'nikov interpreted it to mean restoration of Gosbank's authority and supervision of the economy through monetary controls.[38] In his private notes Trotsky wrote that the Finance Commissar 'on all occasions counterposes the falsely interpreted interests of the countryside . . . to the vital interests of industry'. If permitted he would 'injure the interests of industry and of the monopoly of foreign trade in the name of reviving commodity circulation in general'. On 22 December Trotsky portrayed Sokol'nikov as 'a theoretician of the economic disarmament of the proletariat vis-à-vis the countryside'.[39]

Interpreting the two coalitions in terms of their class backgrounds Trotsky decided that their struggle represented a distorted attempt to review the existing relations between the proletariat and the peasantry. But the conflict was taking place 'without opposing . . . platforms of principle'.[40] The origins of the goods famine were traced to the Twelfth Party Congress in 1923. The fact that Zinoviev had been intimately involved in sabotaging the report on industry suggested there was little reason to expect a thorough change of attitude in 1925. Yet Leningrad, Zinoviev's bailiwick, was a key focus of hostility towards the *kulak*. It seemed that Zinoviev was unconsciously articulating the grievances of the Leningrad workers.[41] If this were the case Sokol'nikov's affiliation with Bukharin's critics could only be viewed as 'an example of the purest personal lack of principle and at the same time of the greatest careerism'.[42] The setbacks experienced during the grain procurement campaign shocked Trotsky out of his brief flirtation with Bukharin and the *kulak*; but so long as the Leningraders tolerated the Finance Commissar in their midst he believed they could not be trusted.

Their careless references to state capitalism indicated that Zinoviev and Kamenev were drifting; neither of them had any clear conception of the proper relationship between the NEP and socialism. In his haste to deride Bukharin's agricultural policies Zinoviev behaved with such reckless abandon as to suggest that the whole economy was state capitalist in nature rather than socialist. As Trotsky wrote on 14 December 1925:

Kamenev, Zinoviev and others continue to treat industry as a component part of the system of state capitalism. This point of view was common two or three years ago. . . The essence of this outlook is that industry is one of the subordinate parts of a system which includes . . . the peasant economy, finances, co-operation, private capitalist enterprises regulated by the state and so forth. . . In this scheme of things the regulating role of industry completely vanishes. The planning principle is almost entirely squeezed out by financial-credit regulation, which assumes the role of an inter-mediary between the peasant economy and state industry, treating the two as litigants with each other.[43]

'Financial and credit regulations,' Trotsky summarized, '. . . do not and cannot guarantee a development toward socialism.'

Had it not been for Sokol'nikov's misleading notions of financial control as a substitute for genuine planning Bukharin's idea of 'agrarian co-operative socialism', with its insensitivity toward industry, would never have arisen. Kamenev was right to criticize Bukharin. It had to be admitted though that Bukharin was on firm theoretical ground when he insisted that Russia's industry was truly socialist rather than state capitalist. In their own way both sides were tearing apart the programme devised in 1923 by Sokol'nikov. Kamenev, for instance, had made certain unexpected remarks in favour of industry, which Trotsky took as 'an undoubted step forward'. But Kamenev had yet to link industry's needs with current agricultural difficulties: he did not understand that rural stratification and the power of the *kulak* were derivatives of scarcity, lack of agricultural equipment, and industrial underdevelopment in general. A fundamental change in priorities was necessary. Before any reconciliation could be brought about Kamenev and Zinoviev would have to repudiate the stand they had taken at the Twelfth Congress. 'It is imperative,' Trotsky wrote in his notes, 'to liquidate the position of 1923, not in bits and pieces but in its entirety.' Otherwise a continuing lag in industrial growth would be inevitable; agriculture would race ahead and the goods famine would critically worsen.

Faced with a choice between two amorphous policy outlooks, neither of which was satisfactory, Trotsky hesitated to support either side. Even if he avoided personal commitment, however, he could not escape involvement: his silence would be taken to indicate tacit approval of Stalin and the party leadership. Bukharin was the unpredictable factor in the one alliance; Sokol'nikov in the other. Of the two, Trotsky believed Sokol'nikov to represent the greater threat. The sympathies of Stalin and Rykov for industry were thought likely to outweigh Bukharin's folly in agriculture. Bukharin's mistakes were simply a *reductio ad absurdum* of Sokol'nikov's concepts. In the wake of the procurement crisis a change of policy was probable in any case. Weighing the two evils Trotsky tentatively decided to endorse Stalin against Zinoviev. Discussing this decision Antonov-Ovseenko, one of Trotsky's supporters, later wrote the following:

I know that you planned to come out at the [Fourteenth] Party Congress [in December 1925] against Zinoviev–Kamenev. I deeply regretted and still do regret the fact that short-sighted factionalist-friends convinced you (after no small opposition on your part) to refrain from this action (which had already been decided upon). You know that I was against your [later] bloc with Zinoviev–Kamenev, considering it completely unprincipled.[44]

The fact that Trotsky never denied the validity of the Antonov-Ovseenko letter can be taken as sufficient evidence that it was genuine. Nevertheless, Trotsky's ultimate indecisiveness was probably less related to arguments put forth by his colleagues than to

his concern for the trade monopoly and his desire to import producers' goods. On 6 November *Pravda* had published a Central
Committee resolution dealing with the monopoly for the first time
since 1922. The precise reasons for the resolution are not clear,
although the question appears to have been raised by Krasin in
order to evade responsibility for the export failure. Whatever
the case Lenin's remarks from 1922 were deliberately cited, evok-
ing memories of Trotsky's earlier clash with the Finance Commissar. Particular attention was also drawn to the relationship
between machinery imports and industrialization:

> a solution of the problem of basic capital for our industry is closely tied up
> with the future of foreign trade. We must vigorously develop our ex-
> ports... [The development of exports means increased] possibilities for
> purchasing equipment abroad for our industry, together with machines
> and implements for agriculture; that is, it permits an acceleration of our
> economy's transition to a new technical base.

Later in the same month the Foreign Trade Commissariat was
abolished as a separate ministry and combined with the Commissariat of Internal Trade. But the principle of state control was
strictly maintained, and the Central Committee's resolution would
not have differed substantially had it been written by Trotsky
himself. The decision to preserve the monopoly gave Trotsky
added encouragement to support Stalin in preference to Zinoviev.

The choice became more difficult though, when Bukharin reacted to the procurement crisis by moving one step further in the
direction of conscious isolationism. Refusing to employ administrative pressure against the *kulak* he argued that such a response
would antagonize the countryside and imperil agriculture as a
whole. Furthermore he disputed the contention that the grain
purchase plan had failed because of hoarding by the class enemy.
The real problem, he asserted, had been rainy weather, which
had led to a partial reduction in the harvest. Threshing had been
delayed for the same reason; and the unco-ordinated activities
of the procurement agencies had caused price rises and expectations of subsequent increases, thereby providing the peasant with
an incentive not to sell.[45] Although all these factors had contributed
to the débâcle Bukharin ignored the central problem; namely, the
scarcity of industrial goods.

From the disruption of the import plan he drew the conclusion that Russia must reduce her dependence upon foreign trade.

The more trade grew the more reliant the country would become upon the hostile capitalist world and the more vulnerable to the threat of renewed blockade. Shortly before the Fourteenth Party Congress Bukharin told a meeting in Moscow:

The main dangers are international. We are moving closer now to the world market. We are now entering into a whole series of deals . . . with the world economy and for this reason we are becoming in some measure a participant in the world economy. Our production programme to a certain degree depends upon how much we import from abroad and on how much we export.

But imagine now that a financial and economic blockade develops. . . We would then have to reorganize our entire economic plan. Would this not entail the greatest difficulties?

We are growing on the basis of our ties with the outside world; but on the other hand . . . we are becoming to a certain degree more vulnerable. How can we avoid this danger?

We can avoid it by ensuring that our economy and our country do not become in any manner or degree too dependent economically on the foreign market so long as it is controlled by the bourgeoisie and capitalism.[46]

At the party congress in December 1925 Bukharin repeated the claim that 'we have many new dangers . . . because we are entering the international market; we are becoming more vulnerable'.[47] In the same speech, commenting on Trotsky's alleged belief that Russia's backwardness made it impossible to build socialism, he vowed that construction of a socialist society would continue – even if only at a 'snail's pace'.

Trotsky believed that a 'snail's pace' was precisely what must be expected if the chance to purchase new industrial equipment were lost. Infuriated by Bukharin's apparent spinelessness in face of the *kulak* he predicted that indifference to the tempo of industrial expansion would bring about 'a gradual back-sliding into a *muzhik* (peasant) thermidor'. Bukharin suffered from a 'national-village limitation' and was becoming an undisguised theorist of Soviet *Narodnichestvo* (Populism). In short, through his translation of Socialism in One Country into an economic programme Bukharin had become the architect of the absurd theory 'of a closed (*zamknutoe*) national economy and a closed construction of socialism'.[48] If Stalin and Rykov were seduced into accepting Bukharin's views the goods famine would remain and the peasant would destroy the trade monopoly. Socialism would be lost. The revolution would degenerate. When Stalin's description of industrialization strategy at the party meeting complied with Bukharin's isolationism Trotsky finally resolved that he could lend his support to neither of the former triumvirs.

The Stalin–Sokol'nikov debate

With the exception of the Leningrad delegation the representatives at the Fourteenth Party Congress were hand-picked by Stalin. Having sufficient votes to swamp Zinoviev on any issue the revolution's new *Vozhd* (Leader) used the congress as a forum for his first major venture directly into questions of economic policy. Characteristically he simplified the issues to fit the now established categories of pessimism or optimism and transformed the idea of industrialization into a political rallying cry intended to unite the party under his own leadership.

Russia, he declared, had to choose between two possible avenues of development. The first of these, which Stalin attributed to L. Shanin, was based on the recommendation that the Soviet Union remain an agrarian exporter and an importer of industrial goods. This line, Stalin contended, 'demands that we should wind up our industry'. If the party were to adopt such a course it would mean that Russia could never become 'an economically independent unit', but would be converted into 'an appendage of the general capitalist system'. Foreign trade would grow rapidly; and 'the more our export and import grows the more dependent we become upon the capitalist West, the more vulnerable we become to blows from the side of our enemies'.

The second, and more optimistic alternative, Stalin outlined in the following way:

There is another general line, which starts from the fact that we must exert every effort, so long as the capitalist encirclement exists, to make our country economically independent... This line demands the maximum expansion of our industry... It decisively rejects the policy of converting our country into an appendage of the world capitalist system. This is our line... This line is imperative so long as the capitalist encirclement exists.[49]

To follow the road of socialist independence Russia would first have to provide guarantees against future blockade. Imports would have to be sacrificed to an active trade balance in order that precautionary reserves might be gathered. Without these safeguards 'the camp of struggle against imperialism' would be left economically defenceless against 'the camp of imperialism'. 'We ourselves,' Stalin announced, 'will produce machines and other means of production.'[50] In his proposed resolution the party secretary argued:

[We must] conduct our economic construction in such a way as to convert the USSR from a country which imports machines and equipment into a country which produces machines and equipment... In this manner the USSR ... will become a self-sufficient economic unit building socialism.[51]

On the question whether socialism could in fact be built in one country Stalin restated his new theory:

In the area of economic construction the congress takes as its starting point the fact that our country ... possesses 'all that is necessary for the construction of a full socialist society' [Lenin] ... without so-called 'help' from foreign capital.[52]

The problem would be different when the revolution came in France or in Germany. Then the policy of building a 'self-sufficient economic unit' could be abandoned in favour of 'the inclusion of our country in the general stream of socialist development'. But until that time socialism meant autarchy. In effect Stalin's speech re-established the party line of 1920, when Trotsky had first proposed to build socialism in a state of isolation. The years 1921–4, the years of the integrationist consensus, had been forgotten.

By capturing the initiative in this manner Stalin left Zinoviev to thrash helplessly in his self-created theoretical bog. Flustered, the Leningrad chieftan complained that he had been misunderstood. He had not really meant that Russia could not build socialism:

We are only debating whether it is possible to build socialism finally and to consolidate a socialist structure in one country, and not in a country such as America, but in our peasant country. We are not arguing whether the construction of socialism is impossible in one country: the number of proletarians in the Soviet Union is sufficient for this, the economic prerequisites are present. The general political situation is perfectly favourable for building socialism with great success – remembering that we have the support of the international working class and that our construction of socialism will finally be completed in the international context.[53]

Zinoviev's speech was a rhetorical disaster. The congress had been so thoroughly packed, however, that Stalin had no reason to be more than remotely interested in what Zinoviev might say. A much more intriguing opponent was Sokol'nikov. Stalin had blunted his earlier references to the Finance Commissar by attributing the first general line to Shanin, an economist working with Narkomfin. But there was no doubt that Sokol'nikov was the real target. The response was difficult to predict; in recent months Sokol'nikov had sought desperately to preserve his programme. In the process he had arrived at a number of completely unexpected decisions.

Early in the summer of 1925 he had encountered a book written by Leo Pasvolsky and Harold Moulton entitled *Russian Debts and Russian Reconstruction.* Pasvolsky and Moulton shared the belief that Europe needed Russia both as an outlet for manufactured goods and as a source of raw materials and foodstuffs. They also claimed that a commercial loan to Russia would serve no useful purpose. Neither the country's export–import ratio nor its ability to make interest payments on new credits would be significantly altered.[54] Moreover, on the basis of questionable statistics the two authors maintained that tsarist Russia had for some time been borrowing abroad merely to pay interest on previous loans. Given the attitude of the party after the London negotiations the book made a stunning impression. Without any forewarning Sokol'nikov suddenly and unequivocally disclaimed the basis of his entire strategy since the end of 1921:

At Genoa the Soviet delegation presented a request for a loan of three milliard rubles for Russia's reconstruction. Nothing came of it, and it is very likely a good thing... If it had materialized this loan would have had a whole series of negative economic and political effects for Soviet Russia.[55]

In future foreign loans must not be allowed to assume more than what Sokol'nikov termed 'a supplementary significance'. On several occasions during the later months of 1925 he returned to the same argument, approving of short-term credits, welcoming concessions in the gold-mining industry as a means to expand reserves for the *chervonets*, but rejecting the accumulation of long-term debt. In the period 1894–1913 tsarist Russia's total debt charges appeared to have amounted to five hundred million rubles more than her borrowing.[56] Instead of pathetically chasing after foreign capital the Finance Commissar now proposed to expand the export surplus, which represented a clear gain in foreign currency.

A second and equally important reversal in Sokol'nikov's position concerned the non-monetary purposes which exports were to serve. At the beginning of the NEP he had favoured the import of consumer goods. During 1923, in the debate with Trotsky, industrial raw materials had been given primary emphasis. The need for industrial materials and semifabricates was still evident; but Stalin's intrusion, Gosplan's growing prestige, and the 1925 disaster called for a reappraisal. While the idea of industrialization was too politically charged to be ignored the fact remained that the Russian peasant would no longer tolerate chronic scarcities. Stalin's plan for a self-sufficient economy would increase the danger since the internal production of additional industrial equipment would involve needless delay and unacceptable expense. Besides, Stalin had not offered a single suggestion as to the precise manner in which industrialization should be financed. Becoming more aware of the need for industrial investments Sokol'nikov feared that Stalin's dream would result in the nightmare of uninterrupted inflation and the destruction of three years' work at Narkomfin. One hope was left: if the bulk of Russia's capital goods could be bought in Europe the interests of agriculture, industry and finance might yet be reconciled. Shortly before the congress Sokol'nikov penned one of his last major pronouncements, reviving an argument Rykov had first used against Trotsky in 1920:

According to calculations made before the imperialist war sixty-three per cent of the industrial equipment in the country consisted of machinery imported from abroad... In order to achieve the complete re-equipment of our industry now, without foreign imports, it would be necessary to establish in the USSR those branches of the engineering industry required to renew the technical inventory.

It is perfectly obvious that in this case we would find ourselves in a vicious circle. In order to produce new, more modern machines, it is necessary to make the machines which produce machines.

But an attempt to resolve this task using our own resources ... would presuppose the organization of a series of production and reproduction cycles, which would require decades to complete. For this reason the task of re-equiping our industry must be completed by importing more modern machinery and equipment from abroad. In terms of time this will save us decades.[57]

In one respect Sokol'nikov had permitted himself an overstatement. From forty to sixty per cent of Soviet engineering capacity was still idle and this slack could have been reduced with a some-what smaller volume of new construction than the Finance Com-missar implied. Apart from this polemical simplification his reasoning was sound.

Assuming an indignant tone, at the party congress Sokol'nikov rashly announced that Stalin's exposition of the two general lines was 'entirely mistaken'. There was no question of Russia being reduced to a colony: the pertinent choice was between capital imports and grain sales as vehicles for the import of materials and machinery. Ruling out foreign loans the Finance Commis-sar insisted that advances in agriculture could be sustained without the enormous capital expenditures required by industry. The most rapid possible increase in national income would result from 'a course towards the development of foreign trade relations'.[58]

With Zinoviev disposed of Stalin was in no mood to brook this sort of criticism. 'Everyone knows,' he told the party, 'that we are obliged at present to import equipment. But Sokol'nikov con-verts this necessity into a principle, a theory, a prospect of devel-opment. That is where Sokol'nikov's mistake lies.' Russia had to effect a monumental transition from an 'agrarian country' to an 'industrial country'. 'Can it be,' Stalin asked, 'that Sokol'nikov fails to understand such an elementary thing?' Sokol'nikov was proposing 'the Dawesization of our country'. Playing into the hands of the capitalists he would permit Germany to meet its reparations payments by way of machinery sales to Russia. But Russia had no desire 'to remain an agrarian country for the bene-fit of some other country; . . . we will produce machinery and other means of production ourselves'. That, Stalin affirmed, 'is the essence, the basis of our general line. . . Comrade Sokol'nikov does not wish to understand this simple and obvious fact.'[59]

Soviet industrialization was now firmly identified with the theory of Socialism in One Country. And Socialism in One Coun-try had in turn been defined as economic autarchy. The Four-teenth Party Congress confirmed Stalin's new authority over economic policy, and a number of offices were redistributed to reflect the altered distribution of power. Kamenev was deprived of control over the Moscow Soviet and lost his seat in the Polit-buro. Zinoviev retained his position in the Politburo but lost the Leningrad Soviet. Both the Central Committee and the Politburo were enlarged to accommodate a new influx of Stalin's recruits.

Sokol'nikov sacrificed his candidate membership in the Politburo and was relieved of his duties at Narkomfin. From there he was assigned to work in Gosplan, where he watched the *chervonets* first deprived of its gold parity and later subjected to export prohibitions. As a reward for his reticence Trotsky emerged unscathed. The respite was temporary. Within months, for reasons which I will now consider, he too became involved in a similarly unequal struggle with Stalin.

6

Trotsky's alternative

According to most historical accounts Trotsky's opinions from 1925 to 1927 represented a strange combination of Zinoviev's theoretical abstractions and an amalgam of mythical 'Trotsky-ism', the latter being understood in terms of the definition given by the triumvirs at the end of 1924. Trotsky is portrayed as believing that the success of socialism in Russia presupposed an economic union with socialist Europe. The theory of Permanent Revolution is taken as proof of the need for economic support from the Western proletariat. Because Trotsky's own estimate of the importance of Permanent Revolution does not fit this analysis it is disregarded. Early in 1925 Trotsky wrote that the theory's relevance was 'wholly to the past'. It was a matter for party history. It provided no justification for 'allusions and references to my allegedly "pessimistic" attitude'.[1]

As indicated in the first pages of this study, the real origins of the debate with Stalin were of a more practical nature. In 1922–3 Trotsky had made his peace with the NEP on condition that the market be rendered compatible with socialism through primitive socialist accumulation. At the end of 1924 Bukharin 'solved' the problem of capital scarcity by denying its existence in the short run. Unaware of any contradiction Stalin then committed the party to rapid industrialization while failing to challenge Bukharin's conception of the *smychka*. For a time high taxes on the *kulak* were politically unacceptable. Believing that industrialization could not be financed from Soviet resources while the Bukharin–Stalin partnership survived, Trotsky came to exactly the conclusion Lenin had adopted in 1920–1: Russia would have to augment her capital stock through reintegration into the world economy.

At the most unpropitious of all possible times, in 1925, Trotsky experienced a conversion to integrationism that was both abrupt and total. By an almost unbelievable irony the integrationist–isolationist controversy emerged once again to shake the Bolshevik party to its very foundations. A number of factors contributed to Trotsky's *volte-face*, not the least of which was his appointment to Vesenkha in the spring of the year. Notwithstanding its insights the industrial report to the Twelfth Party Congress had been primarily the intuitive work of a political theorist. The new posting to Vesenkha brought Trotsky face to face for the first time since War Communism with empirical economic questions. Serving on the Main Concessions Committee (a touch of Stalinist humour), the Electro-technical Commission and a special committee on prices and quality, he attempted to reconsider Soviet policy. Almost at once he modified several of his preconceptions concerning such critical questions as concessions, foreign loans, and the relationship between foreign trade and protectionism during industrialization.

In this way the startling theoretical and political realignments of 1925 were concluded. After disdaining Sokol'nikov's policies virtually by force of habit Trotsky now replaced his disillusioned rival as the most emphatic proponent of an accommodation with the West. With Bukharin and Stalin endorsing isolationism the divisions of 1920–1 were reproduced in every important detail. The year 1925 took on an uncanny atmosphere of historical repetition as the Trotsky–Sokol'nikov antithesis gave way to new hostilities between Trotsky and Bukharin. Stalin, with his plans for self-sufficient industrialization, was left to seize and occupy the enviable political middle, a position he later employed to balance Bukharin against Trotsky and to complete the accumulation of unbridled dictatorial power. Having discussed the genesis of Socialism in One Country by reference to the fear of capitalist stabilization, I shall now analyze Trotsky's position in a similar fashion, beginning with his appraisal of recent developments in Europe.

From the theory of *Imperialism* to *Integrationism*

The connections between Trotsky's theory of Imperialism and his political behaviour during and after War Communism have been mentioned on several occasions in this book. In 1925–7 the influence was still at work; Trotsky interpreted the question of stabilization in terms of the analytical framework he had first devised in the

1921 Comintern Report. The methodology was the same; but by taking new factors into consideration it produced answers which directly contradicted those formulated in 1921. The key change in the analysis again involved the problem of the business cycle.

Trotsky recognized that Europe had succeeded in reordering its affairs. However, he still denied that real capital, or the productive forces, had been growing. Because of the causal relations between the two, he believed that a restoration of normal investments would have returned Europe to a regular, traditional cycle. In fact the cycle had not been evident, and Trotsky attributed its absence to a basic alteration in the pattern of capitalist growth. Until 1913 the European countries had enjoyed decades of expansion, colonizing the world in the search for markets. This period ended with the Great War. Marx's theory of a rhythmic cycle had been valid while the era of growth lasted. But by the mid-1920s the barrier of inadequate markets appeared to have halted Europe's recovery causing 'stagnation . . . with sharp fluctuations up and down which make it impossible even to discern a [normal] kon'yunktura'. Marx's theory was due for revision:

At the third congress of the Comintern we . . . showed that conjunctural changes would be inevitable in the future including [the possibility of] an improvement. But there is a difference between the heart beat of a healthy man and that of a sick man. Capitalism has not died, it lives – we said in 1921 – and for this reason its heart will beat and there will be conjunctural changes; but when a living organism finds itself in impossible circumstances its pulse beats irregularly, it is hard to detect the proper rhythm and so forth. This is what we have been witnessing in Europe.[2]

The motivating force of the capitalist system had been paralyzed; new investments had been postponed because existing industry was partially idle. American loans would facilitate currency stabilization and international financial settlements; but they would not mitigate Europe's chronic difficulty. What America gave with one hand it took with the other, multiplying Europe's ills by invading its pre-war markets. In these circumstances the Dawes Plan could not be considered a 'cure'; it was a cosmetic, disguising capitalism's tendency towards inevitable destruction. Like a financier with investments in several trusts America was attempting to squeeze a profit from each of the European countries. None was being allowed to establish even a temporary ascendancy; competition was being regulated from across the Atlantic; markets were being carefully allotted in order to maintain a 'rotten equilibrium'.[3]

The goal of equilibrium was an American chimera. The loss of markets would cause European rivalries to reach pre-war intensity long before comparable levels of production could be attained. Narrower markets would be glutted more quickly with a surfeit of unsaleable goods; a lower national income would incite more violent class struggles.[4] Unless the United States permitted Europe a greater share of world demand the international revolution would resume its course. On the other hand America could not retreat from its new positions without transferring the same contradictions to its own economy. Either way capitalism could not achieve lasting stabilization.[5] The only genuinely stable element in world affairs was 'the uninterrupted, automatic growth of militarism' resulting from capitalism's insurmountable inability to match consumption with production.[6]

Disagreeing with the Bukharin–Stalin prognosis for the West Trotsky saw in Europe's decline not the threat of blockade or isolation, but a unique Russian opportunity. Ever since 1920 those party spokesmen who had stressed capitalism's bleak future had simultaneously pointed to the vast potential of the Soviet market. In 1925 Trotsky conformed to this pattern. The industrial report had already referred to Europe's interest in Russian grain. Now the plight of heavy industry in the West and Europe's struggle for exports were both becoming acute at the very moment when the Soviet Union required new industrial equipment. Since the needs of the two systems were so conveniently complementary Trotsky reasoned that Russia could provide Europe with 'a colossal market which would exceed that of all the British colonies'.[7] If Britain, for example, had invested in Russia the £100 million in sterling spent on armed intervention, 'we should by now without doubt have passed [our own] pre-war level [of production], paid British capital high rates of interest, and what is more important, should have presented a large and continually growing market'.[8] In another place Trotsky wrote: 'there can be no doubt that the British economy would gain great benefits from . . . co-operation . . . with Russia. But this presupposes a great plan, large credits, and the adaptation of an important part of British industry to the needs of Russia.'[9]

Looking at the London negotiations in this perspective Trotsky did not see them as cause for despair. Quite the contrary: the discussions with MacDonald signified a first awakening, a presentiment in the West of the direction in which history was inexorably moving. The occurrence of the socialist revolution in one country had raised political impediments to the United States of Europe. But Trotsky had never abandoned the belief that ultimately objective economic forces would prevail over man-made obstacles. The influence of War Communism had temporarily distorted his judgement. By 1925, however, he shared the view Kamenev had expressed in 1921, when reporting on the question of isolation to the Tenth Party Congress. In Trotsky's words:

> The world division of labour and the exchange which derives from it is not disrupted by the fact that a socialist system prevails in one country while a capitalist one prevails in the others... The fact that the workers and peasants in our country wield state power and own the trusts and syndicates in no way upsets the world division of labour, which results [not from ideology but] from differences in natural circumstances and national history.[10]

In other words, Russia's political isolation need not imply economic isolation. Stalin's intention to insulate Russia from the West until after the international revolution was misleading because it was unhistorical. A change of regime in Europe would be an event, a point in time. The forces of history worked through time; and the future basis of the United States of Europe was inherent in the present requirements of the world economy. Reasoning along these lines Trotsky was completing a personal evolution which had begun with Parvus's theory of the state long before 1917.

MacDonald's fall had impressed Stalin and Bukharin. They considered it a decisive turning point which would adversely affect an entire phase of Soviet development. Trotsky realized that the Tories would not hold office for ever. With their departure the talks might begin again. In the meantime other opportunities would arise. Intermittent financial negotiations had already been under way in Paris for some time. In February 1926, when these were about to be resumed, Trotsky described in *Pravda* the enormous advantages France could derive from machinery sales to Russia. To encourage Soviet purchases he suggested the French should lend Russia 300 million rubles. In return the Soviet government could follow the precedent Rakovsky had established in London. Russia could pay interest in excess of the market rate with the difference going to settle the claims of tsarist creditors. In all Trotsky calculated that the added cost of such an arrangement would be a mere twelve million rubles annually, certainly a meagre price to pay for a loan which would equal three times the sum Vesenkha hoped to invest in new industrial construction during 1925–6.[11]

The prevailing condition of the international economy suggested the hopeful conclusion that even America might be induced to relieve the menace of competition and war with Europe by reaching an agreement with Russia. Although the American bourgeoisie were the world's wealthiest exploiting class, they were no more prepared to abide a falling rate of profit than their European counterparts. Discussing America's world position Trotsky saw no need to revise the analysis he had made in previous years:

America is suffering from plethora. Within the confines of the domestic market it has reached a certain limit. There remains room for only minor developments, whereas until the present America has developed in a continuing spiral with an ever-widening radius. In order to prevent the spiral from being broken by suddenly crashing into the barriers imposed by the world market American capital must push everyone else aside and broaden the market. But it cannot be broadened by economic means alone for it is parcelled out – others must be pushed out, thrown back by force. It is this fact which accounts for the truly frantic development of militarism.[12]

The logical consistency of Trotsky's outlook was too perfect to correspond to the real world. In the summer of 1925 he enthusiastically told a United Press reporter that if American industry provided Russia with credits a joint economic plan could be devised, extending over five years, a decade, or more.[13] The Americans responded in February 1926. An anonymous Washington spokesman noted that the United States had no incentive to enter into a partnership with Bolshevism. American industry was already fully employed and the Soviet government owed the United States 400 million dollars in unsatisfied debts.[14] Irving T. Bush, President of the New York State Chamber of Commerce, was less restrained:

Those in authority [in Russia] sneer at what they name capitalism, and yet they come with empty coffers and outstretched hands asking for capital. They say: 'We have taken what you had invested in Russia, please come

and invest some more.' There are too many other places in the world
Mr Trotsky where obligations are respected... We have refused [to grant
Russia] recognition on moral grounds. We have been accused by those who
know nothing of American ideals of having no ideal but the dollar. England and France and Germany have yielded to the subtle arguments of
trade gains and have recognized Russia. From a sordid business standpoint have they gained profit? Have they reaped anything but trouble?
They have sold their heritage of international law for a mess of pottage.[15]

Trotsky thought moralizing of this kind was as absurd as
Stalin's attempt to thwart history by theoretically dividing the
world into two camps. In the months when Sokolnikov was being
forced to beat a retreat from integrationism his erstwhile antagon-
ist saw new possibilities for concessions. After a time lag of four
years Trotsky decided that the capitalists might be encouraged to
show more sense if Russia took the lead in adopting a more flexible stance. Here too it should be noted that Trotsky's reassessment did not contradict his previous views. In 1920–1 he had
believed that Russia was too poor to attract foreign capital on a
sizeable scale. Since that time recovery had been completed. A
more pronounced imperialist struggle would also be accompanied
by vigorous competition to secure and monopolize raw materials.
With America intruding upon established European sources of
supply it seemed reasonable to suppose that Russia might now
provide a plausible alternative. Speaking to a delegation of German workers, in July 1925 Trotsky argued:

We ourselves have been extremely cautious, one might even say too cautious with respect to concessions agreements. We were too poor and weak.
Our industry and our entire economy were too ruined and we were afraid
that the introduction of foreign capital would undermine the still weak
foundations of socialist industry... We are still very backward in a technical sense. We are interested in using every possible means to accelerate
our technical progress. Concessions are one way to do this. Despite our
economic consolidation, or more precisely, because of our economic consolidation, we are now more inclined than a few years ago to pay foreign
capitalists significant sums for... their participation in the development
of our productive forces.[16]

For more than a year and a half the party's disenchantment
with the concessions programme had been growing unmistake-
ably more pronounced. For Trotsky to ignore this trend was an
act of sheer folly. Only six weeks earlier Stalin had deliberately
associated concessions with the stigma of the old regime and
'enslaving terms' dictated by capitalist fiat:

tsarist Russia ... granted concessions to and accepted loans from the Western powers on such terms and thereby imposed upon herself the yoke of semi-colonial existence. ... It scarcely needs to be proved that this path is ... unacceptable to the Land of Soviets. We did not shed our blood in the three years' war against the imperialists of all countries in order to go into voluntary bondage to imperialism the very day after the victorious termination of the civil war.[17]

From Stalin such comments were to be expected. The theory of Socialism in One Country assumed that industrial investments could be conjured out of nothing. Trotsky was more concerned with the problem Sokol'nikov had raised: how was industrialization to be financed? As he told the German delegation:

The question of concessions assumes a particular significance for us now when we have arrived in earnest at the task of renewing our basic capital. We have succeeded in securing a notable accumulation ... but our savings are not large enough to carry through to the end the renewal and expansion of our factories by our own resources. We are in need of credit, and we need concessions as well in order to speed up our economic growth and thereby to increase the well-being of the masses.[18]

Despite the failure of the concessions programme Trotsky looked hopefully for signs that it might yet prove worthwhile, that 'a period of more lively concessions policy' might be in the offing. He was particularly encouraged by two negotiations which were underway when he was appointed to Vesenkha. One of these, the Lena Goldfields project, was accepted provisionally on 30 April 1925. Included in the agreement were major mining sites, in return for which the Soviet government received seven per cent of total production and commitments from the British concessionaires to provide both smelting plants and extractive equipment. A second important agreement was signed in June 1925, giving W. A. Harriman a twenty-year lease on the Chiatury manganese mines in the Caucasus. When diplomatic relations were restored with Japan disputed possession of the island of Sakhalin was also resolved by means of oil, coal, and timber leases.

If the capitalists could be cajoled into taking part in Russia's industrial construction Trotsky foresaw 'the transfer to our country of foreign plant, foreign productive formulae, and the financing of our economy by the resources of world capitalist savings'.[19] The Dneprostroi combine, one of the largest electrification ventures planned thus far, appeared to be ideally suited to foreign co-operation. Following Lenin's example in 1920–1, Trotsky thought it natural to invite the capitalists to renew and expand the metallurgical and other factories in the Zaporozhya region. The construction of aluminium and chemical plants could be similarly financed. Heavy electrical equipment should be purchased, wherever possible, with foreign credits.[20] 'The dialectics of historical development' would result in capitalism becoming for a time the creditor of socialism. 'Well, has not capitalism been nourished at the breasts of feudalism? History has honoured the debt.'[21] Agreeing belatedly with a policy already about to be rescinded, Trotsky was committing the mistake he had made before in 1920–1 and again in 1923. He was allowing the dialectic of history to obscure a far more important dialectic at present working within the party.

On behalf of the Main Concessions Committee he conscientiously endeavoured to allay foreign fears of expropriation and to convince the West that Russia would fulfil her obligations. Repudiating Stalin's isolationism, he denied that the party had ever intended, indeed, ever thought it possible that Russia might become 'economically a "self-sufficient" country'. Echoing Sokol'nikov he vainly insisted that 'we have [now] economically entered the system of the world division of labour and have thereby become subject to the laws governing the world market'.[22] The idea of consciously detaching Russia from Europe was an atavistic reflection of low levels of trade in the past. 'However, with the rapid growth of exports and imports the position was radically changed. We are becoming a part, a highly individual but nevertheless component part of the world market.'[23] 'We have arrived at a new stage,' he wrote in *Ekonomicheskaya Zhizn'*, 'from a closed national economic organism we are crossing over to the position of a component part of the world economy.'[24] The future growth of industry would entail an enormous increase in foreign trade and 'a gigantic expansion of imports'. If national income were to double Trotsky predicted that total foreign trade turnover might increase tenfold.[25]

Only an incredible case of political myopia could have induced any party member to identify with such objectionable opinions in 1925. Sokol'nikov's actions were understandable. He was defending an established position of his own creation against critics whom he took to be insolent upstarts in the realm of economic theory. But Trotsky had been so battered politically that any view he expressed was liable to immediate suspicion simply because it was his. Sokol'nikov could claim to have enjoyed Lenin's support, but it was precisely over the implications of trade and foreign investments that Lenin and Trotsky had found themselves in outright conflict. Trotsky himself had originated the entire theoretical arsenal currently being employed by Stalin. In 1921–2 he had discredited concessions and expounded the earliest version of the theory of stabilization. In 1923 he had embraced the concept of primitive socialist accumulation, arguing, as during War Communism, that Russia's capital requirements must be met internally. When Stalin and others began to find fault with Sokol'nikov's integrationism Trotsky had prepared the way with his repeated prophecies of military intervention. The man's whole image had become that of a die-hard revolutionary, defending fortress Russia against real and imaginary foreign threats until the European proletariat lifted the seige. By 1925, however, even Trotsky's appraisal of the military danger had been completely reformulated.

Military power depended upon industry; and industry depended upon foreign machinery. Russia was therefore to diversify foreign trade relations to the utmost: 'The more multiform our international relations,' Trotsky explained, 'the more difficult it will be . . . for our possible enemies to break them. And . . . even if [war or blockade] . . . were to come about, we should still be much stronger than we would have been under a "self-sufficient" and consequently belated development.'[26] Germany was said to offer an instructive example. During her period of industrialization Germany had vigorously expanded foreign trade. Yet when the hostilities of 1914–18 resulted in almost total blockade Germany possessed an exceptionally adaptable productive apparatus, which was ultilized to the full for military purposes. An attempt to plan for a self-contained economy would be reasonable if Russia were at war. During peacetime, however, Trotsky now felt it was imperative to imitate the German experience and to take full advantage of the international division of labour. To show how this might be done he transformed integrationist concepts into a systematic strategy for industrial growth – and committed political suicide.

Trotsky's proposed industrialization strategy

From the first phase of the debate on industrialization Stalin and Trotsky were at odds not over the question of *whether* socialism could be built in Russia, but over the far more important matter of *how* the task should be conceived. Arguing from isolationist premises Stalin contended that heavy industry must grow more quickly than the consumer goods sector. Investments in light industry were to be delayed until the domestic engineering industries were able to provide the required capital equipment. Trotsky took this to be an inverted order of priorities. His dissatisfaction was clear by the spring of 1925, when the party learned of Vesenkha's plans for metallurgy. In a letter to Dzerzhinsky Trotsky complained that the planned commitments were excessive: they were based on 'unreal credits' and they would lead to a crisis.[27] Obliquely commenting on the later monetary expansion he warned that the securities involved did not represent real savings. They were only 'auxiliary instruments for the calculation and distribution of real values'; they added nothing to 'the actual volume of goods which serves as the basis for the expansion of production'. In 1924–5 deposit and current accounts averaged eleven per cent of the pre-war level, 'one of the striking indications of the small amount of our savings'.[28]

Trotsky and Sokol'nikov were both aware that a precipitous attempt to expand the engineering and metallurgical industries would not only risk inflation; it would also interfere with future grain procurements, disrupt exports, reinforce the irrational drive to self-sufficiency, and lead to a critical neglect of other branches of industry. Looking ahead Trotsky realized that during the gestation period 'basic capital' would be immobilized in construction work and light industry would suffer. The goods famine would intensify and 'proportionality' would be destroyed:

If we were suddenly to shift our resources ... to the making of new machinery we would either destroy the necessary proportion between the different branches of the economy, and between the basic and circulating capital in a given branch, or if we maintained the proportion we should be greatly decreasing the whole coefficient of development. And for us a decrease in the rate of development is infinitely more dangerous than the import of foreign machinery and of the foreign goods we require in general.[29]

The last sentence of this excerpt provides the essential key to understanding the historic confrontation. It cannot be emphasized too strongly that by 1925 Trotsky believed Russia must return to the traditional trade patterns he had discussed in *Results and Prospects*. On this point he was in complete accord with Sokol'nikov:

We must not ... forget for a moment the great mutual dependence which existed between the economies of tsarist Russia and world capital. We must just bring to mind the fact that nearly two-thirds of the technical equipment of our works and factories used to be imported from abroad. This dependence has hardly decreased in our own time, which means that it will scarcely be economically profitable for us in the next few years to produce at home the machinery we require, at any rate, more than two-fifths of the quantity, or at best more than half of it.[30]

At various meetings of the Electro-technical Commission Trotsky provided more specific illustrations of the alternative he envisaged to Stalin's policies. Already worried over the lengthy gestation period involved in the construction of power stations, in July 1925 he suggested that the programme would be further delayed if the need for protectionism was interpreted too rigidly. Instead of requiring domestic industry to produce the diverse varieties of necessary equipment, Russia should concentrate on the items in greatest demand, importing the more complex and expensive. Where mass production was not practicable at least part of the work might be done domestically if components could be purchased in the West and assembled by Soviet trusts. 'The electrical industry,' Trotsky declared, 'must not hold back electrification by measures of blind protectionism. . . Above all . . . the electrical industry must not . . . immediately undertake too many new tasks.' 'We must,' he continued, 'concentrate on the necessary minimum of products, but in their production strive for a maximal achievement of quantity and quality.'[31]

As in the tsarist period Russia should import technical 'know-how', modernizing industry through 'concessions of technical help', or technical assistance agreements. Early in 1927 Trotsky cited an example of the advantages such arrangements could offer. Foreign patents, blueprints and instruction reduced the planning costs of a turbine from 7 to $2\frac{1}{2}$ per cent of the total. He admitted that foreign supervision in a socialist industry represented a 'cruel dependence'. But he asked: 'Which is better; the independent production of a poor and costly turbine, or the dependent production of a better one? The question is its own answer.' With respect to Stalin and Bukharin he wrote: 'The type of independence which slows us to a snail's pace, with optimism thrown into the bargain, is a reactionary independence. The philosophy of this independence is a reactionary philosophy.'[32] Russia was obliged to leap into the future 'by a clever use of the resources emanating from the . . . world division of labour.'[33]

Investment plans were a case in point. Socialist planners, Trotsky urged, should learn from the behaviour of capitalist trusts. To guard against the danger of excessive capital expenditure the trusts deliberately allowed small competitors to grow up during periods of boom. When contraction subsequently set in, the smaller and less stable enterprises collapsed and fell into the hands of the industrial giants. In this way the trusts expanded their production capacity at an entirely fictitious cost. 'In other words, a capitalist trust endeavours to cover the existing demand only and then expands according to the growth of the latter, as far as possible transferring the risk connected with fluctuating conditions to the weaker and casual enterprises, which form, as it were, a productive reserve.'[34] Trotsky thought the world market could perform exactly the same reserve function for Russia, permitting the most economical employment of domestic savings and guarding against inflationary over-expenditures.

The purpose of the analogy was to show how the whole tempo of Soviet growth might be enhanced. And it was this emphasis on speed and tempo which prompted Trotsky's enemies to charge that he was a 'super-industrializer', an indiscriminate proponent of industrialization who would not scruple to impinge upon the welfare of the peasantry. In this regard it is worth noting, however, that Trotsky's anxiety to increase grain exports also caused him to consider the world market's potential as a 'reserve' for the consumer goods industries. To sustain the *smychka* he was now prepared to adopt a more or less permanent programme of 'commodity intervention'. In 1923 he had been critical of a prospective *smychka* between the Russian peasant and European capitalists. But by April 1924, when objecting to the policy of an active trade balance, he commented: 'we cannot blockade ourselves; we must have recourse to foreign commodities, although in this instance we must, of course, behave strictly in accordance with the interests of the corresponding branches of our own industry.'[35] A month later he implied that there might be justifi-

cation for certain 'changes' and 'improvements' in the trade
monopoly with the aim of making it more 'flexible' and 'elastic'.[36]
In 1925 he expressed the same sentiments in terms of a new,
externally oriented interpretation of 'proportionality':

> The problem is one of preserving the proportion of progress between the
> main branches of industry and the economy as a whole by means of an
> opportune inclusion in the proportion of such elements of world economics
> as will help to speed up development all round.[37]

This emphasis on the role of foreign trade during industrialization brings out the differences between Trotsky and Zinoviev and
clarifies the misunderstandings in the traditional interpretation of
Trotsky's position. Zinoviev fretted over the fate of the *smychka*
unless the international revolution brought Russia access to the
industrial resources of Europe. Trotsky agreed that Russian agriculture must be balanced for a time by European industry. But
he saw no reason why the complete restoration of trade should be
forestalled by Europe's retarded political development. Whether
Europe was capitalist or socialist was of little practical consequence in economic terms. The same division of labour would
prevail if the revolution came tomorrow. A socialist Europe might
be more liberal in the extension of credits; otherwise there would
be no substantial difference. To embark upon a programme of
autarchic development would be inconsistent with scientific socialism.

As for the party's mistrust of commodity intervention, Trotsky
attributed the attitude to 'a passive fear of the foreign market . . .
[which] led to the theory of a closed (*zamknutoe*) national
economy'.[38] Believing that the negative consequences of all types
of imports would only arise if trade were not properly planned,
he now looked upon complete *internal* proportionality as a false
objective:

> Above all we must settle what is meant by independence: a closed (*zam-
> knutoe*) economy, which is self-sufficient, or a strong economy. . . What
> do we understand by independence or self-sufficiency?
>   Naturally. . . It is impossible to acquire economic strength without the
> development of all the basic branches of industry and without electrifi-
> cation.
>   But this does not in any way mean that we must assume the task in the
> coming years of acquiring such a proportionality of all the branches of the
> economy that we will not need the foreign market. . .

If we were to take this road we should have to distribute our savings between too great a number of new products, new enterprises, and new branches of industry, which would really lower the tempo of our development to a snail's pace.

On this road ruin inevitably awaits us. The basic criterion of our economic policy must be tempo – the speed of accumulation, the speed of growth in material values.[39]

The real problem was to determine how a trade plan might be devised in such a way as to benefit Russia's own industry. The answer was to be provided by a system of comparative coefficients, which would relate Russian production to world standards of price and quality. If a Russian commodity compared with a similar foreign product in terms of quality in a ratio of 1 : 3, while the corresponding cost price ratio was 3 : 2, the coefficient would be derived by multiplying the two ratios, giving $\frac{1}{2}$; that is, a measure of the efficiency of Russian production compared with that of foreign countries. It would not be necessary, Trotsky maintained, to establish a coefficient for every single commodity, only for the 'junction articles', which might be taken as representative. A coefficient of quality would be more difficult to derive than a comparable figure for costs, but the problem could be solved. In the case of textiles, one of the main items in the peasant budget, quality could be measured in terms of durability and fastness of colour. The result would be 'a . . . description of quality in terms of quantity'.[40] The import plan would focus on those goods where Soviet industry showed the least satisfactory coefficients.

In order to preserve the trade monopoly the coefficients were also to serve as a guide for investment decisions. Soviet industry, Trotsky wrote, was 'a fighting front under attack by world capital'.[41] A poor coefficient would signify a weak point in the industrial front and alert the planners to the need for capital reinforcements. The process would work as follows:

If in the main branches of industry the comparative coefficient is particularly unfavourable for us, it will necessitate the import from abroad of ready-made commodities, patents, formulae, and new plant; or we may apply to foreign specialists or invite foreign interests to take up concessions. The . . . concessions policy can only . . . be properly planned if based on a widely elaborated system of comparative industrial coefficients.[42]

Once the coefficients were in operation it would be a simple matter to measure the pressure of contraband on the country's economic defences:

A comparative coefficient is the same for us as a pressure gauge for a mechanic on a locomotive. The pressure of foreign production is for us the basic factor of our economic existence. If our relationship to this production is 1 : 8 or 1 : 5, then foreign production will sooner or later pierce the trade monopoly.[43]

While the coefficients would function as a warning system, in the final analysis the domestic market would have to be secured by a genuine effort to provide the peasantry with low-cost consumer goods of an acceptable quality. Trotsky worried that Stalin's disregard of light industry would have the effect of breaking off commercial relations with the countryside altogether. The 1925 procurement campaign demonstrated that grain and raw materials would only be brought to market willingly if adequate incentives were at the government's disposal. And the incentives would have to be real; the peasant would not credit the state endlessly by hoarding useless cash. Illicit imports were now reaching an estimated 150 million rubles annually, approximately twenty per cent of the recorded import figures for 1924–5.[44]

The idea of discouraging contraband by using foreign trade as a reserve for light industry proves the falseness of the allegation that Trotsky ignored the peasantry. His desire to husband scarce capital, to maximize the political and economic return from investments in the shortest possible time, actually led straight to the conclusion that a major share of investments should be devoted to the less capital-intensive consumer goods industries. The same reasoning also had important political implications which would exert a considerable influence on Trotsky's later views in exile. The incipient totalitarianism of War Communism had resulted from an attitude of indifference towards the consumer. Yet when the 1925 goods famine enabled industry to continue manufacturing shoddy merchandise, Trotsky stubbornly tried to impress upon administrators the need to recognize 'the consumer point of view'.[45] His immediate motivation, of course, was to safeguard the monopoly. Nevertheless, by acknowledging the interests of the consumer he became aware that Russia's political degeneration was connected with faulty procedures for economic decision-making:

We must not build socialism by the bureaucratic road, we must not create a socialist society by administrative orders; only by way of the greatest initiative, individual activity, persistence and resilience of the opinion and will of the many-millioned masses, who sense and know that the matter is their own concern ... – only in these conditions ... is it possible to build socialism. This is why bureaucratism is a deadly enemy of socialism... Socialist construction is possible only with the growth of genuine revolutionary democracy.[46]

In his personal notes Trotsky wrote that an effective economic policy was 'impossible without the active participation and control of the public opinion of the country, above all of the party'.[47] There was an obvious similarity between these comments and the position Trotsky's critics had taken during the debate over *udarnost*'.

However sympathetically one looked upon the consumer though, a compromise of sorts had to be made with Russia's objective circumstances. Trotsky conceded that consumer demands would still have to be modified by technical necessity. The most important aim was not to satisfy every whim of the individual, but to mitigate intolerable scarcities. Russia did not require an aristocracy of products to suit the states of different social classes: 'mass' products were needed, 'democratic' products.[48] As in 1920 Trotsky urged that products be standardized and factories specialized.[49] Ideally he looked forward to 'the standardization of products on a national scale, a rationalization of the productive process, a specialization of enterprises [and] the conversion of whole factories into huge parts of one single manufacturing body of the entire Union'.[50] Raw materials and semi-fabricates were to be prepared according to predetermined norms. Standardized production was to facilitate the manufacture of inexpensive farming equipment, thus giving an impetus to socialized agriculture. The basic pattern of the standardization campaign was to be governed, and its success measured, by reference to the world market through the comparative coefficients.

Given the weakness of his personal political position Trotsky attempted to enhance the persuasiveness of his proposals by investing them with the inviolability of an historical law – the law of labour productivity. The key to raising the standard of production was said to lie in the productivity of labour: 'every social regime is measured by the productivity of labour.'[51] Externally imposed necessity would force Russia first to match and ultimately to exceed the growth rates of the West. Historically this was a familiar Russian problem, as Trotsky had attempted to demonstrate in *Results and Prospects*. In 1925 he wrote: 'we are not free to choose the rate of development, as we live and grow under the pressure of the world market.'[52] 'We know the fundamental law of history – in the end that regime will conquer which ensures human society a higher economic standard.'[53]

If we return now to the question of Socialism in One Country, it will be clear that Trotsky viewed Stalin's theory as a speculative diversion, as an attempt to find certainty in an area where no *a priori* answer was possible. The purpose of the various policies we have been discussing was to give Russia whatever advantage was possible in the international competition between capitalism and socialism; but history would eventually decide which system would be the victor, and which the loser. Trotsky allowed that 'socialism in a backward country would be very hard pressed if capitalism had the opportunity not only to germinate, but to embark upon a long period of development of its productive forces in the advanced countries'. On the other hand he saw 'no reasonable grounds to presume a variation of this kind'. Only one conclusion could follow: 'it would be senseless first to develop a fantastically optimistic future for the capitalist world [i.e. the theory of stabilization] and then to break our heads trying to find a way out of it.'[54]

Although he considered the debate between Stalin and Zinoviev to be essentially inane, Trotsky was disturbed by its possible consequences. The creation of a socialist society was an economic problem. If Stalin persisted in treating Russia's future as a matter for child-like faith and quasi-theological casuistry the party might lose the historical competition by default. In his own appraisal of the decisions imposed by Stalin upon the Fourteenth Party Congress Trotsky stressed two points above all others. First he wrote:

It would be incorrect . . . to think that the path of economic independence on a high industrial level leads to the political economy of a state-economic unit which is closed-in upon itself (*zamknutovo v sebe gosudarstvenno-khozyaistvennovo tselovo*). On the contrary, it is only possible to equal and surpass the world economy by using its resources.[55]

Secondly, he argued that while the doctrine of the two camps correctly described the current political division of the world, it bore no relation to economics:

The international division of labour flows from both economic and historical causes. The fact that our country has gone over to a socialist organization of its economy, while the rest of mankind lives in capitalist conditions,
in no way eliminates the international division of labour or the bonds and
dependencies which result from it. One of the causes of our economic
collapse during the first years of the revolution was the blockade. Escape
from the blockade means a restoration of economic links, which grow out
of the world division of labour; that is . . . out of the different economic
levels of the various countries.[56]

Had it not been for a purely opportunistic political coalition
with Zinoviev in 1926 Trotsky's analysis of industrialization
might not have been so readily identified with the former trium-
vir's pedantry. As it happened, the alliance merely provided
additional fuel for a continuing campaign of misrepresentation.
With every means possible Stalin's propagandists drove home the
charge that the country's two leading evangelists of pessimism
had entered into a natural and inevitable collaboration. This
alleged pessimism was said in turn to account for the frantic
demand that the country's industrial base be expanded at an
impossible rate. The charges became all the more convincing
when Trotsky's proposals were likened to those of Preobrazhensky, the most fervent of all industry's advocates. While it is
not my intention to examine here the writings of Trotsky's own
supporters in any detail, a few observations are in order, if only
for purposes of additional clarification.

Of the numerous secondary figures with whom Trotsky co-
operated, probably Krasin, the Commissar of Foreign Trade,
shared the integrationist viewpoint most consistently. In the
Council of Labour and Defence he and Trotsky were in frequent
personal contact, periodically exchanging handwritten notes on
topics under review. One such note, written by Krasin in July
1924, indicates that capital imports were one of the subjects the
two men had been discussing:

An increase of labour productivity in the state sphere is first and mainly
a question of the radical re-equipment of almost all industry. Our means
of production are already incapable of providing a cheap product even
with good management. Without [foreign] loans, and without a radical
change of concessions policy we will not solve this question.[57]

Since the end of War Communism Krasin had not missed an
opportunity to promote foreign loans and concessions. The above
communication is especially interesting, however, for it suggests

that Krasin might have played some part in encouraging Trotsky to take a second look at many of his earlier opinions. Even more noteworthy is that fact that by the summer of 1925 the two most prominent defenders of the trade monopoly agreed on the need for what Krasin termed 'chronic commodity intervention'.[58] If Krasin's death had not intervened in the early autumn of 1926 there are good grounds for suspecting that he might eventually have joined Trotsky in open opposition to Stalin.

Pyatakov, the talented chairman of Vesenkha's committee on industrial investments, was similarly critical of the current drift into isolationism. Estimating that a five-year industrial plan would necessitate 250 million rubles' worth of machinery imports annually, he believed that Russia's dependence on Europe was above dispute:

The party must not forget for a minute that the economy of the USSR can only develop as a part of the world economy. A correct directive ... concerning the adoption of decisive measures aiming at a systematic increase of [our] exports can only be interpreted to mean an increase of our ties ... with the world economy... The dependence of the economy of the USSR on the world economy will therefore have to ... grow in the future... The growth of [our] ... dependence ... on the world economy does not mean a growth of colonial or semi-colonial dependence, but primarily an increase of trade connections ... with other countries ... this means an expansion of the USSR's dependence on other countries as a buyer and as a seller. These other countries are ... capitalist.[59]

Preobrazhensky, being a more prolific writer than either Pyatakov or Krasin, provided a full-scale discussion of industrialization policy in his recently translated book *The New Economics.* Essentially be believed that the concept of socialist accumulation could not be considered merely a programme; it was an economic 'law', which he contrasted with the 'law of value' operating on the market. He agreed with Trotsky that socialism was inconceivable without the trade monopoly, but his exact opinion of the role of foreign trade, and particularly his attitude towards imports, is difficult to ascertain. In one place he approved of machinery purchases abroad, arguing that a rapid expansion of heavy industry would require investments in enterprises 'whose construction is by no means of first rate importance, given the existence of connections with the world economy'.[60] Yet on another occasion he wrote:

The thought that we might limit our capital expenditures and develop light industry more quickly is a reactionary utopia. This thought is sustained ... by an analogy with 1921, that is, with a period when our industry had scarcely begun to recover from an unprecedented collapse.[61]

While this remark was intended to enlighten the Bukharin-Sokol'nikov school it still implied an important difference of emphasis from Trotsky. There are other reasons too for thinking that the affinity between the two men was not quite so close as is commonly supposed. In 1923 Preobrazhensky had been one of the first to endorse Larin's proposal for commodity intervention. By 1925–6 his enthusiasm was less evident; unlike Trotsky he felt that the import of consumer goods was likely to have a predominantly negative effect. In principle the admission of foreign commodities was a threat to Soviet industry even though profits from their sale could provide a source of badly needed revenue. Where Trotsky searched for a safety valve Preobrazhensky feared the opening of a flood-gate under the pressure of peasant demand.[62]

Moreover, his views on concessions had scarcely altered since the period before the Genoa conference: 'The result of this [policy] may be ... that a too large dose of concessions taken into the organism of the state economy may begin to undermine it, just as in its time capitalism disrupted the weaker natural economy.'[63] Having participated in the Paris and London loan negotiations Preobrazhensky was equally sceptical of the prospects for more direct financial support. He reacted to the Pasvolsky–Moulton work with the same apprehension as Sokol'nikov. If Soviet appeals had been successful at Genoa he believed the resulting interest payments would have been intolerable. Russia 'would not only be prevented from developing, but would economically regress even in comparison with the present position'.[64] For these reasons *The New Economics* placed an inordinate stress on internal accumulation. Trotsky might have shared this attitude in 1923; he certainly did not by 1925.

A number of documents in Trotsky's archives tend to confirm the suspicion that he and Preobrazhensky worked together in a state of latent tension. In May 1926 Trotsky wrote that the concept of a domestic struggle between the law of primitive socialist accumulation and the law of value was 'in the highest degree productive, more accurately, the only correct way' of studying

the Soviet economy. But unless it was given the proper interpretation Preobrazhensky's approach was remarkably compatible
with isolationism. As Trotsky noted: 'It was necessary to begin
this investigation within the limits of a closed Soviet economy.
But now the danger is growing that this methodological approach
will be converted into a finished economic perspective for the
development of "socialism in one country".' An effort had to be
made to show that 'the growth of economic ties and interdependencies prepares industrial "independence".' The threat to the
trade monopoly arising from high industrial prices within Russia
also had to be carefully explored:

The interaction of the law of value and the law of socialist accumulation
must be put in contact with the world economy. Then it will become
clear that the law of value, within the confines of the NEP, is supplemented by a growing pressure from the external law of value, which
emerges on the world market.[65]

In January 1927 Trotsky's concern could once more be detected:

We are part of the world economy and find ourselves in the capitalist
encirclement. This means that the duel of 'our' law of socialist accumulation with 'our' law of value is embraced by the world law of value, which
... seriously alters the relationship of forces between the two laws.[66]

In many respects Trotsky's partnership with Preobrazhensky
resembled his earlier association with Lenin in 1920. During the
first stage of labour mobilization Lenin and Trotsky advocated
many of the same policies, although they started from different
theoretical premises. In much the same way Preobrazhensky
zealously applauded Trotsky's demand to accelerate industrial
growth; but he did not share Trotsky's integrationism. At best, he
thought the notion of comparative coefficients was a 'fruitful
framing of the question' of how to relate Russia to the world at
large.[67] Trotsky's irritation was understandable therefore, when
his enemies consistently asserted that he wished to follow Preobrazhensky's famous analogy in *The New Economics*, financing
industrialization by exploiting the peasants just as a metropolis
exploited its colonies:

Almost all of Bukharin's polemics against me ... are of this type. Instead
of taking my own thoughts as I have described them in their internal
connections, he resorts to a method which can only be called literary
marauding: he seizes a phrase or a fragment from Preobrazhensky, adds

to it, and announces that Preobrazhensky's phrase, together with a Bukharinist twist, is genuine Trotskyism. He tears out a few words from one of my uncorrected stenograms – ignoring the perfectly obvious meaning of my speech – and then builds a system out of all this. At best the system represents Bukharin's views turned inside out; it certainly doesn't represent my own.[68]

Trotsky's concealed differences with Preobrazhensky eventually had tragic consequences. Preobrazhensky interpreted the problem of the peasant, of the relation between industry and agriculture, almost exclusively with reference to Russia's internal economy. Trotsky viewed the same question in a larger international context, relating it to the danger of contraband and to forces operating on Russia from beyond her own frontiers. It was quite logical that he should resist any measure which might result in price increases on Soviet industrial products. As in 1923 he thought industrialization (to the extent that it was internally financed) had to be based upon lower production costs and higher agricultural taxes. In exchange for these direct subsidies the peasant was to enjoy reductions in industrial prices made possible in part through commodity intervention. Preobrazhensky's narrow attachment to industry and his virtually total commitment to internal accumulation made Trotsky's behaviour seem increasingly inscrutable, if not perverse. When Stalin finally recognized that high industrial prices should be viewed as a major instrument of socialist accumulation, Preobrazhensky deserted the opposition. Before considering the disastrous political effects of Trotsky's new views, however, some mention should first be made of their possible economic implications.

An assessment of Trotsky's integrationism
Although Trotsky worked from historical rather than theoretical insight his discussion of the comparative coefficients revealed a competent understanding of the potential economic gains inherent in foreign trade. In so far as Soviet production costs reflected factor endowments and social costs the coefficients would have resulted in a rational trade pattern, maximizing returns on the basis of comparative advantage. Producing for herself those commodities in whose manufacture she was most competitive, and importing others, Russia would have secured many of those advantages normally ascribed to free trade. Because Soviet costs

were in many cases unrealistic a strong argument could also be made for a transitional period of moderate protectionism, giving existing industries an opportunity to regain lost efficiencies and permitting newer 'infant industries' to expand and achieve economies of scale. On one important point, however, Trotsky's logic failed him. The coefficients were intended, among other things, to encourage a more systematic planning of foreign trade, thus aiding in the development of an overall planned economy. If the latter were to result in price structures determined in such a way as to favour priority sectors, the cost aspect of the coefficients would have become completely artificial. In short, to function rationally the system required the combination of a domestic market with planned trade. Trotsky had long ago contended that the purpose of a socialist policy must be to swallow the market and eliminate it.

A more serious objection involves Trotsky's proposal that the coefficients be allowed to influence investment decisions. Capital expenditures were to be arranged in a strict order of sequence, guarding against the temptation to spread resources too thinly. So long as Trotsky employed this kind of reasoning in order to discredit investments in heavy industry he was in no danger of being inconsistent. In general the producers' goods industries were to be accorded a secondary priority with the world market acting as a reserve. The problem lay in defining a clear approach to light industry. Here too imports were to alleviate domestic scarcities. But being concerned with the likelihood of attempts to sabotage the trade monopoly, Trotsky had spoken of the coefficients as a 'pressure gauge', implicitly advocating a 'broad front' strategy in light industry. The general state of Soviet industry was such that the majority of the light industrial coefficients would have been unsatisfactory, with the result that in this sector a temptation would arise to spread capital very thinly indeed – in fact, so thinly that without the exercise of considerable discretion the system could very well have manifested a tendency towards at least a limited form of autarchy. Even if a rigid sequence of investments were established and adhered to, the successive elimination of 'weak points' in the industrial front would have had precisely the same effect.

Regardless of these logical difficulties Trotsky's stated objective was perfectly creditable. By importing the major share of new industrial machinery he would have avoided the complications which were destined to grow out of Stalin's programme for self-sufficiency. Investment in heavy industry took from three to five years to mature, delaying any serious attempt to mitigate the goods famine. While Soviet engineering capacity was under-utilized in 1925, the fact remained that many types of heavy industrial equipment had never before been produced in Russia and would require costly new construction. Indivisibilities, or the technical need to initiate construction projects on a scale sufficiently large to be economical, were most pronounced in the heavy industrial sector. Complementarity phenomena also operated to augment expenses. New industries had to be provided with vital services. Related manufacturing processes frequently had to be located, or relocated, within reasonable proximity of each other. To extend the engineering industries therefore ultimately required considerable supplementary investments, all of which could have been either avoided or postponed through imports. Even to provide the necessary materials for a programme of industrial self-sufficiency depended upon important initial capital allocations to metallurgy for the sake of modernization.

The most unique feature of Trotsky's strategy was its elaboration of a middle way between Stalin and Bukharin; that is, between a policy of heavy industrial investments and one which supported light industry in word if not in deed. Possibly Trotsky's recommendations would have permitted a high rate of industrial growth without unduly antagonizing the majority of the peasants. The collapse of the grain market by 1927–8 finally removed any doubt as to how long the villages would continue to market food and materials without an increasing volume of consumer goods. In the mid-1920s grain sales reached only one-half the volume which prevailed before the revolution; and until areas traditionally specializing in technical crops could be provided with foodstuffs from other parts of the country, raw materials production could not be fully restored. The roads to socialism advocated by both Bukharin and Stalin logically led to an impasse which had to be surmounted after 1929 by forced collectivization and a resurgence of class warfare in the countryside.

Trotsky's arguments were motivated by his current belief that after eight years of Soviet power the interests of industry and agriculture, like those of Europe and Russia, had at length converged. At the same time he thought that Russia was trapped in a vicious circle. The peasant would not provide grain and other export products without receiving manufactured goods in return. And domestic manufacture of consumer goods could not be increased satisfactorily without imports of machinery paid for by exports. At some point the circle had to be broken. Trotsky shared the hope that the year 1925, with its abundant harvest, would provide the necessary breakthrough. Commodity intervention, concessions, and other forms of capital imports were intended to serve the same purpose. The essential problem appeared to be one of setting an appropriate trade cycle into motion, thereafter allowing it to gain its own momentum. Trotsky summarized the basic outline of the proposed cycle in a manner strongly reminiscent of Sokol'nikov's remarks in 1923 to the Twelfth Party Congress:

Our economic system has become part of the world system. This has made new links in the chain of exchange. Peasant grain is exchanged for foreign gold. Gold is exchanged for machinery, implements, and other requisite articles of consumption for town and village. Textile machinery acquired for gold and paid for by the export of grain provides new equipment for the textile industry and thus lowers the prices of fabrics sent to the rural districts. The circle becomes very complicated, but the basis remains the same – a certain economic relation between town and village.[69]

If Russia had followed such a strategy industrialization might well have taken place without a return to repression and grain requisitioning. It was possible, however, that the situation had deteriorated so far by the end of 1925 that even Trotsky's programme would have encountered serious obstacles. Both industry and agriculture had reached pre-war levels of production, yet a goods famine remained together with the growing menace of a grain strike. The old pre-war 'proportions' were no longer adequate. By comparison with the pre-war period Russia was experiencing a considerably higher rate of rural consumption of agricultural products. Poor peasants, who consumed the major share of their output and frequently were net buyers in the market, had increased substantially in number, creating a barrier to expansion of the marketed grain surplus. As suppliers of marketable produce the landed estates had been replaced by vastly more numerous *kulak* and middle-peasant farms. The *kulak* and the *serednyak* (the middle peasant) had grain to sell, but they were unwilling to do so given the terms of trade prevailing between industrial and agricultural products. Consequently the market alone would not suffice both to place adequate food at the disposal of industry and the cities and to leave a surplus for export as well. In these circumstances agricultural taxes might have been adjusted upwards until trial and error determined the proper level. Commodity intervention and lower industrial prices would have made fiscal pressure more tolerable to the *kulak*, perhaps sustaining exports and helping to provide an answer. No doubt the whole process of industrialization could have been enormously facilitated by a large-scale foreign loan.

During 1926–7 Russia did achieve some success in the quest for a loan, receiving 140 million rubles from Germany, 50 million rubles from the Viennese Municipal Government, and various other short- and medium-term credits, amounting to a total of 600–700 million rubles.[70] The concessions policy brought an insignificant capital inflow, predominantly into mining. Joffe, on behalf of the Main Concessions Committee, put the total sum at 48.8 million rubles by the autumn of 1926.[71] The true potential for capital imports is impossible to establish. Comparing concessions and loans with slavery and colonialism Stalin effectively dissuaded most investors from taking the risk of renewed losses through nationalization or debt repudiation. Thus the decision of how to pay for industrialization remained to be taken. This problem, together with the more fundamental debate concerning resource allocation between industry's different branches, provided the main source for the political struggles of 1926 and led to Trotsky's public denunciation of the theory of Socialism in One Country.

7

Trotsky's attack on socialism in a 'separate' country

At the end of 1925 Trotsky had avoided a direct commitment either to Zinoviev or Stalin, hoping that Stalin's favourable attitude towards industry would cause him to see the threat in Bukharin's isolationism. Instead, Stalin reacted to the failure of the export plan by enthroning Russia's projected self-sufficiency in party dogma. For some time before the Fourteenth Congress the implications of the 1925 goods famine had already been apparent. Early in December Rykov told a party meeting in Moscow that Gosplan's targets would be reduced. At the congress Rykov struck a note of limited optimism, but in February 1926 Dzerzhinsky explained in some detail the need to retrench. While Dzerzhinsky foresaw orderly cutbacks throughout industry, he specified that the most severe impact would be felt in light industry. To Trotsky, having witnessed Stalin's debate with Sokol'nikov and fearing a worsening of the goods famine, it seemed that the *kulak* had thwarted the planners and raised the prospect of a genuine 'snail's pace'.

The economic crisis inevitably acted as a political catalyst and encouraged Trotsky to make the decision he had attempted to sidestep. The league with Kamenev and Zinoviev resulted. Although the coalition brought together an impressive collection of Bolshevik notables, its heterogeneity worked against its survival. For Zinoviev Stalin's defeat meant one thing – a return to power. Trotsky believed a change in party leadership was necessary in order to reorient Soviet thinking over the long run. By his criticism of Russia's isolation, however, Trotsky only reinforced his own. The other members of the opposition would condemn Stalin for his half-hearted resistance to the *kulak*: with few exceptions they were much less convinced of either the political or the economic wisdom of Trotsky's integrationism.

Offensive and counter-offensive in 1926

In the early months of 1926 Trotsky took his first steps towards exile. The Central Committee was scheduled to convene in plenary session in April. In an effort to alter party opinion while the crisis atmosphere lasted, Trotsky proposed that the forthcoming agenda be devoted to economic questions. His own notes indicate the matters he wished to raise. First, high industrial costs had to be lowered by increasing the volume of production:

At the basis of our export difficulties lies the disproportionality between agricultural and industrial production. This does not mean that the village is producing too much, but that the city is producing too little. The high cost of industrial production is closely connected with its inadequate volume.[1]

Until industrial output expanded, the NEP-men would continue to thrive on scarcity prices, reselling the products of socialist industry for purposes of capitalist accumulation. Investments would also have to be patterned in such a way as to minimize the danger to the trade monopoly. 'The question of comparative quantitative and qualitative coefficients,' Trotsky wrote, '. . . is a question of the fate of our economic development. In the present circumstances the tempo is determined not merely by the speed of movement, but also by its direction.'[2] Domestic resources would have to be diverted from less essential government departments, and 'real steps' would have to be taken to attract foreign technology. A failure to appreciate the need for a high tempo would be 'madness'. 'The world market will not wait. Nor will the peasant wait.'[3]

When Rykov presented the Central Committee with the party's official position early in April, Trotsky thought his worst suspicions were confirmed. Although the resolution formally acknowledged both the goods famine and the need to purchase foreign machinery, it also demanded 'systematic measures to free our economy from its dependence on the capitalist countries'. 'Particularly energetic measures' were to be taken 'to develop those [heavy industrial] branches of the economy in which our dependence on foreign countries is most strongly felt'. A sharp increase in the rate of progression applying to agricultural taxes was scheduled. However, Stalin's call for 'reserves' was also ratified to provide some flexbility in the event of future planning errors.[4] Discreetly understating the difficulties of 1925 Rykov had recently explained that taut plans would have to be avoided, 'since previously the slightest inconsistency in the plan [produced] strain in the whole economic environment'.[5]

Trotsky took the resolution to be a covert retreat in the face of *kulak* speculators. Presenting what amounted to his own report he warned that a repetition of the events of the previous autumn would result in 'a socialist development with a minus sign. In other words, capitalism will assume predominance over socialism.' In order to compete with private manufacturers state industry required new equipment. Rykov had blindly incorporated 'a contradiction in the resolution between the demand to develop exports (and imports) on the one hand, and "independence" on the other'. 'The tempo of industrialization,' Trotsky told the Central Committee, 'is not something arbitrary but is internationally conditioned.'[6]

In fifteen pages of typewritten amendments he listed his objections point by point. The disruption of the foreign trade plan had produced over-reaction in slowing the pace of industrial growth. If industry were allowed to continue marking time the result would be 'a struggle of the peasant against the monopoly of foreign trade, that is, against socialist industry'. The goods famine was 'obvious and incontestable proof that the distribution of national economic resources and savings between state industry and the rest of the economy has not . . . acquired the necessary proportionality'. Progressive taxes and the state budget were to become the primary levers for redistributing national income in favour of industry. The 'village uppers', or the *kulaks*, should be forced to provide a larger share of the resources needed to secure industry's leading role. As an inducement to accept this added burden the peasantry should be allowed to enjoy the benefit of commodity intervention, which was now becoming 'inevitable'. An attempt could also be made to divert profits from the NEP-men by an experimental increase in certain wholesale prices. But any rise in retail prices would be completely inadmissible; the party would have to 'strive in every way for their reduction'. Apart from commodity intervention the export–import plan was to be constructed primarily with a view to hastening the technological re-equipment of industry.[7]

The most controversial section of the proposed amendments dealt with the question of reserves. Looking upon the world market as the only genuine reserve Trotsky accepted the view that a foreign currency fund was a valid 'guarantee of our rights to world production', particularly when exports depended upon unpredictable harvests. For the moment though, Russia could not afford an active trade balance; the currency reserve would have to be sacrificed. A budget surplus, the second form of reserve considered, would be superfluous with a proper financial policy. Reserves of spare parts and materials, intended to avoid tension in the plan, were similarly intolerable. Current plans were already too slack for a period of goods famine. Any further change would be 'minimalism' and would needlessly retard the rate of growth: 'A further advance towards socialism will only be guaranteed if the gap separating our industry from that of the leading capitalist countries – in terms of volume of products, cost, and quality – is clearly and tangibly reduced.'[8]

It was a foregone conclusion that Trotsky's amendments would be rejected. Stalin could not afford the spectacle of being convincingly outbid in his support for industrialization. To preserve his connection with Bukharin he was still forced in some measure to straddle the fence between industry and agriculture, leaving Trotsky to distinguish himself as a radical industrializer and a threat to party unity. With Rykov as his spokesman Stalin planned to adopt a pose of moderation and compromise, to expose Trotsky as an incorrigible enemy of the peasant. But for a single complication this tactic might have succeeded entirely by the spring of 1926. The problem was that Stalin neglected to make alowance for Zinoviev and Kamenev.

Unwilling to be left on the sidelines in the new crusade for industry and socialism the two former triumvirs produced their own amendments to Rykov's resolution, once again, as at the Fourteenth Congress, placing the danger of the *kulak* in the forefront. Now, however, the two men who since 1923 had insisted on the need to begin with the peasant economy, argued that the *kulak's* strength was the obverse of industry's weakness. Trotsky had received support from a most improbable quarter. So obvious was the similarity between the two positions that Stalin immediately asked: 'What's this? A bloc?'[9] The question was premature in that Trotsky still thought the alternatives proposed by Kamenev were flawed by 'certain concessions to Comrade Sokol'nikov'.[10] Nevertheless, Rykov's resolution was even less acceptable. When his own proposals were dismissed Trotsky voted, with reservations, for Kamenev's. A short while later Trotsky met with his old enemies to discuss their common ground. Before the discussions could be concluded, however, a new attack of fever took him to Berlin for medical treatment lasting six weeks.

The party leaders at once seized the opportunity to revise their strategy. In May 1926 Vesenkha, with the support of the trade commissariat and approval from the Council of Labour and Defence, launched a well-publicized campaign to lower retail prices by administrative orders. In this way it was to be proved that the opposition had exaggerated the extent of the goods famine. As editor of *Pravda* Bukharin supported the manoeuvre, vigorously condemning the 'super-industrializers' who had de-manded extortionate agricultural taxes.[11] More important, Stalin saw a chance to split the unlikely coalition in its infancy by ex-ploiting Zinoviev's hostility to any compromise with the West. In a speech to a Leningrad audience on 13 April the party secretary railed against 'enslaving loans' and 'enslaving concessions'. Repeating the argument he had set out at the Fourteenth Con-gress he claimed that:

The country of proletarian dictatorship, finding itself in the capitalist encirclement, cannot remain economically self-sufficient if it does not produce for itself equipment and means of production, if it lingers at that stage of development where it must keep its economy tied to the strings of the developed capitalist countries... To linger at this stage would be to abandon ourselves and submit to world capital.[12]

Only a week later a comprehensive counter-offensive was underway, concentrating on the theme of Soviet independence and obviously referring to Trotsky. On 21 April *Pravda* carried an important article by Milyutin. An 'opinion' was said to exist, according to which Russia's industrial growth was subject to 'the comparative control of the world capitalist economy'. 'The com-rades' who adhered to this opinion were wrong. Russia would manipulate the capitalist world to stimulate her own develop-ment:

to say that the tempo of our development must be determined by the development of the capitalist countries means to recognize a dependence ... of 'our economic development' on the external encirclement, a de-pendence which does not in fact exist and which, it is to be hoped, never will exist. Our goal and task is to achieve a greater self-reliance ... for our economy ... by way of developing ... our industry.

Rykov expounded the same line in a speech published on 23 April. 'Certain comrades', he observed, had suggested that the Central Committee's resolution was contradictory when it advocated both a development of trade and economic independence. Explaining that exports and imports would enable Russia to develop her own heavy industry he concluded: 'the course towards the industrialization of the country does not in the least exclude, but in a sense presupposes an expansion of the bonds between our economy and the world economy. It would be incorrect to think that the process of industrialization implies the necessity for some kind of economic "self-blockade".' It would be equally incorrect to overlook the need to develop within the country 'those branches of the national economy whose growth guarantees the greatest possible economic independence of the USSR in relation to the world capitalist market'.[13] In May Bukharin supplemented Rykov's remarks with the claim that 'if we were to import products from abroad permanently in the final analysis we would fall into slavish dependence on the outside world'.[14]

On 10 July the press campaign reached a dramatic climax with a *Pravda* editorial entitled 'The Right Danger in our Party'. Ostensibly attacking the Workers' Opposition, the party organ revealed the contents of a letter written in 1924 by Medvedev, one of the group's leaders. The letter had urged that industrial contraction and unemployment resulting from the sales crisis be counteracted by the encouragement of concessions.[15] Indignant that such defeatist measures should have been contemplated, *Pravda* exclaimed that Medvedev's policy would lead to 'the liquidation of [our] independent state industry by allowing it to be squeezed out by concessions capital'. The inevitable consequence would be 'a growing economic influence of concessionaires and foreign bankers in our country; . . . international capital would begin to command our economy. "Our" industry would become the private domain, a subsidiary of international finance capital, and our many-millioned proletariat would become the object of exploitation by foreign capitalists.' Of course the party was not opposed to all concessions, only to 'unlimited concessions . . . [to] the surrender of our industry to international capital'. This would be a policy of 'Dawesization . . . which is a prologue to the return of capitalism.' The country must make a choice between socialist construction, as provided for in the April resolution, and 'Urquhartist slavery'. The reference to Urquhart seems to have been deliberately intended to remind Zinoviev of the position he had taken in 1924 when discussing the negotiations with MacDonald.

On the surface the carefully contrived propaganda ploy met with something less than complete success. By 1926 character assassination had become one of the main tasks of the party press, and Trotsky and Zinoviev had both had ample opportunity to grow insensitive to *Pravda*'s insults. The assault was not limited, however, to propaganda alone. From the first week of January 1926 Molotov, heading a team of Stalin's agents, had purged and replaced the Zinovievists at every level of the Leningrad party organization. Frunze, Zinoviev's supporter who had replaced Trotsky as War Commissar, had died in October while undergoing surgery. As rumours circulated that Frunze had been forced to agree to the operation, the remaining Trotskyists were also being removed from the military. At a special party conference held in Leningrad in mid-February, Bukharin refuted all talk of the leadership's degeneration. All Zinoviev's errors, he contended, came from one source:

We believe it is necessary to struggle decisively against one position which was put forth by comrade Zinoviev and comrade Kamenev ... the position that we will perish because of our technical backwardness if economic help does not arrive in time from the victorious Western European proletariat.[16]

Abusing both the Trotskyists and the Zinovievists for the same crimes and shortcomings, Stalin and Bukharin helped to weld the two groups together. When the party's Central Committee reconvened in the middle of July 1926 Trotsky, Zinoviev and eleven other supporters presented the Declaration of the Thirteen. Demanding 'energetic tax pressure' against the *kulak* the leaders of the new joint opposition warned that the wealthiest peasants now controlled 'hundreds of millions of rubles'.[17] A second document echoed the charge and argued that 'industry's lag behind the development of the national economy as a whole . . . has increased the role and political self-confidence of the petty-bourgeoisie'.[18] Zinoviev denounced Stalin's 'factional' misuse of the party machine and declared that Trotsky had been right in

1923 when he warned against the threat of an apparatus regime. On specifically industrial questions Pyatakov renewed Trotsky's appeal for a system of comparative coefficients. Tempers flamed in the ensuing debates. Dzerzhinsky delivered a scathing indictment of his critics, collapsed, and died of a heart attack. Recalling the plenum Trotsky tersely wrote that 'a correction concerning the comparative control of worldwide development was rejected'.[19]

Although the opposition leaders struggled to sustain their attack, the furor caused by *Pravda's* editorial on the Right Danger clearly had some impact. As part of his price for the alliance Zinoviev appears to have demanded that Trotsky retract his provocative opinions on concessions. In a joint statement the opposition leaders disclaimed any intention to accept 'the surrender of state industry' to foreign capital. 'It would be unthinkable,' they declared, 'to base our calculations to any degree on foreign concessions, which cannot be given . . . a leading, or . . . an important place in our economy without undermining the socialist character of our industry.'[20] A manuscript written by Trotsky in September 1926 provided additional evidence of a tactical retreat: 'Concessions can and must occupy a strictly limited and subordinate place in our economy. Any attempt to extend the limits of concessions beyond a certain point, to give foreign capital a leading or even a very important influence on our economy, would be a direct betrayal of the affairs of socialism.'[21]

The effort to refute the charge of disloyalty to socialism served to incite more venemous attacks. On 28 July Bukharin told a Leningrad audience that Medvedev's position was tantamount to 'demanding the surrender of our socialist industry to foreign capital without reservation'. Trotskyism, he asserted, was an intermediary stage leading to 'outright liquidationism on the basis of a lack of faith in the socialist construction taking place in our country'. Trotsky believed that 'if the international revolution is not victorious, the counter-revolutionary peasant will throw off the dictatorship of the proletariat. That is the basic position which he developed in his theory of Permanent Revolution.'[22]

During the summer and autumn of 1926, apparently to placate Zinoviev, Trotsky avoided the question of capital imports and concentrated his fire on the *kulak*. The decision had serious consequences, for events now worked to weaken further the opposition's credibility. In anticipation of the coming harvest the *kulak* released his stocks of grain. Recent reductions in government spending contributed to a decline in agricultural prices, and by August official party statements were bullishly optimistic. Gosplan's control figures for 1926–7 foresaw an expenditure of 845 million rubles on state industry. A few weeks later the government raised the projection to 900 million, over 1,000 million with the inclusion of electrification. The import plan was expressly drawn up to satisfy industrial requirements, and machinery imports were to treble. Assuming Dzerzhinsky's post at Vesenkha Kuibyshev claimed that eighty per cent of the import bill would be devoted to industry and raw materials for industrial production. In October 1926, when the party was to assemble in conference, grain prices were a full twelve per cent lower than they had been a year earlier. Procurements were running well in advance of last year's figures. There was every indication that the opposition had panicked at the very moment when the crisis was passing. To the public and to the party rank-and-file it seemed that Trotsky's reconciliation with Zinoviev constituted a purely unprincipled attempt at mutual rescue.

Believing that the current improvements represented merely a conjunctural change Trotsky was appalled by the smugness of the party leaders. Stalin's doctrine of Socialism in One Country had given birth to criminal complacency based upon a false and dangerous sense of security, upon the conviction 'that once the proletariat has seized power in one country it can exclude itself from the economic and political development of the rest of the world'. The party secretary had authored 'a depressing theory', 'an ideological masquerade'.[23] Moreover, Stalin was not speaking of an empirical fact, that thus far socialism was limited to 'one' country; he was speaking of 'socialism in a separate country (*sotsializm v otdel'noi strane*)'.[24] 'The defenders of the new theory,' Trotsky wrote, '. . . start . . . with the assumption of a closed (*zamknutoe*) economic and political development.' They saw nothing but 'the isolated accumulation of economic successes', remaining oblivious to events 'in Europe and in the world economy in general'. Their 'scheme for a self-contained socialist development' was the result of 'a national limitation supplemented by provincial conceit'; it led inevitably to Bukharin's 'philistine, tailist relationship to industrialization'.[25] On the eve of the Fifteenth Party Conference Trotsky wrote:

Actually the most essential line of our economic growth is precisely the fact that we are at last leaving behind our closed (*zamknutoe*) state-economic existence and are entering into increasingly profound ties with the European and world markets. To reduce the whole question of our development to the internal relation between the proletariat and peasantry in the USSR, and to think that correct political manoeuvering ...frees us from world economic dependencies, means falling into a dreadful national limitation. Not only theoretical considerations, but also the difficulties with exports and imports provide the evidence of this fact.[26]

If Russia's ties with the world economy were not utilized to the advantage of socialism, 'the pressure of European industry on our economy, in the form of cheap commodities, would ... acquire an unbearable character'.[27]

For almost two years Trotsky had maintained his silence on the key theoretical issue of the period. In the late autumn of 1926 he at last decided to give battle. It is hard to imagine a decision more badly timed. In July 1926 Zinoviev had been expelled from the Politburo. Shortly before the conference Trotsky was similarly removed. Kamenev lost his candidate membership; Bukharin replaced Zinoviev as head of the Comintern; and Pyatakov was dismissed from Vesenkha. From this point on the war would be limited to words. Constrained by Kamenev and Zinoviev, and faced with an obvious (if temporary) improvement in the economy, Trotsky failed even to choose his words wisely.

The Fifteenth Party Conference

When the conference gathered, Kamenev led the opposition attack. The only novel element in his speech was his discovery that 'a lag in the tempo of development can do us harm not only in the form of dreadnoughts and shells, but . . . [also] in such a simple thing as the question of prices and . . . of exports and imports'.[28] Likewise Zinoviev asked: 'Is it possible to say that we are threatened only by armed intervention? No and no again. The laws of the world market exercise a certain force over us.'[29] In spite of these efforts neither man succeeded in concealing a natural discomfort at being associated with the theorist of Permanent Revolution. Kamenev meekly promised that he would never support Trotsky's views against those of Lenin and concluded by stressing his preparedness to accept party discipline.

Trotsky's long-awaited speech was equally uninspired. The change of super-industrialism, he exclaimed, was inconsistent with his alleged belief that Russia could not build socialism: 'I ask you, if we don't believe in the construction of socialism in our country, . . . and if we suggest passively waiting for the European revolution, I would like someone to tell me – why do we suggest robbing the peasantry? What would be the purpose? It is impossible to understand.' The entire myth of 'Trotskyism' was based on the theory of Permanent Revolution, a theory which had no relevance to the present disagreements:

Comrades I have absolutely no intention of raising the question of the theory of Permanent Revolution. This theory has no relation to the present argument – whether it was true, or whether it was false and incomplete – it has no relation to the present argument. I have said this tens of times. In any case neither the opposition of 1923 nor that of 1925 has . . . the slightest responsibility for this theory of Permanent Revolution . . . which I myself long ago considered a question relegated to the archives.[30]

Deflected from a consistent statement of integrationism Trotsky reverted to the scholastic technique of quotation-collecting which his dubious supporters, Zinoviev and Kamenev, had done so much to popularize. Lenin, he pointed out, had argued that 'the full victory of the socialist revolution is unthinkable in one country, but demands the active co-operation of at least several of the leading countries, among which we cannot include Russia'. The recent wave of propaganda over the problem of 'independence' precluded any effort to explain that such 'co-operation' might presently be achieved through an interim settlement with capitalist Europe. Instead of developing this theme, Trotsky defined a full socialist society as one in which rural-urban contradictions, the housing shortage, and unemployment had been eliminated.

Not until the closing section of his address, when he turned to Bukharin's theory of the snail's pace, did he make any attempt to clarify his real opinions on policy.

It is impossible to opt out of the world economy. What is export? . . . And what are imports? . . . There you have it. On the question of imports and exports the whole theory of Comrade Bukharin . . . at once falls to pieces. The success of socialist construction depends on the tempo, and the tempo of our economic development is presently most directly . . . determined by the import of materials and equipment. Of course, one can 'opt out' of a lack of foreign currency and order a large quantity of cotton and machines, but this could only be done once. Such an 'opting out' could not be repeated. Our entire construction is internationally conditioned.

To ignore the world economy, Trotsky added, would be as foolish as walking naked in the streets of Moscow in mid-winter – trying to ignore the cold.[31]

At the very least Trotsky's supporters might have expected him to deny the charge of pessimism with a forceful expression of confidence in the revolution's future. Refusing to view the matter so categorically, he suggested that the proletarian revolution would probably take place in the West before the construction of socialism was carried through to the end. On the other hand, if capitalism were to survive for another fifty years, Russia would be smothered. In an initial draft of his speech Trotsky had outlined this reasoning more carefully. A lasting economic recovery in Europe, he thought, would expand grain exports, increase peasant purchasing power, and bring the trade monopoly under irresistible pressure. If Europe were to decline – but to do so only gradually – then Soviet exports would contract, the pace of development would decelerate, and socialist industry would be left vulnerable to American competition.[32] By giving the conference an inadequate explanation of his position Trotsky left the impression that he, like Zinoviev, did not 'believe' in the revolution. The fact was that he thought the supposed options of 'belief' or 'disbelief', 'faith' or 'pessimism', were too contemptible to discuss. In March 1927 he wrote:

What is the general significance of the debate over tempo, over the 'snail's pace' on the one hand and 'super-industrialism' on the other? *This is not a debate over whether or not socialist construction is possible or impossible, but over which policies promise success.* Setting forth and underlining our dependence on the world market seems necessary to me in the first place because it corresponds to reality, and secondly because it is the only way to clarify the question of tempo... Where is there capitulation ... if my basic belief is that we can only ... accelerate our own development by wisely using the resources of the world economy?[33]

Trotsky's diary notes, dating from November 1926 made the following analysis:

The correlation of industrial and agricultural prices (the scissors) must be the decisive factor in the question of the peasantry's relation to capitalism or socialism. The export of agricultural products places the internal scissors under the control of the world market.

The products of our industry are $2\frac{1}{2}$ to 3 times more expensive than foreign products. With a correction for quality our industrial products are 3 to 4 times less attractive than the products of the world market.

The preservation of the foreign trade monopoly is only possible if this relationship changes...

This in itself is adequate proof of the bankruptcy of a theory which suggests opting out of the world market and looking at the question of building socialism in isolation, within the confines of a single country.[34]

On another occasion Trotsky observed: 'it is . . . impermissible . . . even to raise the question of whether it is "possible or impossible" for any given country to build socialism independently. The question is decided by the dynamics of the struggle between the two systems, between the two world classes.'[35] Stalin had gone beyond the pale of scientific prediction, concocting a mystical creed and setting himself up as an inquisitor to root out heretics. By refusing to debate on Stalin's level at the Fifteenth Conference Trotsky wasted his last opportunity to ridicule his enemy before a full party audience. His speech was more an apology than an attack, and it invited a pedantic reply.

Osinsky, a former oppositionist who had recently returned to respectability, claimed Trotsky had underestimated the extent of Russia's pre-war growth. Capital imports over four decades had prepared all of the necessary conditions for continuing development. Trotsky was wrong to see an obstacle in the world economy: 'Comrade Trotsky forgets the fact that this limitation on development by the world market exists for each capitalist country. But it does not deprive them of the possibility for an independent economic growth.'[36] Larin deliberately added to the confusion with the claim that the opposition's demand for 'super-industrialization' logically suggested 'an increased pliability with respect to foreign capital'. The proof of this fact was to be seen in the failure of the opposition leaders to disown Sokol'nikov, 'with his negative approach to the monopoly of foreign trade and with his ideas of converting state trusts into mixed . . . enterprises with . . . foreign capital'.[37]

The conference resolution served propaganda purposes too, mindlessly repeating the charge that the opposition's policies would raise industrial prices and cause a new sales crisis. When the same resolution called for machinery purchases to strengthen the engineering industries and to reduce Russia's 'dependence on the capitalist countries', the local party representatives found it incomprehensible that a super-industrializer should object. Was this not the surest way to guarantee Russia's survival regardless of what took place in the West? Trotsky's answer was categorically negative. One month after the party conference he made a more energetic effort to explain why.

Trotsky appeals to the International

Early in December 1926 the Executive Committee of the Communist International met in Moscow for its seventh plenum. In theory the Comintern was a court of final instance for each of its member parties. After his expulsion from the Russian Politburo on charges of factionalism Trotsky demanded and received the right of appeal. Arguing from his theory of Imperialism he compensated for the weaknesses of his conference speech by setting out a comprehensive case against economic isolationism.

Industrial societies, he explained, tended to be fundamentally alike. Moreover, they were inevitably bound to one another through growing international trade. As the more backward countries industrialized they could not avoid being drawn into the world economy: 'This is the basic fact, and for this reason even the attempt to look at the economic and political fate of a separate country (*otdel'naya strana*), tearing this country away from its links and interdependencies with the world economy as a whole, is basically false.' The imperialist war had been caused by a rebellion of the productive forces against the nation-state. 'The road back to the isolated state no longer exists.' Russia's own historical evolution, benefitting from imports of French capital during the tsarist period, was a perfect illustration. And Russia's past would leave its imprint upon the socialist future:

The precondition of socialism is heavy industry and machine-building – these are the most important levers of socialism. On this ... we are all agreed. But let us ask ourselves how things really stand with the technical equipment in our factories and works. According to statistical calculations ... before the war 63 per cent of our industry's equipment consisted of imported machines. Only a third was of domestic manufacture, and even this third consisted of the simplest machines; the most important and complicated items came from abroad. Consequently when you look around at the technical equipment of our factories you see with your own eyes the materialized dependence of Russia – and also of the Soviet Union – on the world economy.[38]

Stalin's isolationism derived from the assumption that capital goods were some kind of natural resource. During the reconstruction period, when the revolutionary legacy from the old regime had yet to be put into motion, such primitive naiveté was excusable. Now that the reconstruction period had ended the party conference was right in recognizing the need for machinery imports. However, these would have to be planned for the most part with light industry in mind:

> We must renew our basic capital, which is presently passing through a crisis. Whoever imagines that we will be able to build all of our equipment in the coming years, or even the greater part of it, is a dreamer. The industrialization of our country . . . means . . . not a decrease, but on the contrary a growth of our connections with the outside world, which means . . . our growing dependence . . . on the world market, on capitalism, on its technical equipment and its economy.

As a product of historical forces Soviet Russia's industry constituted an empirical embodiment of the world division of labour. A refusal to fill the 'gaps' in Soviet equipment with imports would be the equivalent of a socialist Munroe Doctrine. Certainly in ten or twenty years Russian metallurgy and engineering might make self-sufficiency feasible. But 'this would inevitably mean an extraordinary lowering in the tempo of our economic growth. . . Moreover, the tempo of development is the most decisive factor: . . . thus far an isolated socialist state exists only in the dreams of journalists and resolution-makers.' In the long run the world economy would assert control over all its component parts 'even if one part stands under the proletarian dictatorship and is building socialism'. 'Whoever discusses the theory of Socialism in One Country,' Trotsky concluded, 'ignoring the fact of "co-operation" and struggle between our economy and the world capitalist economy, is occupying himself with empty metaphysics.'

The appeal to the Comintern provided a true indication of Trotsky's thinking, but it did not win any converts. Bukharin and Rykov both insisted that Trotsky had seen only one half of a dialectical contradiction, that he had not grasped the manner in which 'dependence' would engender 'independence'. Stalin resumed much the tone he had taken in his exchange with Sokol'-nikov a year earlier: 'No-one denies that there exists a dependence of our economy on the world capitalist economy. No-one denies this or has denied it.' Still less did anyone intend to forget about exports and imports: 'To depict a socialist economy as something absolutely self-contained and absolutely independent of the surrounding national economies is to talk nonsense.' On the other hand, Russia was not Montenegro or even Bulgaria; and the USSR, the vanguard of the proletarian revolution, would avoid becoming 'a cog in the international capitalist economy'. When Trotsky spoke of capitalist control did he mean that the banks should be denationalized, that industry and transport should be surrendered? To Stalin's knowledge such policies had not been advocated. But then he admitted: 'I don't know . . . what they are thinking in the Main Concessions Committee.'[39]

The last public word in the present phase of the conflict went to Bukharin. In a speech published in *Pravda* on 13 January 1927 he again argued that 'the growth of our dependence on the capitalist world is at the same time the growth of our independence'. Trotsky had counterposed the international division of labour to autarchy, as if autarchy were an end in itself. This was not true; ultimately a planned economy would emerge embracing the entire world and governing even the division of labour. When the dictatorship of the proletariat was established in all the leading countries there would be no need to insist that a particular factory or plant be constructed on our 'Russian street'. 'Our task will then be to conduct and rationalize our production in such a way as to take into consideration the most favourable geographical, climatic, transportation, technical and other conditions.' With an international socialist economy industry could be located according to purely economic criteria:

But matters do not stand that way now. Now the world economy, unfortunately, is not under the dictatorship of the proletariat. . . We are struggling and we must struggle to become more independent of this world capitalist economy. And when we hear . . . that our 'national limitation' lies in this [belief] we can only chuckle. Our independence is independence of a class type, an independence of the capitalist states.

Bukharin was now convinced that Russia's isolation might last even longer than the theory of stabilization had first seemed to suggest. The international revolution had been halted by a new division of the world into 'three vast spheres': 'the imperialist world, the rising East, and the Union of Socialist Soviet Republics'. Before the three spheres could be reunited 'a great historical epoch' might pass. Soviet Russia must therefore make preparations for the increasing likelihood of war or blockade.[40]

Trotsky's personal notes indicate that of all the accusations made against him both at the Comintern meeting and before, he was most resentful of the claim that he, the architect of the Red Army, had not appreciated the threat of further military clashes. Disgusted with histrionic references to his 'hopelessness, scepticism, lack of faith and all the rest', he recalled that he had already explained the relation between trade and defence in 1925:

In my book *Towards Socialism or Capitalism?* I explained that we have reconstructed our dependence on the world economy, that this dependence will grow, and that with a proper policy on our part this is the natural road for ... strengthening our position against the possibility of military intervention as well as against the permanently operative 'intervention' of cheap commodities. I explained that in contemporary circumstances the question of national economic self-sufficiency cannot be resolved by building a Chinese Wall, and as an example I cited the case of Germany... What is the lesson for us? The lesson is that we do not need 'independence' of the world economy, but a high productivity of labour, which can only be achieved with a rapid tempo of development, and which in turn requires a broad and knowledgeable exploitation of the world market's resources.[41]

To avoid any possible provocation and to facilitate loans and other agreements with Europe, Trotsky had recently advocated non-interference in the British General Strike. The strike had erupted in May 1926, inspiring Soviet hopes that the revolution was again on the move. The Anglo-Soviet Trade Union Committee, which had been created a year earlier, was used to channel financial support to the fraternal strikers. Trotsky ridiculed the committee, claiming that it sustained the power of moderate British unionists.[42]

Turning to the issues Stalin had raised, he defended himself as follows:

The world market controls our backwardness from day to day both with respect to production as a whole and with respect to each branch in particular. How? By the movement of prices. Comrade Stalin attempted to interpret my opinion regarding the control of the world economy ... in the sense of ... some kind of extraordinary retreat ... in the form of concessions and so forth. When the question is phrased that way one can only shrug one's shoulders. The issue is decided ... by the Marxist law of value. Lenin said that the world market will examine us.[43]

As for Bukharin's mention of the dialectical connections between dependence and independence, Trotsky believed that it was really Bukharin who had seen only one half of the problem, continuing to think in terms of his 'fantastic scheme of isolated development'. 'It is true,' he wrote, 'that if you press Bukharin for an answer he begins to "recognize" our dependence on the world economy; but all his arguments, conclusions and perspectives are built on the scheme of a closed (*zamknutoe*) economy.' Bukharin did not see that nations are like business firms – they compete or they perish. In his analysis of capitalism Marx had shown that technical equipment wears out in two senses, physically and technologically. Both forms of wear had to be amortized. A capitalist who made adequate provision for the installation of new technology received more than an equal return in the form of low costs. Those capitalists who did not slipped from the first rank to the second, to the third, and finally into liquidation. Even without a new imperialist war the law of labour productivity meant that socialism could only triumph if 'we measure up not only to our own discoveries and inventions, but also to the progress of world technology'.[44]

The law of labour productivity, expressed in the form of technological change, determined the forward movement of civilization. Capitalism had come into conflict with the nation-state because there was 'a lack of correspondence between technological innovation and the national state frontiers'. Since socialism would be superior to capitalism in every respect, and since international trade was the visible result of technological progress, it followed that it was in the very nature of socialism to expand and perfect the world division of labour. The alternative was to rely on 'the curbed and domesticated productive forces, that is . . . [on] the technology of economic backwardness'.[45] In November 1928 Trotsky *defined* socialism in terms of international trade:

The victory of the proletariat in the leading countries would mean for us a radical restructuring of the very economic foundation in correspondence with a *more productive international division of labour, which is alone capable of creating a genuine foundation for a socialist order.*[46]

A short while later Trotsky moved from this argument to the open assertion that the bureaucratically degenerated Soviet state could not in fact build socialism before the international revolution. But that is to anticipate.

Believing that the revolution was inevitable, in the spring of 1927 he asked whether there was any sense in the Stalin–Bukharin suggestion that Russia should remain isolated until *after* the proletariat took power in Europe. His answer completed the parallel with the ideas of the first integrationists. In 1920 Rykov had objected to labour mobilization; he suggested that the restoration of trade would prepare the way for Russia's later collaboration with socialist Europe. Trotsky's position was now identical:

the further development of the productive forces will increase our interest in international exchange within the capitalist encirclement from year to year. This exchange will be strictly regulated by the methods of the foreign trade monopoly. With a European socialist federation exchange will acquire a planned character. [But] there is no abyss between these two systems... On the contrary, *a properly regulated growth of export and import with the capitalist countries prepares the elements of the future commodity and product exchange* [which will prevail] *when the European proletariat assumes power and controls production.*[47]

By developing foreign trade with the West Russia would both anticipate and prepare for the world revolution. Overlooking Trotsky's integrationism, later Trotskyists have found it embarrassingly difficult to reconcile rejection of Socialism in One Country with the demand that Russia industralize in all haste. Countless articles and tracts have suggested that Trotsky thought Russia could begin to build socialism on her own, but could not complete the process. To Trotsky this whole scheme of analysis was foreign (at least during the period we are now considering). Russia's reunification with Europe was to begin far in advance of the revolution in the West; Russia would 'grow' into Europe, and this economic symbiosis would later find political expression in an international socialist federation.

In order to promote industrialization Russia would systematically have to exploit her enormous and untouched natural resources. In isolation this was impossible. 'The Kursk deposits of magnetic iron, the Ural potassium deposits, and all our gigantic resources in general demand the application of international savings and world technology.' Harnessing the economic potential of Siberia would be a 'gigantic international task'.[48] Again the role of concessions was obvious. In spite of the propaganda campaign of recent months, in March 1927 Trotsky renewed the demand for concessions in industry as well: 'Other conditions being equal foreign capital must be attracted to those branches of industry which show the greatest backwardness . . . by comparison with the corresponding branches of world industry.'[49] Institutionalizing her relations with Europe, Russia would simultaneously come into contact with Europe's colonies in Asia, India, and the East as a whole. The preconditions would be created for a gigantic Eurasian commonwealth with the Soviet Union as its pivot:

We . . . believe that the United States of Europe and our Soviet Union are coming together in one single economic unit. We believe . . . that the Soviet Union is a gigantic bridge between the [future] socialist federation of Europe and a federation of Asia. We do not believe . . . that free India and socialist England will exist in a shut-in manner, independently of each other. The exchange of values between them is a necessary condition for economic progress. This exchange of values will continue even after the overthrow of the British bourgeoisie and will be completed within the limits of a great federation. The same applies to our India of the north – to Siberia.[50]

The theory of imperialism, the problem of scarce capital, awareness of Russia's past and a vision of her future: together they drove Trotsky's imagination beyond the horizons of his contemporaries. On 1 March 1927 Stalin once again equated concessions with tsarism and slavery.[51] Meanwhile, the opposition had already experienced its first split, over the question of how to finance industrialization.

Divisions and defeat
The problem of an industrial pricing policy was the counterpart of divisions within the opposition concerning the role of concessions. Although the various factions were all prepared to tax the *kulak* more progressively, many of those who followed Trotsky into the grand alliance simultaneously called for increases in industrial wholesale prices. The less confidence they placed in concessions or loans, the more vocally they tended to advocate internal accumulation. Trotsky himself had agreed to experimental changes, but in September 1926 he wrote that 'the rise in wholesale prices must strike a blow at private capital, not at the consumer. . . If retail prices begin to rise as well we must hold back.'[52] I have already mentioned this cautious appraisal of pricing problems as a source of possible disagreement between Trotsky and Preobrazhensky. Pyatakov and Smirnov repeatedly argued that wholesale prices must be raised at once. Zinoviev, in contrast, appears to have been equally persistent in his refusal to contemplate such a policy under any circumstances.[53] To stress the need to tax the *kulak* directly though, as Zinoviev preferred, was to invite the charge of super-industrialism and an anti-peasant bias.

Trotsky's chief interest, as leader of the opposition, was to disprove this allegation and at the same time to keep his own colleagues united. In February of 1927 (as in the summer of 1926 following the editorial on concessions and the Right Danger) he appears to have decided on a tactical change of course, answering his critics by voting with the party leaders for wholesale price reductions. Justifying this decision he wrote in his notes that the opposition's 'strategic line' had always been to lower market prices. 'The whole of the present economic situation,' he continued, 'has made it *tactically* impossible to postpone price reductions.'[54] The difficulty was that Trotsky's willingness to embrace this particular tactic was more than several of his supporters could tolerate.

Smirnov and the Democratic-Centralists immediately abandoned the coalition they had first entered in 1923. In Smirnov's opinion Trotsky's speech to the February plenum of the Central Committee was 'the most colourless' of all:

All the sharp questions were deliberately avoided. Not a single word was uttered about unemployment, not a single word about the inadequacies of the plan. On the contrary . . . it was underlined that . . . the Central Committee had accepted the opposition's plan [put forth] in April [1926].[55]

With the success of the latest procurement campaign investment targets had been raised to a figure approximating the sum advocated by Trotsky at the April plenum a year earlier. Biding his time, Trotsky asserted that the party leaders had begrudgingly vindicated the opposition. Smirnov was more candid, maintaining that the plan could never be realized with current government revenues. He interpreted Trotsky's manoeuvre as ideological backsliding, opportunism and capitulation: 'Trotsky can suggest only one thing to the opposition – wait, wait while "the candidate for gravedigger of the revolution", as he called Stalin . . . begins to struggle for proletarian interests and then join him. How can one say . . . [it] is a manoeuvre and not capitulation?'[56] In July 1927 the split was finalized. The Democratic-Centralists published their own programme, substituting wholesale price increases for capital imports as a source of investment resources.

The defection of the Democratic-Centralists raises an important point concerning Trotsky's general view of tactics after the Fifteenth Party Congress. The idea of 'waiting' was based on an analysis made in mid-September 1926, when he had described the ruling group in the party as an insecure coalition between the centre and the right wing. From this standpoint Stalin did not appear to be a threat. Devoid of ideas, Stalin was a plagiarist, a 'combiner' of other people's proposals. Politically he served as spokesman for the apparatus and the wavering political middle. His usefulness was restricted to his performance as 'a brake on the bloc, whose tendencies pull to the right'. The *kulak* deviationists, with Bukharin as their chief representative, were taken to be the main enemy. Even if Stalin did not understand industrialization he did express proletarian interests. Trotsky did not doubt that the centrifugal forces within the ruling clique would cause it ultimately to fly apart: 'The logic of class interests is more powerful than apparatus diplomacy.'[57] The opposition was to serve the party and the proletariat by rendering positive support from the left for the constructive moves of Stalin and the centrists, while continuing to criticize errors of principle. Although his perception of the still latent contradictions in the relationship between Bukharin and Stalin was commendable, Trotsky's pathetic misunderstanding of the party secretary's true importance could only lead to personal disaster.

In the spring of 1927 the pace of events suddenly quickened. In China Stalin's policy of co-operation with the Kuomintang collapsed, as Chiang Kai-shek massacred his Communist 'allies'. To the opposition the time now seemed right to renew the struggle on all fronts. On 15 April Trotsky wrote to the Central Committee, *Pravda* and the Central Control Commission about economic policy, protesting against the recent plenum's isolationist decisions.[58] 'Our foreign trade,' he declared, 'will not only grow absolutely but also relatively; the same applies to our dependence on the world market.'[59] One month later Russia's relations with Great Britain took a severe turn for the worse. Following a search of the Soviet trade mission, diplomatic ties were severed altogether. Overnight Trotsky was politically destroyed. His enemies moved quickly to interpret Russia's misfortune as their own success. Rykov cried that Britain had confirmed 'the falseness of the position of those comrades who assert the need . . . to start from a strengthening of our economy's dependence on the world market'.[60] Bukharin imprudently exclaimed that the West was preparing to launch a preventive war.[61] Rykov supported this view, and alleged that England was financing white guard and monarchist conspiracies.[62] Bukharin answered with the assertion that the breathing space was ended, that a new period had opened, fraught with the danger of war and attacks.[63] Early in August a joint meeting of the Central Committee and the Central Control Commission decided that the sharpening contradictions between Russia and the West were 'the main tendency' of the present period.[64]

The *coup de grace* came with the collapse of financial discussions in Paris. In July 1926 the French had accepted a provisional agreement involving a total sum of 450 million rubles and exports of Russian oil. Then the French government had fallen. Poincaré, a traditional enemy, returned to power and the negotiations were delayed. By May 1927 a further agreement had been concluded but Poincaré raised the familiar demand for settlement of war debts and indemnification for French losses through nationalization. The Soviet representative, Rakovsky, endeavoured to keep the issue before the French public and became an embarrassment. In October 1927 Paris demanded his recall to Moscow on the grounds that he had signed an opposition document calling on foreign soldiers to be loyal to proletarian Russia in the event of war. For all practical purposes Rakovsky's return marked the termination of diplomatic relations with the second most powerful capitalist country in Europe. A new wave of near-hysteria ensued in the Soviet press.

Finding themselves in an impossible situation the opposition leaders decided their only defence lay in attack. In August Zinoviev had alleged that the party leaders were planning to recognize Russia's debts and to abolish the trade monopoly in order to buy their way out of the war danger. Shortly before Rakovsky's recall Stalin did suggest the possibility of 'certain concessions to the French'.[66] Trotsky and Zinoviev replied that Stalin was attempting to buy Soviet security, thereby compensating for the miserable failures of the Comintern. A Leninist policy did not exclude partial retreats, but Stalin was said to be planning a retreat 'in general'.[67] On 12 October a collective opposition declaration announced that general debt recognition would be a 'shattering blow for socialist construction . . . since it would inevitably lead . . . to an even greater delay . . . of industrialization, to a threatened growth of the forces of foreign capital in the economy of our country . . . [to] the enslavement of our country by foreign capital'.[68] Stalin should have come to terms with the French when a respectable compromise was being offered.

The declaration was transparently a political move. The document was submitted to the Politburo five days after Rakovsky had been declared *persona non grata* in Paris and on the day Chicherin acceded to the French demand to withdraw his envoy. The opposition knew there was nothing to lose; they hoped a political advantage might be gained. Stalin answered the charges by emphasizing how reasonable he had been: he had based his decisions on the formula: 'you give – we give. You [France] provide credits – and you receive something from us with respect to the pre-war debts; if you don't give – you don't receive.'[69]

At the end of September Trotsky addressed the Comintern Executive Committee for the last time. On 23 October he defended himself before the Central Committee. 'Expel me,' he challenged, 'but you will not prevent the victory of the opposition.'[70] Both he and Zinoviev were expelled. On 7 November, the anniversary of the revolution, they attempted to appeal to the public in Leningrad and Moscow. The workers looked on with apathy; the party activists resorted to organized repression. On 15 November 1927 both men were dismissed from the party on charges of inciting counter-revolutionary demonstrations. As a political force the opposition ceased to exist.

In the autumn of 1927 the party's xenophobia knew no restraint. On 12 October Bukharin applauded Trotsky's fate as proof of the need for economic isolation.[71] On 26 October he denounced 'the orthodox wing of our Trotskyist opposition' for their objections to the so-called 'national limitation'.[72] In both speeches he facetiously argued that those who advocated Russia's dependence on capitalism were logically committed to abolishing the trade monopoly. How else would they develop maximal trade links with the West? A foreign loan of tens of milliards of rubles would not justify the sale of Russia's socialist primogeniture in exchange for bondage to foreigners.

By this time, however, Bukharin had also debated himself into a corner. Promoting a war scare in order to discredit Trotsky he had simultaneously alarmed the nation in general. Panic hoarding resulted; the goods famine intensified; and the *kulak* went on strike. The flow of food to the cities dwindled to a trickle. Suddenly Bukharin realized that his own policies had led to a dead end. In a speech which foreshadowed his coming break with Stalin, he attributed the crisis to the structure of the invest-ment programme:

If we were to invest capital . . . in the light industries, where returns are more quickly realized . . . in the form of finished products, thus speed-ing the turnover of capital . . . and alleviating the goods famine – this would provide us with a way out of the present situation . . . investments in very large-scale factories, for example in metallurgy and so forth, only yield a return after several years. As a result we collect money and invest it; but the market for consumer goods does not feel the effects as quickly or as directly as we would wish.[73]

A year later the disagreement with Stalin led to an open breach. In his famous 'Notes of an Economist' Bukharin warned that Stalin was building industry with 'bricks of the future', ignoring the need to maintain a 'dynamic economic equilibrium'. The party was forgetting the peasantry, the goods famine, and its negative impact on agricultural exports.[74] Stalin took note of Bukharin's 'panic' and 'bewilderment', attributing these pessi-mistic attitudes to a failure to understand that industrialization required new methods of class struggle.

Bukharin was not alone in embracing the new right deviation. In December 1927 Rykov told the Fifteenth Party Congress that Russia's *de facto* isolation implied the need to develop heavy in-dustry. But this policy would mean neglecting light industry and would bring the danger of 'a crisis in our entire commodity turn-over'. There was one solution. Russia must rely heavily on im-ports of machinery:

The weakest point in the whole economic development is foreign trade. In the five-year plan it is necessary to start from the fact that . . . the process of the country's industrialization will depend very heavily on trade with the outside world. This dependence will be expressed in the need to import foreign machines to equip our factories.[75]

Concern to expand imports was shared at the time by most Soviet planners. Nevertheless, Rykov's remarks were a political event in that he, like Bukharin, was beginning to link the danger of a peasant retribution to the kind of investment structure which seemed implicit in Stalin's speeches. Thus an attitude, which in Trotsky's case had been labelled 'super-industrialism', was soon transformed into 'rightism', providing the ideological background for charges against the alleged Bloc of Rights and Trotskyists during the great purges of the 1930s.

At the Fifteenth Congress Stalin refuted his critics by maintaining that self-sufficiency was more necessary now than ever
before. Current plots against the USSR indicated that the period
of stabilization was finally coming to an end. Borrowing a leaf
from Trotsky he continued:

The contradiction between the growth of the productive forces and the
relative stability of markets lies at the base of the fact that the problem of
markets is now the fundamental problem of capitalism. . . Strictly speaking this explains why the under-utilization of factories and plants is becoming a universal phenomenon [in the West]. A strengthening of tariff
barriers only throws the fat into the fire. Capitalism has become too
crowded within the confines of the present markets. . . Peaceful attempts
to solve the problem of markets cannot save the capitalist system.[76]

The last official pronouncements of the opposition, calling for
a compulsory grain loan from the *kulak*, had hinted at the only
possible remedy for the grain problem. Stalin announced that
agriculture would have to be collectivized (by means of 'demon-
stration and persuasion'). The goods famine, he acknowledged,
was inevitable; light industry must wait. By measures of revolutionary legality the peasant must be forced to sell grain – 'But
this does not exclude, of course, the application of certain necessary administrative measures.'[77] From the early months of 1928
the necessary administrative measures were freely used.

In the spring of 1928 Stalin argued that the use of force was
unavoidable: 'we need reserves for export. We need to import
equipment for industry.' Having long since given up the attempt
to lower industrial prices he now took Preobrazhensky's position:
the price scissors were 'a supplementary tax . . . in the interests of
industrialization'.[78] Hearing this comment Bukharin exclaimed to
Kamenev that 'Stalin is an unprincipled intriguer who subordinates everything to the preservation of his power. He changes
theory to suit the needs of the moment.'[79] The insight was
several years too late. The revolution had turned full circle; and
the cataclysmic rush into political and economic totalitarianism
was about to begin.

8

Integrationism in defeat and exile

At the beginning of this study it was proposed that Trotsky's appraisal of Soviet economic policy should be seen in terms of two periods: War Communism and the mid-1920s. In both of these periods, as we have now shown, the uniqueness of Trotsky's views centred on the question of Russia's relation with Europe. At each stage of the revolution's development he found himself either tacitly or explicitly in conflict with the majority opinion in the Bolshevik leadership. When Trotsky thought Russia had no alternative but isolation, his opponents favoured integration. When Trotsky endorsed integration, others advocated Russia's isolation.

Taking into consideration the political tensions of the time it is tempting to attribute this odd dialectic to either conscious or unintentional personal perversity on Trotsky's part. Several of the more prominent members of the opposition eventually came to this conclusion, believing that collectivization and the first five-year plan removed all of the substantive causes of earlier disputes. Systematic repression of the *kulak*, the elimination of the NEP-men, and massive investments in industry: together these policies seemed not merely to fulfil the opposition's demands, but also to guarantee Russia's march to socialism. Even Isaac Deutscher, in his well-known biography, suggested that Trotsky had become 'the authentic inspirer and prompter' of Stalinist industrialization.[1] To most contemporaries it seemed that Stalin had seen the error of his own, and particularly of Bukharin's ways, thus making possible a political reconciliation between the party's left and centre. The problem with this interpretation was that it concentrated exclusively on internal questions. In exile first at Alma Ata in Soviet Central Asia, and after January 1929 on the Turkish island of Prinkipo, Trotsky believed the basic issues remained unchanged. Sickened by the revolution's slide into

despotism he would not be moved from his conviction that Stalin
was leading the nation to a catastrophe which might have been
avoided.

A complete study of Trotsky's economic writings in exile would
range far beyond the plan of this book. On the other hand,
because the themes I have been considering did not suddenly disappear at the end of 1927, it would be misleading and inappropriate to end the discussion here. Many of the supreme ironies of
Trotsky's career only became apparent during the first five-year
plan, when the forms and the methods, indeed, even the attitudes
of War Communism, were revived. Rapid technological change
introduced important qualitative differences, but the historical
parallels were not difficult to detect. With the similarities of
approach came similar social contradictions and antagonisms.
Viewing these from the perspective of the mid-1920s Trotsky
went one step beyond the position set out in preceding chapters.
Essentially criticizing Stalin for those policies which had once
provoked his own clash with Lenin over *udarnost'* and the trade
unions, he concluded that socialism could not be fully achieved
in Russia until the country's *political* isolation ended. Political
degeneration was taken to be the major cause of economic mis-
takes. And political recovery required the rejuvenating inspiration that would come from a successful international revolution.

Assessing Stalin's 'left course'
Psychologically conditioned by the doctrine of *partiinost'*, or
party-mindedness, even the most stalwart oppositionists were
poorly prepared for exclusion from the Bolshevik ranks. Zinoviev
and Kamenev recanted their errors before the end of 1927. By
March 1928 Preobrazhensky described Stalin's 'left course' as 'a
new political fact of enormous importance' and urged Trotsky to
tell *Pravda* that current decisions were correct.[2] Stalin's critics
had once risked error on the side of 'pessimism'. In April Preobrazhensky argued that 'we must now take a risk on the side of
optimism . . . and move towards rapprochement with the party;
otherwise [we face] conversion into a small sect of 'true Lenin-
ists', like the many . . . [religious] sects of the past'.[23] 'A reduction
of our disagreements with the Central Committee on a number
of real questions of international and internal policy' was plainly
evident, and Preobrazhensky thought the time was right 'to make

peace with the party majority on the basis of the new course'.[4] An important influence on this decision was his belief that Stalin's adoption of socialist accumulation ruled out any further chance for a foreign loan: 'The anti-*kulak* policy of the Soviet power, being accompanied by pressure on the NEP-men, cannot but sharpen our relations with the whole of world capitalism, diminishing the already insignificant chances of foreign credits for industrialization.'[5] Pyatakov had made his peace with Stalin in February 1928. Karl Radek thought the opposition should offer Stalin 'support' against the right wing and loosely endorsed Preobrazhensky's summons to accept 'responsibility for the left course in the countryside'.[6] Early in 1929 a humiliating surrender on Stalin's terms brought both former 'Trotskyists' back into the party's embrace.

In vain Trotsky warned that Stalin's change of front was a mere 'zig-zag, that 'a sharp turn to the right' would result if the opposition were to become lax in its criticism.[7] Continuing struggle for the opposition platform, he advised, was 'the only proper, serious and honest support that can be rendered to any kind of progressive steps by the centre'.[8] In a letter to Rakovsky he wrote:

Support . . . consists in the first place of a redoubled struggle by Marxists for a Marxist framing of real questions; secondly in merciless criticism of the half-heartedness of centrist leftism, with the intention of helping the best elements of the centrists . . . to move over more rapidly to a Bolshevik position. There can be no other support. . . It is not only completely inadmissible to take upon ourselves responsibility before the party for the left-centrist line (this was in Preobrazhensky's note), but is it equally inadmissible to try to convert ourselves into ingratiating persuaders as Radek hints. . . In the same way as a monkey without a tail is still not a man, a centrist who puts his tail aside on the basis of good advice is still not a Marxist. Moreover, Stalin's articles show that there has been no request for good advice.[9]

With his customary political acumen Trotsky thought his prophecy of a zig-zag was being fulfilled as early as July 1928. A Central Committee decision to ease the pressure on the *kulak* seemed to signal Rykov's triumph over Stalin, thus proving that the left course was an 'episode'. As collectivization raced ahead with dizzying speed, however, it was clear early in 1930 that the zig-zag had become a programme of ultra-left bureaucratic adventurism.[10] Stalin had decided to eliminate the *kulak* as a social class.

Trotsky objected to collectivization for reasons I have already mentioned in another context. When the peasants resisted the campaign by slaughtering their livestock the government was unable to provide new supplies of mechanical equipment as compensatory horsepower. Trotsky believed labour productivity would critically decline; individual incentives would vanish; and the party would ultimately be forced to beat an ill-prepared retreat. 'It is impossible,' he wrote, 'to create large-scale agriculture out of peasant wooden ploughs . . . just as it is impossible to create a ship by adding up fishing boats.'[11] All-round collectivization would result in 'all-round weeds in the fields'.[12] Should Stalin persist in the adventure resources would be diverted from industry with no prospect of a reasonable return for decades. Only large-scale imports of tractors, ploughs, and other machinery could place the few farms with the potential for profitability on a sound footing. In the spring of 1930 Trotsky claimed that with foreign machinery 'collectivized agriculture could pass far more easily through the period of infantile illness and be able, almost in the next few years, to realize a greatly improved harvest, with such stocks for export as would radically change the picture of the grain market of Europe. . . The menacing disproportion between the swing of collectivization and the state of technology flows directly from the economic isolation of the Soviet Union.'[13]

When Stalin attempted to reconstruct a system of agricultural incentives in the spring of 1932, he did so by creating a collective farm market. Once deliveries to the state were completed, the peasants were allowed to sell whatever remained of their products. Trotsky, the most inveterate critic of the NEP during the 1920s, hailed the decision as necessary and inevitable: 'All-round collectivization . . . extraordinarily lowered the labour incentives available to the peasantry. . . The answer to this threat was the legalization of trade. In other words, . . . it was necessary partially to restore the NEP, or the free market, which was abolished too soon and too definitely.'[14] To be consistent Stalin should also dissolve those farms which were currently exhausting government funds for no useful purpose:

Il faut reculer pour mieux sauter. It is imperative to correct past errors. The peasants must be helped to strengthen and develop viable, stable collective farms, which stand the test of practice. Those peasants who have been disappointed by the collective farms must be given, as soon as possible, the right to return to individual farming.[15]

Up to eighty per cent of rural families should be permitted to return to commercial agriculture.

The partial frustration and chaotic consequences of the plan's industrial provisions evoked a similarly hostile critique. The disproportionate emphasis on heavy industry raised anew the question of comparative coefficients and the trade monopoly. As 'narrow spots' or bottlenecks grew in number Trotsky asserted that with commodity intervention it would be possible 'to overcome partial crises, weaken partial disproportions, equalize the dynamic equilibrium of different branches, and guarantee in this way a high tempo of development'.[16] In October 1932 he suggested that even minimal imports of scarce goods could rectify supply breakdowns and reactivate vastly greater Soviet resources. To forego these advantages in the pursuit of autarchy was to follow Hitler rather than Marx.[17] A minimum concession to common sense would require that the year 1933 be used as a buffer between the first and second plan. The purpose of a buffer year would be to complete the work of crises in a capitalist economy, 'to liquidate inopportune construction; to concentrate means and resources on construction of first-rate importance; to balance the different branches of industry on the basis of experience; to bring the factories into order; to restore the equipment'.[18] 'We would consider it a grandiose success,' Trotsky wrote, 'to fulfil the five-year plan in six, seven, or even eight years or more, if the disproportions could be eased, if the well-being of the masses could be raised, clearing the way for an economic *smychka*.'[19]

If Trotsky's estimate of the plan's practical difficulties grew out of the industrialization strategy he had developed in 1925 the same could not be said of his attitude to planning *per se*. Shocked by the human and economic costs of the current wave of 'planomania' he began to consider the possibility of combining the plan with a market in the form of 'market socialism'. During War Communism he had attempted to balance central directives with a measure of decentralization and local initiative. But the five-year plan was blind; it made no provision for feedback, for adjusting to the consequences of its own operations. Hence the remorseless attack on the *kulak* had fed on its own excesses, and had led directly to the famine of 1933. Responsibility lay squarely with the bureaucracy, which Trotsky ridiculed mercilessly for its attempt to produce plans 'beginning with the number of hectares of wheat and ending with buttons on a waistcoat'.[20] The experience of the 1930s indicated that with the given state of knowledge total plans were a figment of the bureaucratic imagination. In an article entitled 'The Soviet Economy in Danger' Trotsky stressed the need to establish an interaction between the plan on the one hand, and supply and demand on the other:

The innumerable living participants in the economy, state and private, collective and individual, must announce their needs and their respective intensities not only through the statistical calculations of the planning commissions, but also by the direct pressure of supply and demand. The plan . . . [must be] verified, and in an important measure must be achieved through the market.[21]

Before a comprehensive and internally consistent plan could be devised the Soviet Union would have to pass through a lengthy transition period. Gosplan and the ruble would have to exercise dual control over socialist construction. The capitalist system of monetary accounting would have to be perfected not merely to ensure economic rationality, but also to build into socialism a broad system of incentives. 'The personal interest of the producer and consumer' had to be activated by material encouragement measured in cash. Inflation had become one of the main instruments for the bureaucratic disorganization of the Soviet economy.

In an unpublished manuscript, written in 1933, Trotsky paid the ultimate compliment to Sokol'nikov's views regarding state capitalism. In a capitalist system, he argued, the volume of money had to be determined by both gold reserves and 'the speed of the commodity–money turnover'. As planning methods improved, the issuing of money could be successfully co-ordinated with production and exchange plans, and the currency could be detached from its gold basis. A completed socialist society would do away entirely with both gold and money. The existing disproportions in the Soviet economy proved, however, that throughout the entire transitional epoch the currency must remain 'a universal equivalent, and consequently must be grounded in precious metal'. Gosplan's material balances and administrative prices could not substitute for the impartiality of gold:

Cast iron can be measured in tons; electricity in kilowatts; cloth in metres. But it is impossible to create a universal plan without reducing all its branches to one and the same value denominator. If the denominator is itself fictitious, if it is the product of bureaucratic discretion, then it eliminates the possibility of testing and correcting the plan in the process of its implementation. Fixed prices which are not controlled by a stable currency open up unlimited room for bureaucratic subjectivism in the area of planning.[22]

Calling for market socialism on economic grounds Trotsky did not shrink from recognizing such a system's political implications. If the centralized monopoly of decision-making was to be compromised by the market a certain pluralization of political influence would be inevitable. The regeneration of Soviet society depended upon a two-way flow of communication between party and people and the creation of a controlled political market in which divergent social interests might compete. Russia had not yet achieved a classless society. Accordingly the basic questions of policy – the division of the national income, the relation between investment and consumption, and the determination of wage schedules – would have to be settled by 'the direct action of class struggle and the struggle of social groups, including the different layers of the proletariat itself'. Eventually the 'interested millions' would use the institutions at their disposal to impress their demands upon decision-makers:

The struggle of vital interests, in the form of a new factor of planning, brings us to the role of politics, which is concentrated economics. The equipment of the social groups of Soviet society is (and must be); the soviets, the trade unions, the co-operatives, and above all the ruling party. Only the interaction of the three elements; of state planning, of the market, and of soviet democracy, can provide the economy with proper leadership in the transitional epoch.[23]

Just as the currency would provide a common denominator for the regulation of economic decisions, so Marxism–Leninism would establish the boundaries within which political competition should take place. For the consciousness and will of the masses, for 'collective economic experience, tested, discussed, and criticized on a day-to-day basis by the working people themselves', Stalin's bureaucrats had sought to substitute their own commands. 'This,' Trotsky decided, 'is the main political cause of the mistakes that have been committed.'[24]

Not realizing that these errors were inherent in the system of teleological planning itself Stalin was attempting to overcome social resistence by the use of brute force. To scrutinize the behaviour of the peasants he had created a network of 'political departments' attached to the new machine tractor stations. In 1920 the question of political departments had played a key role in the controversy provoked by the mobilization of labour. Thirteen years later, in 1933, Trotsky blithely condemned Stalin's move, characterizing it as 'a strengthening of compulsion and command-giving (*komandovanie*) in accordance with the [current] party line'.[25]

With the soviets losing their last remnants of independence, and with the party itself being suffocated, there was little hope that the industrial proletariat would fare any better than the peasants as long as the Stalinist regime lasted. In 1920 another major political issue had involved the question of equality; 'equalization' had been demanded by Trotsky's critics in preference to *udarnost'*. Now Stalin was leaping backwards to War Communist methods, treating equality as a bourgeois prejudice and instituting a rigorous system of piece-work in the factories. According to Trotsky this measure too was a manifestation of 'the contradictions of economic backwardness'. Russia was not making bold strides towards a socialist future; rather, 'economic development has entered into a contradiction with the political conditions within whose limits it takes place'.[26]

The final blow to the trade unions came with their official 'statification' in 1933. The Commissariat of Labour was abolished, and the Central Council of Trade Unions absorbed its functions and many of its personnel. Labour discipline and increases in production became the unions' official responsibility, taking priority over traditional protective functions. Organized labour became an instrument of the state, virtually the same policy Trotsky had advocated month after month in the latter stage of War Communism. Yet in 1933 Trotsky revived the arguments originally put forth by the Workers' Opposition and the Democratic-Centralists:

The relative independence of the trade unions is a necessary and important corrective in the Soviet state system, which finds itself under pressure from the peasantry and the bureaucracy. Until such time as classes are liquidated the workers – even in a workers' state – must defend themselves with the help of their professional organizations. In other words: *the trade unions remain trade unions just as long as the state remains a state, that is, an apparatus of compulsion. The statification of the trade unions can only take place parallel with the de-statification of the state itself.* Consequently, in the same measure as the elimination of classes deprives the state of its functions of compulsion, causing it to dissolve itself into society, the trade unions lose their special class functions and dissolve into the state, which is withering away.[27]

Trotsky had conveniently forgotten his own answer to the original defenders of trade union independence. In the context of the earlier debate he had contended that before the state withers away it must adopt the form of the proletarian dictatorship, 'that is, of the most merciless state, which imperiously embraces all sides of life'.[28] Only in the limited sense that Stalin was reviving War Communist policies could it be said with Deutscher that Trotsky was the inspirer of Soviet industrialization. Still concerned with the paramount problem of isolation, Trotsky himself would have greeted such faint praise with total disdain.

Final judgements of the Soviet experiment

By the beginning of his exile Trotsky's fear of Thermidorian degeneration converged with his belief that the task of socialism was to perfect the world division of labour. Together these two approaches to the question of Socialism in One Country acted to harden his already acute hostility both to Stalin's doctrine and its practical consequences. Uncertain of his future, suspicious of possible designs against his person by the GPU, vilified and slandered by Stalin's puppets in all countries, and deserted by his friends, at this point in his life Trotsky was anxious to define his legacy to posterity, to secure his place in history. No doubt was to be left about the differences between his point of view and that of the 'epigones'. To demarcate his contribution to Marxism, to prove that in the world of ideas he had left a mark which dwarfed his detractors, Trotsky now made the most ironical decision of a lifetime: he personally endorsed the myth of 'Trotskyism' which his enemies had used to destroy him.

Even before his departure from Alma Ata he had criticized a new Comintern programme, claiming that 'we will enter on the path of *real* socialist construction only when the proletariat of the most advanced countries will have conquered power'. Russia's internal contradictions might be 'regulated and abated by a correct internal policy'; but they could only be finally resolved in an international context.[29] Once abroad, one of the first works he published was an essay with the inflammatory title *The Permanent Revolution*. His aim, he declared, was 'not at all ... to say that my conception of the revolution follows, in all my writings, one and the same unswerving line'. But the disclaimer was superfluous; Trotsky set out to do precisely this, to show that 'the theory of Permanent Revolution, even as presented in my earliest works, primarily in *Results and Prospects* (1906) is immeasurably more permeated with the spirit of Marxism and consequently far closer to the historical line of Lenin ... than ... the present Stalinist and Bukharinist retrospective wisdom'.[30] Whereas his opponents in 1905 and afterwards had considered that Russia was not ripe for socialism, Trotsky now claimed to have foreseen the inevitability of proletarian dictatorship as well as the limitations of 'national socialism'.[31] In his autobiography, also written in 1929, he confessed: 'I like and appreciate discipline and system ... I cannot endure disorder'.[32] In the effort to impart order to his own thought he now proclaimed that the revolution must be permanent in an international sense: 'Thus the socialist revolution becomes a permanent revolution in a newer and broader sense of the word; it attains completion only in the final victory of the new society on our entire planet.'[33]

Co-ordinating the theory of Permanent Revolution with the theory of Imperialism he asserted that because 'the productive forces . . . can no longer be reconciled with the framework of the national state', it followed that 'the construction of an independent socialist society in any single country in the world [is] impossible'.[34] The class struggle took place on a world scale. The revised interpretation of Permanent Revolution meant that a solution could not be found on national foundations:

The maintenance of the proletarian revolution within a national framework can only be a provisional state of affairs, even though, as the experience of the Soviet Union shows, one of long duration. In an isolated proletarian dictatorship the internal and external contradictions grow inevitably along with the successes achieved. If it remains isolated, the proletarian state must finally fall victim to these contradictions. The way out for it lies only in the victory of the proletariat of the advanced countries.[35]

While many of Stalin's policies were qualitatively correct, they were quantitatively wrong. Russia had no choice but to industrialize; however, Stalin was expanding industry too quickly and in the wrong directions. Similarly, socialist agriculture was inevitable; but again Stalin was behaving idealistically, attempting to transform the whole of Soviet agriculture at once with no regard for objective, material limitations. If properly guided and rescued from Stalin's excesses many of the current initiatives being taken in the Soviet Union would ensure a movement towards socialism. Given Russia's political degeneration, however, errors were impossible to correct. As a result Trotsky saw the country being helplessly caught up in a maelstrom of catastrophic contradictions and antagonisms: between town and country, between heavy industry and light, between the party and the working class, between the party and its own secretarial apparatus, and even within the apparatus itself. In his *History of the Russian Revolution* he insisted that the Soviet experience proved beyond any doubt that socialism's future lay in the international arena:

From the world-wide division of labour, from the unevenness of development of different countries, from their mutual economic dependence, from the unevenness of different aspects of culture in the different countries, from the dynamic of the contemporary productive forces, it follows that the socialist structure can only be built by a system of economic spiral, only by taking the inner contradictions of a separate country out into a whole group of countries, only by a mutual service between different countries, and by a mutual supplementation of the different branches of their industry and culture – that is, in the last analysis, only on the world arena.[36]

'Rural Russia,' he added in the same work, 'needs . . . a mutual industrial plan with urban Europe.'[37] The task of socialism was 'to carry the international exchange of goods and services to its highest development'.[38] Stalin did not see that foreign trade was one way to minimize Russia's domestic contradictions. In Trotsky's opinion Stalin's continuing isolationism was rooted in a total inability to grasp the significance of fluctuating international phenomena; in particular Stalin had monstrously misinterpreted the meaning of capitalism's Great Depression.

In 1920 Trotsky had linked isolationism and the mobilization of labour with his prediction of the rapid collapse of capitalism. Stalin was now doing the same. Disenchanted with the theory of stabilization, after 1928 Stalin interpreted capitalism's future in terms of the doctrine of the Third Period. The decade after the first world war was divided into three phases: (1) the period of crisis which came with the end of the war; (2) the period of gradual stabilization; and (3) the final period of 'rapid development in the contradictions in the world economy', of 'maximum sharpening in the general crisis of capitalism', which would inevitably result in a new series of wars and revolutions.[39]

Making a final amendment to his own theory of Imperialism Trotsky shrilly denounced Stalin's entire argument. In the international character of the depression he saw evidence that the disjointed developments of the 1920s, when one country had experienced recovery while another underwent a slump, had come to an end. Economic unity had been restored in adversity; the universality of capitalism's affliction indicated that the world economy had at last returned to a normal pattern of cyclical growth. A revival would therefore follow the decline. In Trotsky's words:

The present crisis has a world character. This means that the world economy, which ceased to exist in the war years, has carved its way through the customs walls and is indicating, in an extremely painful manner, that it is a powerful reality. There is every basis for assuming that the next change of *kon'yunktura* in the direction of recovery will also assume . . . a world character. In other words, the cyclical nature of capitalism has been restored.[40]

The probability that capitalism would survive demonstrated that the conditions for long-run co-operation were still at hand. The onset of new marketing problems in the West provided ideal circumstances in which to solicit foreign credits. In an article on 'World Unemployment and the Five-Year Plan' Trotsky admitted that 'systematic and all-embracing economic co-operation' would only be possible with Europe after the international revolution. Nevertheless, the crisis was likely to expand Russia's access to world reserves: 'If the crisis develops further the reformist governments [i.e. Social-Democratic] which base themselves upon millions of organized workers, can be wedged into such a vice that they will be compelled – to one extent or another – to yield to economic collaboration with the Soviet Union.'[41] In a letter to the remnants of the Russian opposition he recommended using 'the threatening growth of unemployment, especially in Germany and England, for the acquisition of credits for planned orders of agricultural equipment, machinery and so forth in exchange for the products of collectivized agriculture'.[42] When the Comintern rejected these ideas as counter-revolutionary, Trotsky

answered that such 'stupid absurdities' were the natural consequence of the theory of Socialism in One Country.[43]

From this brief survey of Trotsky's later writings it can be seen
that his growing theoretical intransigence on the question of
Socialism in One Country served only to reaffirm his integrationism. By constructing an artificial dichotomy between Stalin's
theory and *Results and Prospects* however, Trotsky subscribed
to official Soviet mythology. By seeking to define his place in history he succeeded in confounding it. To his successors and to
history he bequeathed an enigma.

Recent Soviet histories have done nothing to reduce the confusion; they have failed to go beyond the bounds of established
orthodoxy.[44] Leonid Brezhnev summarized the current Soviet
understanding of the Trotsky–Stalin debate with the following
comment:

Resolving these tasks [of socialist construction] the party conducted an un-
compromising struggle against the Trotskyists, the right opportunists, and
other opposition groups, whose views reflected the pressure of bourgeois
and petty-bourgeois elements. The oppositionists denied the possibility of
initially building socialism in our country, by itself; they did not believe
in the strength of the working class, in the stability of its alliance with the
peasantry, and thus they sought to deflect the party from its Leninist
course.[45]

In December 1966, in reply to a question on the prospects for
rehabilitating Trotsky, the Soviet Prime Minister, Mr Kosygin,
declared. 'Our party, which conducted a victorious struggle
against Trotskyism, condemned it and still does condemn it. That
is how matters stood in the past, and that is how they stand in
the present.'[46] Such is the party's judgement on Trotsky.

Trotsky's own definitive evaluation of the Stalinist party and
its works was given in *The Revolution Betrayed*. The book was
written in 1936, shortly before the treason trial and execution of
Smirnov, Zinoviev, and Kamenev; published in 1937, in the
same year as Pyatakov, Radek, and Sokol'nikov were consumed
by the Great Terror; and in wide circulation by 1938, when
Bukharin, Rykov and Rakovsky met the same end. Its theme
was that the revolution had degenerated into a totalitarian dictatorship, supported by what seemed to be a new class of bureaucrats. The cause of the degeneration, Trotsky reasoned, was the

contradiction between the low level of productive forces and the advanced socialist forms which had been imposed upon them. The bureaucracy functioned as supreme arbiter in conditions of poverty and scarcity. Controlling the distribution of goods, it had created a workers' aristocracy based on piece-work and premia.

Trotsky did not normally interpret social phenomena in terms of definitions. But now the time had come to pass judgement on the Soviet experiment. He concluded that the Stalinist system could not possibly be socialism. Marx had written that even the lower stage of communism would stand at a higher level than capitalism. This could not be said of Russia. 'It would be truer,' he decided, '... to name the present Soviet regime, in all its contradictoriness, not a socialist regime, but a preparatory regime transitional from capitalism to socialism.'[47] For such a meagre achievement Trotsky had exchanged a lifetime.

Bibliography

PRIMARY SOURCES

UNPUBLISHED

Trotsky Archives (Houghton Library at Harvard University).
Bukharin, N. Program of the Communist International [draft], 1924 (Type-written text in New York Public Library).

PUBLISHED

Bukharin, N. *Mirovoe Khozyaistvo i Imperializm*. Moscow, Moskovskii Rabochii, 1927.
Programm der Kommunisten. Berlin. Verlag 'Rote Fahne', 1919.
Ekonomika Perekhodnovo Perioda. Moscow, Gosudarstvennoe Izdatel'stvo, 1920
Novyi Kurs Ekonomicheskoi Politiki. Petersburg, Gosudarstvennoe Izdatel'stvo, 1921.
Krizis Kapitalizma i Kommunisticheskoe Dvizhenie. Moscow, Izdatel'stvo 'Krasnaya Nov', 1923.
Tekushchii Moment i Osnovy Nashei Politiki. Moscow, Moskovskii Rabochii, 1925.
K Voprosu o Trotskizme. Moscow, Gosudarstvennoe Izdatel'stvo, 1925.
Tsesarizm pod Maskoi Revolyutsii. Moscow, Izdanie Gazety '*Pravda*', 1925.
Building up Socialism. London, Communist Party of Great Britain, 1926.
Kritika Ekonomicheskoi Platformy Oppozitsii. Leningrad, 'Priboi', n.d.
Tri Rechi – k Voprosu o Nashikh Raznoglasiyakh. Moscow, Gosudarstvennoe Izdatel'stvo, 1926.
K Itogam XIV S'ezda VKP (B) – Doklad na Sobranii Aktivnykh Rabotnikov Moskovskoi Organizatsii. Moscow, Moskovskii Rabochii, 1926.
Doklad na XXIII Chrezvychainoi Leningradskoi Gubernskoi Konferentsii VKP (B). Moscow, Gosudarstvennoe Izdatel'stvo, 1926.
Mezhdunarodnoe i Vnutrennee Polozhenie SSSR. Moscow, Moskovskii Rabochii, 1927.
Put' k Sotsializmu i Raboche-Krest'yanskii Soyuz. Moscow, Gosudarstvennoe Izdatel'stvo, 1927.
Kapitalisticheskaya Stabilizatsiya i Proletarskaya Revolyutsiya. Moscow, Gosudarstvennoe Izdatel'stvo, 1927.
Ob Itogakh Ob'edinennovo Plenuma TsK i TsKK VKP (B). Moscow, Gosudarstvennoe Izdatel'stvo, 1927.
V Zashchitu Proletarskoi Diktatury. Moscow, Gosudarstvennoe Izdatel'stvo, 1928.

The Programme of the Communist International. London, Modern Books, 1929.

Kamenev, L. B. *O Vnutrennem i Mezhdunarodnom Polozhenii v Svyazi s Novoi Ekonomicheskoi Programmoi.* Moscow, Izdanie Vserossiiskovo Tsentral'novo Soyuza Potrebitel'skikh Obshchestv, 1921.

Kautsky, K. *Terrorism & Communism.* London, George Allen & Unwin, 1920.

The Dictatorship of the Proletariat. Ann Arbor, University of Michigan Press, 1964.

Kollontai, A. *The Workers' Opposition in Russia.* London, Dreadnought Publishers, n.d.

Kossior, V. *Nashi Raznoglasiya – O Roli i Zadachakh Profsoyuzov.* Moscow, Gosudarstvennoe Izdatel'stvo, 1921.

Krasin, L. B. *Vneshnyaya Torgovlya SSSR.* Moscow, Izdanie RIO NKVT, 1924.

Planovoe Khozyaistvo i Monopoliya Vneshnei Torgovli. Moscow, Izdatel'stvo 'Planovoe Khozyaistvo', 1925.

Voprosy Vneshnei Torgovli. Moscow, Gosudarstvennoe Izdatel'stvo, 1928.

Kristman, L. *Geroicheskii Period Velikoi Russkoi Revolyutsii.* Moscow, Gosudarstvennoe Izdatel'stvo, n.d.

O Edinom Khozyaistvennom Plane. Moscow, Gosudarstvennoe Izdatel'stvo, 1921.

Krzhizhanovsky, G. M. *Izbrannoe.* Moscow, Gosudarstvennoe Izdatel'stvo Politicheskoi Literatury, 1957.

Khozyaistvennye Problemy RSFSR i Raboty Gosudarstvennoi Obshcheplanovoi Komissii (Gosplana). Moscow, Tipografiya Moskovsk. Gorodsk. Soveta Narod. Khoz., December 1921.

Labry, Raoul, ed. *Une Législation Communiste.* Paris, Payot & Cie., 1920.

Larin, Yu. *Trudovaya Povinnost' i Rabochii Kontrol'.* Izdatel'stvo 'Kniga', 1918.

Proizvodstvennaya Propaganda i Sovetskoe Khozyaistvo na Rubezhe 4-vo Goda. Moscow, Gosudarstvennoe Izdatel'stvo, 1920.

Larin, Yu. and Kritsman, L. *Ocherk Khozyaistvennoi Zhizni i Organizatsiya Narodnovo Khozyaistva Sovetskovo Soyuza.* Moscow, Gosudarstvennoe Izdatel'stvo, 1920.

Larin, Yu. *Uroki Krizisa i Ekonomicheskaya Politika.* Moscow, Moskovskii Rabochii, 1924.

Lenin, V. I. *Selected Works* (3 vols). Moscow, Foreign Languages Publishing House, 1960.

Collected Works, vols 27–33. London, Lawrence & Wishart, 1965–6.

Leninskii Sbornik, vol. 20. Moscow, Partiinoe Izdatel'stvo, 1932.

Leninskii Sbornik, vol. 35. Moscow, Gosudarstvennoe Izdatel'stvo, 1945.

Leninskii Sbornik, vol. 36. Moscow, Gosudarstvennoe Izdatel'stvo, 1959.

Luxemburg, R. *The Russian Revolution and Leninism or Marxism?* Ann Arbor, University of Michigan Press, 1961.

The Accumulation of Capital. London, Routlege & Kegan Paul, 1963.

Marx, K. and Engels, F. *Selected Works* (2 vols). Moscow, Foreign Languages Publishing House, 1962.

Karl Marx and Friedrich Engels, ed. L. Feuer. New York, Anchor, 1959.

Milyutin, V. *Blizhaizhie Ekonomicheskie Zadachi.* Moscow, Izdatel'stvo Kommunisticheskoi Akademii, 1926.

Osinsky, N. *Stroitel'stvo Sotsializma.* Moscow, Kommunist, 1918.

Mirovoe Khozyaistvo i Krizisy. Moscow, Izdatel'stvo Kommunisticheskoi Akademii, 1925.
Parvus. *Rossiya i Revolyutsiya*. St. Petersburg, Izdanie N. Glagoleva, n.d.
Preobrazhensky, E. *Finansy v Epokhu Diktatury Proletariata*. Moscow, Narodnyi Komissariat Finansov, 1921.
Voprosy Finansovoi Politiki. Moscow, Gosudarstvennoe Izdatel'stvo, 1921.
Ot Nepa k Sotsializmu. *Moscow*, Moskovskii Rabochii, 1922.
Ekonomicheskie Krizisy pri Nep'e. Moscow, Izdatel'stvo Sotsialisticheskoi Akademii, 1924.
The New Economics, trans. Brian Pearce. London, Oxford University Press, 1965.
Rykov, A. *Stat'i i Rechi* (3 vols). Moscow, Gosudarstvennoe Izdatel'stvo, 1927–9.
Neurozhai i Narodnoe Khozyaistvo SSSR. Moscow, Gosudarstvennoe Izdatel'stvo, 1924.
Smilga, I. *Promyshlennost' v Usloviyakh Novoi Ekonomicheskoi Politiki*. Moscow, Gosudarstvennoe Izdatel'stvo, 1924.
Sokol'nikov, G. *Gosudarstvennyi Kapitalizm i Novaya Finansovaya Politika*. Moscow, Narodnyi Komissariat Finansov, 1922.
Problemy Finansovovo Stroitel'stva. *Moscow*, Narodnyi Komissariat Finansov, 1923.
Denezhnaya Reforma. Moscow, Narodnyi Komissariat Finansov, 1925.
Finansovaya Politika Revolyutsii (3 vols). Moscow, Narodnyi Komissariat Finansov, 1925–8.
Stalin, J. V. *Problems of Leninism*. Moscow, Foreign Languages Publishing House, 1954.
Sochineniya, vols 1–10. Moscow, Gosudarstvennoe Izdatel'stvo, 1946–9.
Strumilin, S. G. *Emkost' Nashevo Rynka*. Moscow, Izdanie Kommunisticheskovo Universiteta Imeni Ya. Sverdlova, 1924.
Problema Promyshlennovo Kapitala v SSSR. Moscow, Izdanie 'Ekonomicheskaya Zhizn' ', 1925.
Trotsky, L. D. *Do Devyatovo Yanvarya*. Geneva, 1905.
The Permanent Revolution and *Results and Prospects*, trans. John G. Wright and Brian Pearce. London, New Park Publications, 1962.
1905. Moscow, Gosudarstvennoe Izdatel'stvo, 1925.
1905, Before and After. trans. and ed. M. J. Olgin, Ceylon, Lanka Samasamaja, 1953.
V Zashchitu Partii. St Petersburg, Elektropechatnoe Tovarishchestvo 'Delo', 1907.
A Paradise in This World. Ceylon, Lanka Samasamaja, 1957.
The Trotsky Papers 1917–1922, vol. 1, ed. Jan. M. Meijer, The Hague, Mouton & Co., 1964.
Mezhdunarodnoe Polozhenie i Krasnaya Armiya. Moscow, Izdatel'stvo Vserossiiskovo Tsentral'novo Ispolnitel'novo Komiteta Sovetov R., C., K., i K. Deputatov, 1918.
O Zadachakh Proizvodstvennykh Soyuzov. Moscow, Narodnyi Komissariat Putei Soobshcheniya, 1920.
Terrorism and Communism. Ann Arbor, University of Michigan Press, 1963.
Rol' i Zadachi Professional'nykh Soyuzov. Moscow, Gosudarstvennoe Izdatel'stvo, 1920.
Between Red and White. London, Communist Party of Great Britain, 1922.

The First Five Years of the Communist International, vol. 1. New York, Pioneer Publishers, 1945.

The First Five Years of the Communist International, vol. 2. London, New Park Publications, 1953.

Na Proizvodstvennyi Put'. Moscow, Gosudarstvennoe Izdatel'stvo, 1921.

Voina i Revolyutsiya (2 vols). Moscow–Petrograd, Gosudarstvennoe Izdatel'stvo, 1923.

Kak Vooruzhalas' Revolyutsiya, vols 1; 2; 3, pt. i & ii. Moscow, Vysshii Voennyi Redaktsionnyi Sovet, 1923–5.

The New Course. Ann Arbor, University of Michigan Press, 1965.

Voprosy Byta. Moscow, Izdatel'stvo 'Krasnaya Nov'', 1924.

Pokolenie Oktyabrya. Moscow, Molodaya Gvardiya, 1924.

Literature and Revolution. Ann Arbor, University of Michigan Press, 1960.

Lenin. New York, Capricorn Books, 1962.

Zapad i Vostok. Moscow, Izdatel'stvo 'Krasnaya Nov'', 1924.

Sochineniya, vol. 1, pt. i & ii; 2; 3, pt. i & ii; 4; 6; 8; 9; 12; 13, 15, 17, 20; 21. Moscow, Gosudarstvennoe Izdatel'stvo, 1925–7.

Europe and America. trans. John G. Wright. Ceylon, Lanka Samasamaja, 1951.

Where is Britain Going? London, Plough Press, 1960.

Towards Socialism or Capitalism? London, Methuen & Co., 1926.

Problems of the Chinese Revolution. New York, Pioneer Publishers, 1932.

The Platform of the Left Opposition (1927). London, New Park Publications, 1963.

The Third International After Lenin, trans. John G. Wright. New York, Pioneer Publishers, 1957.

My Life. New York, Grosset & Dunlap, 1960.

The History of the Russian Revolution, trans. Max Eastman. London, Victor Gollancz, 1965.

Three Articles on Workers' Control of Production. London, Socialist Labour League, 1932.

The Stalin School of Falsification. New York, Pioneer Publishers, 1962.

The Suppressed Testament of Lenin and *On Lenin's Testament*. New York, Pioneer Publishers, 1946.

Whither France? trans. John G. Wright. Ceylon, Lanka Samasamaja, 1961.

World Unemployment and the Five Year Plan. New York, Communist League of America, 1931.

Germany – the Key to the International Situation. Ceylon, Lanka Samasamaja, 1958.

In Defence of October. Ceylon, Young Socialist Publications, 1962.

The Only Road for Germany. Ceylon, Lanka Samasamaja, 1959.

.The Turn in the Communist International and the German Situation. Ceylon, Lanka Samasamaja, 1958.

The Revolution Betrayed. New York, Pioneer Publishers, 1945.

Ecrits 1928–1940, vol. 1. Paris, Librairie Marcel Riviere et Cie., 1955.

Ecrits 1928–1940, vols 2 & 3. Paris, Publications de 'Quatrième Internationale', 1958–9.

The Death Agony of Capitalism and the Tasks of the Fourth International. New York, Pioneer Publishers, 1964.

Stalinism and Bolshevism. New York, Pioneer Publishers, 1960.

Trotsky's Diary in Exile, trans. Elena Zarudnaya. New York, Atheneum, 1963.

The Age of Permanent Revolution: A Trotsky Anthology, ed. Isaac Deutscher. New York, Dell, 1964.

In Defense of Marxism. New York, Merit Publishers, 1965.

The Living Thoughts of Karl Marx. New York, Premier Books, 1963.

Stalin's Frame-up System and the Moscow Trials. New York, Pioneer Publishers, 1950.

Their Morals and Ours. Mexico, Pioneer Publishers, n.d.

Stalin, An Appraisal of the Man and his Influence. London, Hollis & Carter, 1947.

Varga, E. *Mirovoi Krizis i Taktika Profsoyuzov*. Moscow, Izdanie Otdela Pechati Krasnovo Internatsionala Profsoyuzov, 1921.

Krizis Mirovovo Kapitalizma. Moscow, Vesenkha, 1921.

Mirovoe Khozyaistvo i Politika. Moscow, Moskovskii Rabochii, 1925.

Zinoviev, G. *Novye Zadachi Nashei Partii*. Petrogradskii Soyuz i Sektsiya Poligraficheskovo Proizvodstva, 1921.

O Roli Professional'nykh Soyuzov. Petersburg, Gosudarstvennoe Izdatel'stvo, 1921.

Spor o Professional'nykh Soyuzakh. Petersburg, Gosudarstvennoe Izdatel'stvo, 1921.

Litsom k Derevne. Moscow, Gosudarstvennoe Izdatel'stvo, 1925.

Le Leninisme. Paris, Bureau d'éditions, de diffusion et de publicité, 1926.

Nashi Raznoglasiya: Sodoklad po Politotchetu TsK na XIV S'ezde RKP (B) i Zaklyuchitel'noe Slovo po Sodokladu. Moscow, Gosudarstvennoe Izdatel'stvo, 1926.

Zinoviev, G. ed. *Partiya i Soyuzy*. Petersburg, Gosudarstvennoe Izdatel'stvo, 1921.

OFFICIAL PUBLICATIONS

The Russian [later All-Union] Communist Party (Bolsheviks)

Pyatyi (Londonskii) S'ezd RSDRP: Protokoly. Moscow, Gosudarstvennoe Izdatel'stvo, 1963.

Sed'moi Ekstrennyi S'ezd RKP (B): Stenograficheskii Otchet. Moscow, Gosudarstvennoe Izdatel'stvo, 1962.

Devyatyi S'ezd RKP (B): Protokoly. Moscow, Gosudarstvennoe Izdatel'stvo, 1960.

Desyatyi S'ezd RKP (B): Stenograficheskii Otchet. Moscow, Gosudarstvennoe Izdatel'stvo, 1963.

Vserossiiskaya Konferentsiya RKP (Bol'shevikov): Byulleten' (Nos. 1–5, 19–29 December 1921).

Odinadtsatyi S'ezd Rossiiskoi Kommunisticheskoi Partii (Bol'shevikov): Stenograficheskii Otchet. Moscow, Izdatel'skoe Otdelenie TsKRKP, 1922.

Dvenadtsatyi S'ezd Rossiiskoi Kommunisticheskoi Partii (Bol'shevikov): Stenograficheskii Otchet. Moscow, Izdatel'stvo 'Krasnaya Nov'', 1923.

Trinadtsataya Konferentsiya Rossiiskoi Kommunisticheskoi Partii (Bol'shevikov). Moscow, Izdatel'stvo 'Krasnaya Nov'', 1924.

Trinadtsatyi S'ezd Rossiiskoi Kommunisticheskoi Partii (Bol'shevikov): Stenograficheskii Otchet. Moscow, Izdatel'stvo 'Krasnaya Nov'', 1924.

Chetyrnadtsatyi S'ezd Vsesoyuznoi Kommunisticheskoi Partii (B): Stenograficheskii Otchet. Moscow, Gosudarstvennoe Izdatel'stvo, 1926.

*Pyatnadtsataya Konferentsiya Vsesoyuznoi Kommunisticheskoi Partii (B):
   Stenograficheskii Otchet.* Moscow, Gosudarstvennoe Izdatel'stvo, 1927.
*Pyatnadstatyi S'ezd Vsesoyuznoi Kommunisticheskoi Partii (B): Steno-
   graficheskii Otchet.* Moscow, Gosudarstvennoe Izdatel'stvo, 1928.

*Proceedings of Congresses of Soviets and of the All-Russian [All-Union]
Central Executive Committee*

Vos'moi Vserossiiskii S'ezd Sovetov: Stenograficheskii Otchet. Moscow,
   Gosudarstvennoe Izdatel'stvo, 1920.
Desyatyi Vserossiiskii S'ezd Sovetov: Stenograficheskii Otchet. Moscow,
   Izdanie VTsIK, 1920.
*Vtoraya Sessiya Vserossiiskovo Tsentral'novo Ispolnitel'novo Komiteta,
   X Sozyva: Stenograficheskii Otchet.* Moscow, Izdanie VTsIK, 1923.
*Tret'ya Sessiya Vserossiiskovo Tsentral'novo Ispolnitel'novo Komiteta, X
   Sozyva: Stenograficheskii Otchet.* Moscow, Izdanie VTsIK, 1924.
*Vtoraya Sessiya Tsentral'novo Ispolnitel'novo Komiteta Soyuza Sovet-
   skikh Sotsialisticheskikh Respublik: Stenograficheskii Otchet.* Moscow,
   Izdanie TsIK Soyuza SSR, 1923.
*Tret'ya Sessiya Tsentral'novo Ispolnitel'novo Komiteta Soyuza Sovet-
   skikh Sotsialisticheskikh Respublik: Stenograficheskii Otchet.* Moscow,
   Izdanie TsIK Soyuza SSR, 1924.

Proceedings of Trade Union Congresses and Conferences

*Pervyi Vserossiiskii S'ezd Professional'nykh Soyuzov (7–14 January, 1918):
   Polnyi Stenograficheskii Otchet.* Moscow, Tipografiya M. I. Smirnova,
   1918.
*Vserossiiskii Tsentral'nyi Sovet Professional'nykh Soyuzov, Konferentsiya
   Fabrichno-Zavodskikh i Professional'nykh Soyuzov IV, 1918 Proto-
   koly.* Moscow, 1919.
*Shirokaya Konferentsiya Fabrichno-Zavodskikh Komitetov, Pravlenii
   Soyuzov, i Plenuma M.G.S.P.S.* Moscow, Gosudarstvennoe Izdatel'-
   stvo, 1921.

Proceedings of the Communist International

*Tretii Vsemirnyi Kongress Kommunisticheskovo Internatsionala: Steno-
   graficheskii Otchet.* Petersburg, Gosudarstvennoe Izdatel'stvo, 1922.
· *IV Vsemirnyi Kongress Kommunisticheskovo Internatsionala.* Moscow,
   Gosudarstvennoe Izdatel'stvo, 1923.
*Pyatyi Vsemirnyi Kongress Kommunisticheskovo Internatsionala: Steno-
   graficheskii Otchet.* (2 vols). Moscow, Gosudarstvennoe Izdatel'stvo,
   1925.

Resolutions and Other Works

K Voprosu o Plane Kontsessii. Moscow, Vysshii Sovet Narodnovo Khozyaistva, Redaktsionno-Izdatel'skii Otdel, 1920.
Resheniya Partii i Pravitel'stva po Khozyaistvennym Voprosam, vol. 1.
   Moscow, Izdatel'stvo Politicheskoi Literatury, 1967.
*Vsesoyuznaya Kommunisticheskaya Partiya (Bol'shevikov) v Rezolyutsiyakh
   i Resheniyakh S'ezdov, Konferentsii i Plenumov TsK,* (2 vols). Moscow, Partiinoe Izdatel'stvo, 1931.

Rossiiskaya Kommunisticheskaya Partiya v Rezolyutsiyakh ee S'ezdov i Konferentsii (1898–1922 gg.). Moscow, Gosudarstvennoe Izdatel'stvo, 1923.
Narodnoe Khozyaistvo SSSR za 1922–1923 god, ed. G. I. Krumin. Moscow, Izdatel'stvo 'Ekonomicheskaya Zhizn' ', 1924.
Narodnoe Khozyaistvo SSSR v 1923–1924 god, ed. G. Groman. Moscow. Izdatel'stvo Gosplana SSSR, 1925.
Za Leninizm: Sbornik Statei. Moscow, Gosudarstvennoe Izdatel'stvo, 1925.
Novaya Oppozitsiya: Sbornik Materialov. Leningrad, 'Priboi', 1926.
Ob Ekonomicheskoi Platforme Oppozitsii: Sbornik Statei. Moscow, Gosudarstvennoe Izdatel'stvo, 1926.
Ekonomicheskaya Politika Partii i Oppozitsiya: Sbornik Statei, eds. Sh. Dvolaitskii, A. Katkyn' & S. Strumilin. Moscow, Moskovskii, Rabochii, 1927.
Vl. Sorin, *Partiya i Oppozitsiya*. Moscow, Moskovskii Rabochii, 1925.
Trotskizm – Vrag Leninizma. Moscow, Izdatel'stvo Politicheskoi Literatury, 1968.

NEWSPAPERS AND PERIODICALS

Pravda
Pravda (Vienna)
Izvestiya
Ekonomicheskaya Zhizn'
Nashe Slovo
Vestnik Truda
Krasnaya Nov'
Kommunisticheskii Internatsional
Planovoe Khozyaistvo
Bol'shevik
Ekonomicheskoe Obozrenie
The New International
Vestnik Kommunisticheskoi Akademii
Narodnoe Khozyaistvo
L'Internationale Communiste
Vestnik Finansov
Bulletin Communiste
International Press Correspondence
Sotsialisticheskii Vestnik
Vestnik Promyshlennosti, Torgovli i Transporta
Pod Znamenem Marksizma
Sotsialisticheskoe Khozyaistvo
Na Agrarnom Fronte
Torgovo-Promyshlennaya Gazeta
Byulleten' Oppozitsii

SECONDARY WORKS

Baron, Samuel H. *Plekhanov, The Father of Russian Marxism*. Stanford, Stanford University Press, 1966.
Baykov, A. *The Development of the Soviet Economic System*. New York, Macmillan, 1947.
Borkenau, F. *The Communist International*. London, Faber & Faber, 1938.

Braunthal, Julius. *History of the International: 1914–1943*, vol. 2. London, Thomas Nelson & Sons, 1967.
Carr, E. H. *The Bolshevik Revolution, 1917–1923* (3 vols). London, Pelican, 1966.
  The Interregnum, 1923–1924. London, Macmillan, 1960.
  Socialism in One Country, 1924–1926, vols 1; 2; 3, pt. i & ii. London, Macmillan, 1958–64.
Carr, E. H. & Davies, R. W. *Foundations of a Planned Economy, 1926–1929*, vol. 1, pt. i & ii. London, Macmillan, 1969.
Collette, J. M. *Politique des Investissements et Calcul Economique*. Paris, Editions Cujas, 1964.
Daniels, Robert V. *The Conscience of the Revolution*. Cambridge, Harvard University Press, 1965.
Davies, R. W. *The Development of the Soviet Budgetary System*. London, Cambridge University Press, 1958.
Dennis, Alfred L. P. *The Foreign Policies of Soviet Russia*. London, J. M. Dent & Sons, 1924.
Deutscher, Isaac. *Stalin: A Political Biography*. London, Oxford University Press, 1961.
  The Prophet Armed. New York, Vintage, 1965.
  The Prophet Unarmed. New York, Vintage, 1965.
Dobb, Maurice. *Russian Economic Development Since the Revolution*. London, Routledge & Sons, 1928.
  Soviet Economic Development Since 1917. London, Routledge & Kegan Paul, 1966.
Eastman, M. *Since Lenin Died*. London, Labour Publishing Co., 1925.
Erlich, Alexander. *The Soviet Industrialization Debate, 1924–1928*. Cambridge, Harvard University Press, 1960.
Fischer, Louis. *The Soviets in World Affairs* (2 vols). New Jersey, Princeton University Press, 1951.
Fisher, Arthur, 'Foreign Concessions in Russia', *Soviet Russia in the Second Decade*, ed. Stuart Chase *et al.*, London, Williams & Norgate, 1928, pp. 341–64.
Getzler, Israel. *Martov, A Political Biography*. Melbourne, Melbourne University Press, 1967.
Heitman, S. *Nikolai Bukharin's Theory of Revolution*. Unpublished Ph.D. Thesis, Columbia University, 1963.
Hirschman, A. O. *The Strategy of Economic Development*. Yale, Yale University Press, 1960.
Ignat'ev, V. L. ed. *Bor'ba Partii Bol'shevikov Protiv Trotskizma v Posleoktyabr'skii Period*. Moscow, Izdatel'stvo 'Mysl'', 1969.
Ivanov, V. M. *Iz Istorii Bor'by Partii Protiv 'Levovo' Opportunizma*, Leningrad, Lenizdat, 1965.
Kaplan, Frederick I. *Bolshevik Ideology and the Ethics of Soviet Labou* London, Peter Owen, 1969.
Kemp, T. *Theories of Imperialism*. London, Dobson Books, 1967.
Korey, William. 'Zinoviev's Critique of Stalin's Theory of Socialism in One Country, December 1925–December 1926', *American Slavic and East European Review*, 9 (1950), 255–67.
  'Zinoviev on the Problem of World Revolution, 1917–1927.' Unpublished Ph.D. Thesis, Columbia University, 1960.
Krassin, Lyubov. *Leonid Krassin, His Life and Work*. London, Skeffington & Son, 1929.

Labedz, Leopold, ed. *Revisionism: Essays on the History of Marxist Ideas.* New York, Frederick A. Praeger, 1962.
Laue, Theodore H. von. *Sergei Witte and the Industrialization of Russia.* New York & London, Columbia University Press, 1963.
Lewin, M. *Russian Peasants and Soviet Power,* trans. Irene Nove. London, George Allen & Unwin, 1968.
Lichtheim, George. *Marxism, An Historical and Critical Study.* New York and London, Frederick A. Praeger, 1963.
Makarov, B. I. *Kritika Trotskizma po Voprosam Stroitel'stva Sotsializma v SSSR.* Moscow, 1965.
Mayer, A. J. *Politics and Diplomacy of Peacemaking.* New York, Vintage, 1969.
Meyer, Alfred G. *Leninism.* New York, Frederick A. Praeger, 1962.
Nove, Alec. *An Economic History of the USSR.* London, Allen Lane, The Penguin Press, 1969.
Pasvolsky, Leo & Moulton, Harold G. *Russian Debts and Russian Reconstruction.* New York, McGraw-Hill, 1924.
Ponomarev, A. N., ed. *Moskovskie Bol'sheviki v Borbe s Pravym i 'Levym' Opportunizmom.* Moscow, Moskovskii Rabochii, 1969.
Schapiro, Leonard. *The Communist Party of the Soviet Union.* London, Eyre & Spottiswoode, 1960.
The Origin of the Communist Autocracy. New York, Frederick A. Praeger, 1965.
Schwarz, Solomon M. *The Russian Revolution of 1905.* Chicago & London, University of Chicago Press, 1967.
Shaumyan, S. S. ed. *Bor'ba Partii Bol'shevikov Protiv Trotskizma (1903–Fevral' 1917 g.).* Moscow, Izdatel'stvo 'Mysl'', 1968.
Sutton, Antony C. *Western Technology and Soviet Economic Development.* Stanford, Hoover Institution on War, Revolution and Peace, 1968.
Ulam, Adam B. *The Bolsheviks.* New York, Macmillan, 1965.
Ullman, Richard H. *Britain and the Russian Civil War.* London, Oxford University Press, 1968.
Vyatkin, A. Ya. *Razgrom Kommunisticheskoi Partiei Trotskizma i Drugikh Antileninskikh Grupp.* Leningrad, Izdatel'stvo Leningradskovo Universiteta, 1966.
Wolfe, Bertram D. *Three Who Made a Revolution.* New York, Delta, 1964.
Yufereva, E. V. *Leninskoe Uchenie o Goskapitalizme v Perekhodnyi Period k Sotsializmu* Moscow, Izdatel'stvo 'Ekonomika', 1960.
Zeman, Z. A. B. & Scharlau, W. B. *The Merchant of Revolution.* London, Oxford University Press, 1965.

Notes

1. The myth of Trotskyism

1. Isaac Deutscher, *The Prophet Armed* (New York, 1965), p. 158.
2. George Lichtheim, *Marxism, An Historical and Critical Study* (New York, 1963), p. 342.
3. Robert V. Daniels, *The Conscience of the Revolution* (Cambridge Mass., 1965), pp. 37–8.
4. E. Preobrazhensky, *The New Economics*, intro. Alec Nove (London, 1965), pp. xii–xiii.
5. Leon Trotsky, *The Permanent Revolution* and *Results and Prospects* (London, 1962), p. 196.
6. Trotsky, *Results*, p. 196.
7. *Ibid*, p. 218.
8. *Ibid*, pp. 227–8.
9. *Ibid*, pp. 236–7.
10. *Ibid*, p. 247.
11. Trotsky, *Permanent Revolution*, p. 5.
12. Trotsky, *Results*, p. 170.
13. *Ibid*, p. 194.
14. *Ibid*, p. 233.
15. Parvus, *Rossiya i Revolyutsiya* (St Petersburg, n.d.), pp. 88–9.
16. Trotsky, *Sochineniya* (Moscow, 1925–7), VI, 10.
17. *Ibid*, pp. 38–9.
18. Trotsky, *Voina i Revolyutsiya* (2 vols., Moscow, 1923), I, 75.
19. *Ibid*, p. 76.
20. *Nashe Slovo*, 9 July 1915.
21. Trotsky, *Voina i Revolyutsiya*, I, 162.
22. *Nashe Slovo*, 23 February 1915.
23. Trotsky, *Sochineniya*, III, pt. i, p. 88.
24. Trotsky, *Voina i Revolyutsiya*, I, 153.
25. Trotsky, *Kak Vooruzhalas' Revolyutsiya* (3 vols, Moscow, 1923–5), I, 41.
26. V. I. Lenin, *Selected Works* (3 vols, Moscow, 1960), vol. I, p. 759.
27. Lenin, *Selected Works*, I, 705.
28. Trotsky, *Sochineniya*, III pt. i, 89–90.
29. Lenin, *Selected Works*, I, p. 782.

2. Isolation and the mobilization of labour

1. Lenin, *Selected Works* (Moscow, 1960), II, 341.
2. Trotsky, *Kak Vooruzhalas' Revolyutsiya*, I, 38.
3. *Ibid*, p. 37.

4. *Ibid*, p. 60.
5. Lenin, *Collected Works* (London, 1965–6), xxviii, 424.
6. Trotsky, *O Zadachakh Proizvodstvennykh Soyuzov* (Moscow, 1920), p. 8.
7. Trotsky, *A Paradise in this World* (Ceylon, 1957), p. 28.
8. Trotsky, *Kak Vooruzhalas' Revolyutsiya*, 1, 372–3.
9. *Ibid*, p. 393.
10. Arno J. Mayer, *Politics and Diplomacy of Peacemaking* (New York, 1969), p. 259.
11. Trotsky, *The First Five Years of the Communist International* (2 vols, New York, 1945), 1, 63.
12. Trotsky, *Sochineniya*, iii, pt. i, 223.
13. A. Baykov, *The Development of the Soviet Economic System* (New York, 1947), p. 42.
14. E. H. Carr, *The Bolshevik Revolution* (3 vols, London, 1966), ii, 211.
15. Trotsky, *Sochineniya*, xv, 12.
16. *Ibid*, p. 11.
17. *Resheniya Partii i Pravitel'stva po Khozyaistennym Voprosam* (Moscow, 1967), 1, 159–61.
18. Trotsky, *Sochineniya*, xv, 112.
19. *Ibid*, p. 63.
20. *Ibid*, p. 287.
21. Lenin, *Collected Works*, xxx 332.
22. Trotsky, *Sochineniya*, xv, 554.
23. *Ibid*, p. 35.
24. *Ibid*, p. 96.
25. *Ibid*, pp. 87–8.
26. *Ibid*, p. 44.
27. *Ibid*, p. 51.
28. *Ibid*, pp. 57–8.
29. *Ibid*, p. 107.
30. Lenin, *Collected Works*, xxx, 317.
31. Trotsky, *Sochineniya*, xv, 285–6.
32. *Ibid*, p. 310.
33. *Ibid*, p. 298.
34. *Ibid*
35. *Ibid*, p. 310.
36. *Ibid*, xvii, pt. ii, 357.
37. *Ibid*, xv, 115.
38. Trotsky, *Terrorism and Communism* (Ann Arbor, 1963), pp. 159–60.
39. Trotsky, *Sochineniya*, xv, 126.
40. *Ibid*, p. 133.
41. *Ibid*, p. 181.
42. Lenin, *Collected Works*, xxx, 455.
43. *Devyatyi S'ezd RKP: Stenograficheskii Otchet* (Moscow, 1920), pp. 105–6.
44. *Devyatyi S'ezd RKP: Protokoly* (Moscow, 1960), p. 568.
45. *Devyatyi S'ezd RKP: Stenograficheskii Otchet*, p. 122.
46. *Ibid*, p. 213.
47. *Ibid*, pp. 218–19.
48. *Ibid*, p. 205.
49. N. Bukharin, *Ekonomika Perekhodnovo Perioda* (Moscow, 1920), p. 102.

50. *Trotsky Archives*, No. T–473.
51. *Devyatyi S'ezd RKP: Stenograficheskii Otchet*, p. 123.
52. Trotsky, *Sochineniya*, xv, 136.
53. *Devyatyi S'ezd RKP: Stenograficheskii Otchet*, pp. 111–12.
54. Trotsky, *Sochineniya*, xv, 166.
55. Trotsky, *Terrorism and Communism*, p. 159.
56. Trotsky, *Sochineniya*, xv, 346.
57. *Ibid*, pp. 347–8, 359, 399 and 445.
58. *Pravda*, 28 September 1920.
59. *Rossiiskaya Kommunisticheskaya Partiya (Bolshevikov) v Rezolyutsiyakh ee S'ezdov i Konferentsii* (Moscow, 1923), pp. 291–3.
60. A. Andreev, 'Ocherednye Zadachi Soyuzov', *Vestnik Truda*, 1 (October, 1920), 10.
61. Yu. Lutovinov, 'Udarnost' i Zadachi Profsoyuzov', *Vestnik Truda* 11 (December, 1920), 11–14.
62. Lenin, *Collected Works*, xxxi, 374.
63. J. V. Stalin, *Sochineniya* (Moscow, 1947), v, 10.
64. Trotsky, *Sochineniya*, xv, 410.
65. *Ibid*, p. 414.
66. Trotsky, *O Zadachakh Proizvodstvennykh Soyuzov*, p. 17.
67. *Desyatyi S'ezd RKP: Stenograficheskii Otchet* (Moscow, 1963), pp. 817–18.
68. Trotsky, *Sochineniya*, xv, 431–2.
69. *Pravda*, 29 January 1921.
70. Stalin, *Sochineniya*, v, 11.
71. Trotsky, *Rol' i Zadachi Professional'nykh Soyuzov* (Moscow, 1920), p. 10.
72. Lenin, *Collected Works*, xxxii, 29.
73. *Ibid*, p. 22.
74. *Ibid*, p. 62.
75. A. Kollontai, *The Workers' Opposition in Russia* (London, n.d.), pp. 30–1.
76. Trotsky, *The New Course* (Ann Arbor, 1965), p. 70.
77. I. Deutscher, *The Prophet Unarmed* (New York, 1965), p. 70.
78. Trotsky, *Kak Vooruzhalas' Revolyutsiya*, iii, pt. ii, 241.
79. Trotsky, *Sochineniya*, xv, 228.
80. *Ibid*, p. 236.
81. Trotsky, *The History of the Russian Revolution* (London, 1965), p. 1241.

3. INTEGRATIONISM AND THE NEW ECONOMIC POLICY

1. L. Kritsman, *Geroicheskii Period Velikoi Russkoi Revolyutsii* (Moscow, n.d.).
2. *Trotsky Archives*, No. T–617.
3. Lenin, *Collected Works*, xxxi, 512.
4. *Ibid*, xxxi 514; xxxii, 143.
5. *Leninskii Sbornik* (Moscow, 1932), xx, 111.
6. A. I. Rykov, 'Itogi Sovetskovo Stroitel'stva', *Narodnoe Khozyaistvo* (November 1920), pp. 10–11.
7. *Vos'moi Vserossiiskii S'ezd Sovetov: Stenograficheskii Otchet* (Moscow, 1920), p. 97.

8. Lenin, *Collected Works*, XXXI, 510.
9. *Vos'moi S'ezd Sovetov*, p. 62.
10. Baykov, *The Soviet Economic System*, p. 46.
11. Lenin, *Collected Works*, XXXII, 180.
12. *Ibid*, XXXI, 443.
13. *Vos'moi S'ezd Sovetov*, p. 100.
14. Lenin, *Collected Works*, XXXI, 451.
15. *Ibid*, p. 493.
16. *Ibid*, p. 486.
17. *Vos'moi S'ezd Sovetov*, p. 113.
18. *Ibid*, pp. 100–1.
19. Lenin, *Collected Works*, XXXII, 304–5.
20. *Pravda*, 6 August 1921.
21. Vesenkha, *K Voprosu o Plane Kontsessii* (Moscow, 1920).
22. *Desyatyi S'ezd RKP*, pp. 457–8.
23. *Ibid*, p. 462.
24. Lenin, Collected Works, XXXII, 345.
25. Bukharin, *Novyi Kurs Ekonomicheskoi Politiki* (St Petersburg, 1921),
    pp. 13–14; Preobrazhensky, *Ot Nepa k Sotsializmu* (Moscow, 1922),
    p. 19; cf. Preobrazhensky in *Odinadtsatyi S'ezd RKP (B): Steno-
    graficheskii Otchet* (Moscow, 1922), pp. 72–3; and Bukharin in
    Vserossiiskaya Konferentsiya RKP (B): Byulleten' No. 2, (Moscow,
    December 1921), pp. 50–1.
26. *Trotsky Archives*, No. T–671.
27. *Ibid*, No. T–774.
28. Trotsky, *Pokolenie Oktyabrya* (Moscow, 1924), p. 198.
29. On the trade unions see *Odinadtsatyi S'ezd RKP*, pp. 242–3; for the
    military see *Trotsky Archives*, No. T–716, and *Kak Vooruzhalas' Rev-
    olyutsiya*, III, pt. i, 282.
30. Trotsky, *Sochineniya*, XV, 435.
31. *Ibid*, p. 482.
32. *Ibid*, pp. 481–2.
33. *Ibid*.
34. Trotsky, *The First Five Years*, I, 193.
35. *Ibid*, p. 180.
36. *Ibid*, p. 198.
37. *Ibid*, pp. 206–7.
38. *Ibid*, p. 230.
39. Lyubov Krassin, *Leonid Krassin, His Life and Work* (London, n.d.),
    pp. 180–1.
40. Trotsky, *The First Five Years*, I, 247.
41. Trotsky, *Kak Vooruzhalas' Revolyutsiya*, III, pt. i, 234.
42. Trotsky, *The First Five Years* (London, 1953), II, 253.
43. *Ibid*, p. 243.
44. Trotsky, *Kak Vooruzhalas' Revolyutsiya*, III, pt. ii, 222.
45. *Pravda*, 25 October 1921.
46. *Leninskii Sbornik*, XX, 147.
47. Karl Radek, 'Puti Russkoi Revolyutsii', *Krasnaya Nov'*, IV (December
    1921), 181–2.
48. Preobrazhensky, 'Perspektivy Novoi Ekonomicheskoi Politiki', *Kras-
    naya Nov'*, III (September–October 1921), 205.
49. *Pravda*, 4 December 1921.
50. *Vserossiiskaya Konferentsiya RKP (B): Byulleten' No. 5*, pp. 24–5.

51. *Ibid*, p. 37.
52. *Ibid*.
53. *Ibid*, pp. 48–9.
54. *Odinadtsatyi S'ezd RKP*, p. 280.
55. *Pravda*, 3 March 1922.
56. *Ibid*, 7 December 1921.
57. For the debate see Sokol'nikov, *Gosudarstvennyi Kapitalizm i Novaya Finansovaya Politika* (Moscow, 1922), pp. 14–15; Preobrazhensky, *Finansy v Epokhu Diktatury Proletariata* (Moscow, 1921), p. 43; *Pravda*, 9 June 1922; and 28 July 1922; Sokol'nikov, *Problemy Finansovovo Stroitel'stva* (Moscow, 1923), pp. 3–4; Sokol'nikov, Finansovaya Politika Revolyutsii (3 vols, Moscow, 1925–8), II, 5–22.
58. *Odinadtsatyi S'ezd RKP*, p. 278.
59. *Ibid*, p. 99.
60. Lenin, *Collected Works*, XXXIII, 276–7.

4. The search for a new faith

1. *Pravda*, 5 August 1922.
2. *Ibid*, 24 October 1922.
3. Sokol'nikov, *Problemy Finansovovo Stroitel'stva*, p. 33.
4. Lenin, *Collected Works*, XXXIII, 370.
5. *Ibid*, p. 425.
6. *Ibid*, p. 438.
7. Trotsky, *Kak Vooruzhalas' Revolyutsiya*, III, pt. ii, 62.
8. *Ibid*, p. 65.
9. *Ibid*, p. 69.
10. Trotsky, *Sochineniya*, XXI, 300.
11. Trotsky, *The First Five Years*, II, 242.
12. *Ibid*, pp. 233–6.
13. *Trotsky Archives*, No. T–733.
14. Lenin, *Collected Works*, XXXIII, 354.
15. Trotsky, 'Novaya Ekonomicheskaya Politika' in *Shirokaya Konferentsiya Fabrichno–Zavodskikh Komitetov, Pravlenii Soyuzov i Plenuma M.G.S.P.S.* (Moscow, 1921), pp. 5–7, 25.
16. Trotsky, *The First Five Years*, II, 236.
17. *Trotsky Archives*, No. T–774.
18. Trotsky, *The First Five Years*, II, 228.
19. *Pravda*, 28 May 1922 and 29 June 1922.
20. *Odinadtsatyi S'ezd RKP*, pp. 90–7.
21. *Trotsky Archives*, No. T–764.
22. Trotsky, *The First Five Years*, II, 239.
23. Sokol'nikov, *Gosudarstvennyi Kapitalizm*, pp. 5–6.
24. Lyubov Krassin, *Leonid Krassin*, p. 176.
25. Lenin, *Collected Works*, XXXIII, 370–1, 426, 454.
26. *Ibid*, p. 375.
27. *Ibid*, p. 529.
28. *Trotsky Archives*, No. T–764.
29. *Ibid*, No. T–766.
30. *Ibid*. No. T–765.
31. Lenin, *Collected Works*, XXXIII, 455–8.

32. *Trotsky Archives*, No. T–770.
33. *Ibid*, No. T–773.
34. *Ibid*; cf. No. T–766.
35. *Ibid*, No. T–773, T–774.
36. *Ibid*, No. T–798.
37. *Ibid*, No. T–773.
38. Lenin, *Collected Works*, XXXIII, 427–8.
39. *Trotsky Archives*, No. T–798.
40. *Ibid*, No. T–2962.
41. *Ibid*, No. T–784.
42. *Ibid*, No. T–2964.
43. *Dvenadtsatyi S'ezd Rossiiskoi Kommunisticheskoi Partii (Bol'shevikov): Stenograficheskii Otchet* (Moscow, 1923), p. 23.
44. *Ibid*, p. 25.
45. *Ibid*, p. 36.
47. *Ibid*, p. 304.
48. *Ibid*, p. 313.
49. *Ibid*.
50. *Ibid*, p. 421.
51. *Ibid*, p. 422.
52. *Ibid*, p. 394.
53. A. I. Rykov, *Stat'i i Rechi* (3 vols. Moscow, 1927–9), II, 249.
54. *Dvenadtsatyi S'ezd RKP*, pp. 294–5.
55. *Ibid*, p. 372.
56. *Pravda*, 15 February 1923.
57. *Ibid*, 20 February 1923.
58. *Dvenadtsatyi S'ezd RKP*, p. 381.
59. *Ibid*, pp. 421–2.
60. Sokol'nikov, *Denezhnaya Reforma* (Moscow, 1925), p. 19.
61. Sokol'nikov, *Finansovaya Politika Revolyutsii*, II, 13.
62. *Ibid*, p. 21.
63. Trotsky, *The New Course*, p. 85.
64. Trotsky, 'Pervoe Pis'mo Trotskovo', *Sotsialisticheskii Vestnik*, XI May 1924), 9–10.
65. *Ibid*, p. 11.
66. Trotsky, 'Vtoroe Pis'mo Trotskovo', *Sotsialisticheskii Vestnik, loc. cit.*, pp. 11–12.
67. Trotsky, *The New Course*, p. 89.
68. *Ibid*, p. 93.
69. *Pravda*, 28 December 1923.
70. *Ibid*, 15 December 1923.
71. Rykov, *Stat'i i Rechi*, II, 247–8.
72. Trotsky, *The New Course*, p. 76.
73. See the resolution proposed by Preobrazhensky, Osinsky, Pyatakov and I. N. Smirnov in *Pravda*, 1 January 1924; cf. Osinsky's article in *Pravda*, 10 January 1924.
74. Sokol'nikov, *Finansovaya Politika Revolyutsii*, II, 86.
75. Yu. Larin, *Uroki Krizisa i Ekonomicheskaya Politika* (Moscow, 1924), p. 40; *Pravda*, 4 January 1924.
76. Rykov, *Stat'i i Rechi*, II, 256.
77. *Trinadtsataya Konferentsiya Rossiskoi Kommunisticheskoi Partii (Bol'shevikov)*, (Moscow, 1924), p. 163.
78. *Ibid*, p. 164.

79. *Trinadtsataya Konferentsiya RKP*, p. 165.
80. *Pravda*, 15 April 1924.
81. *Ibid*, 20 April 1924.
82. *Ibid*, 10 April 1924.
83. *Trinadtsatyi S'ezd Rossiiskoi Kommunisticheskoi Partii (Bol'shevikov)*: *Stenograficheskii Otchet* (Moscow, 1924), p. 66.
84. *Ibid*, p. 271.
85. *Ibid*, p. 637.
86. Rykov, *Stat'i i Rechi*, III, 112.
87. *Ibid*, p. 140.
88. Sokol'nikov, *Denezhnaya Reforma*, p. 69.
89. *Izvestiya*, 19 October 1924.
90. Rykov, *Stat'i i Rechi*, III, 338.
91. Sokol'nikov, *Denezhnaya Reforma*, pp. 128–9.
92. *Trinadtsatyi S'ezd RKP*, p. 323.
93. *Pyatyi Vsemirnyi S'ezd Kommunisticheskovo Internatsionala: Stenograficheskii Otchet* (Moscow, 1925), p. 439.
94. *Pravda*, 31 December 1924.
95. *Ibid*, 12 May 1925.
96. *Ibid*, 21 September 1924.
97. *Ibid*, 12 May, 1925.
98. Trotsky, *Voina i Revolyutsiya*, II, 481.
99. *Ibid*.
100. Trotsky, *1905* (Moscow, 1925), p. 4.
101. Kamenev's article 'Partiya i Trotskism' appears in the collection *Za Leninizm: Sbornik Statei* (Moscow, 1925). See pp. 70–1.
102. Zinoviev, 'Bol'shevizm ili Trotskizm' in *Za Leninizm*, p. 148.
103. Stalin, 'Oktyabr' i Teoriya Permanentnoi Revolyutsii tov. Trotskovo' in *Za Leninizm*, p. 328.
104. *Chetyrnadtsatyi S'ezd Vsesoyuznoi Kommunisticheskoi Partii: Stenograficheskii Otchet* (Moscow, 1926), p. 429.
105. 'Oktyabr'', *Za Leninizm*, p. 329; cf. Lenin, *Collected Works*, vol. 33.
106. Rykov, 'Novaya Diskussiya' in *Za Leninizm*, p. 3.
107. Bukharin, *K Voprosu o Trotskizme* (Moscow, 1925), pp. 184–5.
108. Bukharin, 'O Likvidatorstve Nashikh Dnei', *Bol'shevik*, II (15 April 1924), 6.
109. Bukharin, *K Voprosu o Trotskizme*, pp. 164–73 and 181–2.
110. Bukharin, 'O Novoi Ekonomicheskoi Politike i Nashikh Zadachakh', *Bol'shevik*, VIII (30 April 1925), 13.
111. *Ibid*, p. 4.
112. Bukharin, *Tekushchii Moment i Osnovy Nashei Politiki* (Moscow, 1925), p. 4.
113. *Ibid*, p. 20.
114. See in particular Bukharin, *Put' k Sotsializmu i Raboche-Krest'yanskii Soyuz* (Moscow, 1927).

5. SOCIALISM IN ONE COUNTRY

1. *Pravda*, 14 January 1925.
2. *Ibid*, 26 April 1925.
3. *Ibid*, 5 May 1925.
4. *Ibid*, 26 April 1925.
5. *Ibid*, 5 May 1925, 28 June 1925, 6 September 1925.

6. *Ibid*, 5 May 1925.
7. Zinoviev, *Le Leninisme* (Paris, 1926), p. 248; cf. pp. 121–36, 241–76.
8. *Ibid*, p. 273.
9. *Pravda*, 30 April 1925.
10. *Ibid*, 16 May 1925.
11. *Pravda*, 13 May 1925; cf. Rykov in *Pravda*, 16 January 1925.
12. *Ibid*, 16 May 1925.
13. Sokol'nikov, *Denezhnaya Reforma*, p. 143.
14. *Pravda*, 22 March 1925.
15. Sokol'nikov, *Finansovaya Politika Revolyutsii*, III, 162.
16. *Ibid*, p. 105.
17. *Ibid*, p. 155.
18. *Ibid*, p. 154.
19. *Ibid*.
20. *Ibid*, p. 65.
21. *Ibid*, 233–4.
22. Bukharin, *Tekushchii Moment*, p. 35; *Put' k Sotsializmu*, p. 49.
23. *Pravda*, 26–7 May 1925.
24. Zinoviev, *Le Leninisme*, p. 205.
25. Trotsky, *Towards Socialism or Capitalism?* (London, 1926), p. 33.
26. *Izvestiya*, 28 November 1925.
27. *Pravda*, 29 July 1925.
28. *Izvestiya*, 28 November 1925; *Pravda*, 17 December 1925.
29. *Ekonomicheskaya Zhizn'*, 26 September 1925; *Towards Socialism*, p. 90; *Izvestiya*, 28 November 1925.
30. See Vl. Kuz'min, 'Trotsky o Putyakh Razvitiya Sovetskoi Derevni', *Bol'shevik* XXI (15 November 1927), 56.
31. *Ekonomicheskaya Zhizn'*, 26 September 1925.
32. Trotsky, *Towards Socialism*, p. 10.
33. *Pravda*, 16 January 1925.
34. *Ibid*, 20 October 1925.
35. *Pravda*, 27 November 1925; cf. 17 September 1925 and 20 October 1925.
36. Sokol'nikov, *Finansovaya Politika Revolyutsii*, III, 259–60.
37. *Chetyrnadtsatyi S'ezd VKP*, pp. 326–7.
38. *Ibid*, pp. 324–6.
39. *Trotsky Archives*, No. T-2975.
40. *Ibid*, No. T-2972.
41. *Ibid*.
42. *Ibid*, No. T-2975.
43. *Ibid*, No. T-2974.
44. See Rykov in *Pravda*, 26 November 1927; cf. Bukharin in *ibid*, 23 November 1927.
45. Bukharin, *Tri Rechi – k Voprosu o Nashikh Raznoglasiyakh* (Moscow, 1926), pp. 16–18.
46. Bukharin, *Tri Rechi*, p. 20.
47. *Ibid*, p. 68.
48. *Trotsky Archives*, No. T-2975.
49. *Chetyrnadtsatyi S'ezd VKP*, p. 28.
50. *Ibid*, p. 11.
51. *Ibid*, p. 958.
52. *Ibid*.
53. Zinoviev, *Nashi Raznoglasiya* (Moscow, 1926), p. 5.

54. Leo Pasvolsky and Harold G. Moulton, *Russian Debts and Russian Reconstruction* (New York, 1924), pp. 150–5.
55. Sokol'nikov, *Finansovaya Politika Revolyutsii*, III, 28.
56. *Ibid*, p. 27.
57. *Ibid*, pp. 25–6.
58. *Chetyrnadtsatyi S'ezd VKP*, p. 331.
59. *Ibid*, p. 488.

6. TROTSKY'S ALTERNATIVE

1. *Pravda*, 20 January 1925.
2. Trotsky, 'Rech' t. L. D. Trotskovo', *Planovoe Khozyaistvo*, VI (June 1925), 176.
3. *Izvestiya*, 5 August 1924.
4. Trotsky, *Planovoe Khozyaistvo*, VI (June 1925), 173.
5. Trotsky, 'K Voprosu o Tendentsiyakh Razvitiya Mirovovo Khozyaistva', *Planovoe Khozyaistvo*, I (January 1926), 194–6.
6. *Pravda*, 5 November 1924.
7. *Trotsky Archives*, No. T-2966.
8. Trotsky, *Where is Britain Going?* (London, 1960), p. 25.
9. *Ibid*, p. 10; cf. p. 87.
10. *Izvestiya*, 1 August 1925.
11. *Pravda*, 17 January 1926.
12. *Ibid*, 5 November 1924.
13. *Izvestiya*, 1 August 1925.
14. *Current History*, V (1926), 628.
15. *Ibid*, pp. 630–2.
16. *Pravda*, 29 July 1925.
17. *Ibid*, 21 June 1925.
18. *Ibid*, 29 July 1925.
19. Trotsky, *Towards Socialism*, p. 92.
20. *Pravda*, 8 September 1925.
21. Trotsky, *Towards Socialism*, p. 92.
22. *Ibid*, p. 112.
23. *Ibid*, pp. 106–7.
24. *Ekonomicheskaya Zhizn'*, 26 September 1925.
25. *Izvestiya*, 1 August 1925.
26. Trotsky, *Towards Socialism*, p. 120.
27. Trotsky, *Ecrits 1928–40* (vol 1, Paris, 1955, vols 2 & 3, Paris, 1958–9), I, 186; cf. *Trotsky Archives*, No. T-2989.
28. Trotsky, *Towards Socialism*, p. 50; cf. p. 81.
29. *Ibid*, pp. 89–90.
30. *Ibid*, p. 89.
31. *Ekonomicheskaya Zhizn'*, 23 July 1925.
32. *Trotsky Archives*, No. T-3034.
33. Trotsky, *Towards Socialism*, p. 121.
34. *Ibid*, p. 116.
35. *Trotsky Archives*, No. T-2966.
36. *Pravda*, 10 May 1924.
37. Trotsky, *Towards Socialism*, p. 94.
38. *Trotsky Archives*, No. T-2972.
39. *Ibid*, No. T-3034.

40. Trotsky, *Towards Socialism*, pp. 69–71.
41. *Trotsky Archives*, No. T-2971.
42. Trotsky, *Towards Socialism*, pp. 94–5.
43. *Ekonomicheskaya Zhizn'*, 18 August 1925.
44. *Ibid*, 13 September 1925.
45. *Izvestiya*, 7 July 1925; *Economicheskaya Zhizn'*, 18 August 1925; *Izvestiya*, 3 October 1925.
46. *Izvestiya*, 2 June 1925.
47 *Trotsky Archives*, No. T-2984; cf. T-895, T-897.
48. *Pravda*, 20 January 1926.
49. Trotsky, *Towards Socialism*, p. 98; *Pravda*, 2 July 1925.
50. *Ibid*, pp. 47–8.
51. *Ekonomicheskaya Zhizn'*, 13 September 1925; *Pravda*, 29 September 1925, 7 November 1925, 20 January 1926; *Trotsky Archives*, No. T-2977; *Izvestiya*, 2 June 1926.
52. Trotsky, *Towards Socialism*, p. 120.
53. *Ibid*, p. 58.
54. *Ibid*, pp. 127–8.
55. *Trotsky Archives*, No. T-2977.
56. *Ibid*.
57. *Ibid*, No. T-840.
58. L. B. Krasin, *Voprosy Vneshnei Torgovli* (Moscow, 1928), pp. 123, 129.
59. *Trotsky Archives*, No. T-899.
60. Preobrazhensky, 'Khozyaistvennoe Ravnovesie v Sisteme SSSR', *Vestnik Kommunisticheskoi Akademii*, xxii (1927), 46.
61. Preobrazhensky, 'Ekonomicheskie Zametki', *Bol'shevik*, vi (31 March 1926), 64.
62. *Pravda*, 15 December 1925; Preobrazhensky, *Bol'shevik*, vi (1926), 65.
63. Preobrazhensky, *The New Economics*, p. 135.
64. *Pravda*, 7 November 1925. .
65. *Trotsky Archives*, No. T-2984. .
66. *Ibid*, No. T-921.
67. Preobrazhensky, 'Ekonomicheskie Zametki', *Bol'shevik*, xv–xvi (31 August 1926), 81.
68. *Trotsky Archives*, No. T-3034.
69. Trotsky, *Towards Socialism*, pp. 44–5.
70. E. H. Carr and R. W. Davies, *Foundations of a Planned Economy 1926–9* (London, 1969), i, pt. ii, 712.
71. A. A. Joffe, 'Itogi i Perspektivy Kontsessionnoi Politiki i Praktiki SSSR', *Planovoe Khozyaistvo*, i (January 1927), 87.

7. TROTSKY'S ATTACK ON SOCIALISM IN A 'SEPARATE' COUNTRY

1. *Trotsky Archives*, No. T-2977.
2. *Ibid*, No. T-2971.
3. *Ibid*.
4. *Resheniya Partii i Pravitel'stva*, i, 516.
5. *Pravda*, 23 April 1926.
6. *Trotsky Archives*, No. T-2989.
7. *Ibid*, No. T-2983.
8. *Ibid*.

9. E. H. Carr, *Socialism in One Country* (3 vols, London, 1958–64), I, 326.
10. *Trotsky Archives*, No. T-2989.
11. *Pravda*, 13 April 1926.
12. *Ibid*, 18 April 1926.
13. *Ibid*, 23 April 1926.
14. *Ibid*, 28 May 1926.
15. *Trotsky Archives*, No. T-804.
16. Bukharin, *Doklad na XXIII Chrezvychainoi Leningradskoi Gubernskoi Konferentsii VKP (B)* (Moscow, 1926), p. 36.
17. *Trotsky Archives*, No. T-880.
18. *Ibid*, No. T-882.
19. *Ibid*, No. T-3012.
20. *Ibid*, No. T-880.
21. *Ibid*, No. T-3000.
22. *Pravda*, 3 August 1926.
23. *Trotsky Archives*, No. T-3006.
24. *Ibid*, No. T-3017, T-3007.
25. *Ibid*, No. T-3004.
26. *Ibid*, No. T-3017.
27. *Ibid*.
28. *Pyatnadtsataya Konferentsiya Vsesoyuznoi Kommunisticheskoi Partii (B): Stenograficheskii Otchet* (Moscow, 1927), p. 473.
29. *Ibid*, p. 576.
30. *Ibid*, p. 517.
31. *Ibid*, pp. 530–1.
32. *Trotsky Archives*, No. T-3017.
33. *Ibid*, No. T-3034.
34. *Ibid*, No. T-3015.
35. Trotsky, *The Third International After Lenin* (New York, 1957), p. 50.
36. *Pyatnadtsataya Konferentsiya VKP*, p. 614.
37. *Pravda*, 30 October 1926.
38. *Ibid*, 14 December 1926.
39. *Ibid*, 22 December 1926.
40. *Ibid*, 2 February 1927.
41. *Trotsky Archives*, No. T-3034.
42. *Ibid*, No. T-3006.
43. *Ibid*, No. T-3034.
44. *Ibid*.
45. Trotsky, *The Third International*, p. 53.
46. *Trotsky Archives*, No. T-3148.
47. *Ibid*, No. T-3034.
48. *Ibid*.
49. *Pravda*, 25 March 1927.
50. *Trotsky Archives*, No. T-3034.
51. *Pravda* 3 March 1927.
52. *Trotsky Archives*, No. T-3000.
53. *Ibid*, No. T-931.
54. *Ibid*, No. T-3028.
55. *Ibid*, No. T-922.
56. *Ibid*, No. T-931.
57. *Ibid*, No. T-3006.

58. *Pravda*, 13 February 1927.
59. *Trotsky Archives*, No. T-3043
60. *Pravda*, 2 June 1927.
61. *Ibid*, 12 June 1927.
62. *Ibid*.
63. *Ibid*, 18 June 1927.
64. *Ibid*, 10 June 1927.
65. *Trotsky Archives*, No. T-988.
66. *Ibid*, No. T-1015.
67. *Ibid*.
68. *Ibid*, No. T-1028.
69. *Pravda*, 15 November 1927.
70. *Trotsky Archives*, No. T-3100.
71. *Pravda*, 16 October 1927.
72. Bukharin, *V Zashchitu Proletarskoi Diktatury* (Moscow, 1928), p. 221.
73. *Pravda*, 24 November 1925; cf. Bukharin, *V Zashchitu*, p. 225.
74. *Pravda*, 30 September 1928.
75. *Pyatnadtsatyi S'ezd Vsesoyuznoi Kommunisticheskoi Partii (B): Stenograficheskii Otchet* (Moscow, 1928), p. 776.
76. *Ibid*, pp. 40–1.
77. *Ibid*, p. 60.
78. *Trotsky Archives*, No. T-1900.
79. *Ibid*, No. T-1897.

8. INTEGRATIONISM IN DEFEAT AND EXILE

1. I. Deutscher, *The Prophet Unarmed* (New York, 1965), p. 466.
2. *Trotsky Archives*, No. T-1182.
3. *Ibid*, No. T-1497.
4. *Ibid*, No. T-1594. .
5. *Ibid*, No. T-1262.
6. *Ibid*; for Radek see No. T-1521.
7. *Ibid*, No. T-1509.
8. *Ibid*, No. T-3123; cf. No. T-3125.
9. *Ibid*, No. T-1943.
10. Trotsky, 'Noyi Khozyaistvennyi Kurs v SSSR', *Byulleten' Oppozitsii*, IX (1930), 4.
11. *Ibid*, p. 3.
12. Trotsky, 'Sovetskoe Khozyaistvo v Opasnosti!', *Byulleten' Oppozitsii*, XXXI, (1932), 6.
13. Trotsky, *World Unemployment and the Five-Year Plan* (New York, 1931), p. 5.
14. *Trotsky Archives*, No. T-3493–4
15. *Ibid*, No. T-3485.
16. Trotsky, 'Uspekhi Sotsializma i Opasnosti Avantyurizma', *Byulleten' Oppozitsii*, XVII–XVIII (1930), 9.
17. Trotsky, *Byulleten' Oppozitsii*, XXXI (1932), 5.
18. *Ibid*, p. 12.
19. *Trotsky Archives*, No. T-3493–4.
20. Trotsky, *Byulleten' Oppozitsii*, XXXI (1932), 8.
21. *Trotsky Archives*, No. T-3542.
22. *Ibid*, No. T-3493–4.

23. Trotsky, *Byulleten' Oppozitsii*, xxxi (1932), 8–9.
24. *Trotsky Archives*, No. T-3485.
25. *Ibid*, No. T-3493–4.
26. Trotsky, 'Protivorechie Mezhdu Ekonomicheskimi Uspekhami SSSR i Byurokratizatsiei Rezhima', *Byulleten' Oppozitsii*, xxvii (1932), 9–10.
27. *Trotsky Archives*, No. T-3542.
28. Trotsky, *Sochineniya*, xv, 199.
29. Trotsky, *The Third International*, pp. 65–6.
30. Trotsky, *The Permanent Revolution*, p 47.
31. *Ibid*, p. 13.
32. Trotsky, *My Life* (New York, 1960), p. xix.
33. Trotsky, *The Permanent Revolution*, p. 155.
34. *Ibid*, pp. 155–6.
35. *Ibid*, p. 9.
36. Trotsky, *The History of the Russian Revolution*, p. 1252.
37. *Ibid*, p. 1257.
38. *Ibid*, p. 1221; cf. p. 1241.
39. Julius Braunthal, *History of the International* (2 vols, London, 1966–7), ii, 365 *et passim*.
40. *Trotsky Archives*, No. T-3441.
41. Trotsky, *World Unemployment*, p. 7.
42. *Trotsky Archives*, No. T-3279.
43. Trotsky, 'Promblemy Razvitiya SSSR', *Byulleten' Oppozitsii*, xx (1931), 4.
44. See B. I. Makarov, *Kritika Trotskizma po Voprosam Stroitel'stva Sotsializma v SSSR* (Moscow, 1965), pp. 43–7, 93–4; V. M. Ivanov, *Iz Istorii Bor'by Partii Protiv 'Levovo' Opportunizma* (Leningrad, 1965), pp. 59–60 *et passim*: V. L. Ignat'ev (ed.), *Bor'ba Partii Bol'shevikov Protiv Trotskizma* (Moscow, 1969), pp. 190–6; A. Ya. Vyatkin, *Razgrom Kommunisticheskoi Partiei Trotskizma i Drugikh Antileninskikh Grupp* (Leningrad, 1966), p. 157 *et passim*: A. N. Ponomarev (ed.), *Moskovskie Bol'sheviki v Bor'be s Pravym i 'Levym' Opportunizmom* (Moscow, 1969), pp. 97, 153, 171, 197 *et passim*.
45. S. S. Shaumyan (ed.), *Bor'ba Partii Bol'shevikov Protiv Trotskizma (1903 – Fevral' 1917)* (Moscow, 1968), p. 248. .
46. *Pravda*, 5 December 1966.
47. Trotsky, *The Revolution Betrayed* (New York, 1945), p. 47.

Index

administrative philosophy, Trotsky's, 44–5, 79

agriculture, during industrialization (Trotsky on), 113–14, 116, 142, 148, 150–2, 155; see also collectivization, heavy industry, light industry

Allied Council, 27–8

America (U.S.), 20, 57, 60, 65, 121, 164; as source of capital, 54, 96, 131–2; trade with, 26, 131–2; relations with Europe (in Trotsky's view), 56, 91, 100, 128–9

anarchy, 17, 19, 42–3, 59

Andreev, A., 37–8

Anglo-Soviet Trade Union Committee, 169

Antonov-Ovseenko, V. A., 117

'Arakcheyevshchina', 25

Austria, 9, 15

autarchy, 6, 121, 124, 139, 149, 168, 183

'backwardness', economic, 3, 7, 10, 33, 46, 108; Bukharin on, 159; Kamenev on, 100, 107; Trotsky on, 8, 99, 132, 169, 170, 186

Baldwin, S., 95, 100

Bavarian Soviet, 21

Bernstein, E., 12, 57

blockade, economic, 17, 21, 54, 74, 97, 110, 129; Bukharin on, 119, 168; Rykov on, 158; Stalin on, 120; Trotsky on, 26–8, 34, 60, 83, 135, 138, 144

Bogdanov, P., 74

Brest-Litovsk, treaty of, 18, 20, 61

Brezhnev, L., 191

buffer group, 40, 42–3

Bukharin, N. I., 6, 89, 91, 106, 126, 150, 156; and buffer group, 40, 42,

43; compared with Sokol'nikov, 102, 110, 116, 117; denounces Stalin, 178; difference with Stalin over investments, 177; editor of *Pravda*, 157; head of Communist International (1926), 162; in Politburo, 98; in trade monopoly debate (1922), 75–6; isolationism of, 118–19, 127, 153, 158, 160, 168, 176; member of Left-Communists, 20; on theory of class struggle, 101; on theory of Socialism in One Country, 101–4, 105, 111–13, 159, 167; on theory of stabilization, 96; on trade unions, 31; purged, 191; raises war scare, 174–5, 176; Trotsky on, 119–20, 137–8, 147–8, 161, 163, 169–70, 174; see also capital, state capitalism

Bullitt, W. C., 21

Bush, I. T., 131–2

capital: Bukharin on turnover of, 101–4, 177; substitution of for labour, 47–55

Central Control Commission, 174–5

centralism, in Trotsky's view, 32, 72, 183–4

Chamberlain, A., 95, 97, 100

chervonets, 70, 82, 86, 87, 95, 122, 125

Chiang Kai-shek, 174

Chicherin, G. V., 51, 64, 176

collectivization, 4, 150, 178, 179; Trotsky's view of, 113–14, 182–3

Comintern (Communist International), 61, 88, 107, 175, 190; Bukharin as head of, 162; report to by Lenin, 70; report to by Trotsky, 55–8, 91, 128; Trotsky

National Economy), 44, 52–3, 74, 83, 131, 157; and industrialization, 108–9, 145, 161; creation of (1917), 18; criticism of by Trotsky, 23, 32, 36, 78, 84, 89, 136; Kollontai on, 42; Trotsky appointed to, 127, 133

War Communism, 5, 14, 23–46, 59, 65, 70, 78, 80, 87, 91, 94, 101, 127, 130, 135, 141, 144, 179; and political struggles of 1920s, 69, 73; compared with five-year plan, 180, 183 *et seq*; Sokol'nikov on, 61–2
workers' control, 18, 53
workers' democracy, Trotsky on, 39, 87–8, 142, 185
Workers' Opposition, 31, 38, 42–3, 158, 186

zamknutoe khozyaistvo (shut-off economy), 6, 119, 139, 143, 161–162, 170
Zinoviev, G., 3–4, 70, 80, 95; allies with Trotsky, 144, 153, 156, 159–160, 162, 175–6; and British loan negotiations, 91–7, 159; and origins of 'triumvirate', 75–7; and Socialism in One Country, 107–108, 121, 159, 164; attacked by Trotsky (1924), 98; clashes with Trotsky over planning (1923), 81–82; compared with Trotsky, 139; dissolution of triumvirate, 105–6, 124; on *kulak*, 112, 113, 114, 115, 172; on Permanent Revolution, 100; opposition to Trotsky's labour policies, 36–7, 40–1; purged, 191; recants 'errors', 180; Trotsky on, 116–17, 143, 156